Barnes & Noble Critical Studies

General Editor: Anne Smith

Lost Bearings in English Poetry

Against the Cruel Frost (Poetry)
The Case Against Pornography (ed.)
Children's Writing
Dylan Thomas: The Code of Night
English for Maturity
English for the Rejected
English in Australia Now
The Exploring Word
Flesh Wounds (Fiction)
Gustav Mahler and the Courage to Be
Human Hope and the Death Instinct
Imaginings (Poetry)
The Masks of Hate
Object Relations (Poetry)
Old World New World (Poetry)
The Pseudo-revolution
The Quest for Love
The Secret Places
Sylvia Plath: Poetry and Existence

LOST BEARINGS
IN ENGLISH POETRY

David Holbrook

BARNES & NOBLE

Barnes & Noble Books
Harper & Row, Publishers, Inc.
10 East 53rd Street
New York

ISBN 0–06–492934–5

*This volume incorporates the
substance of the Sir D. Owen
Evans Memorial Lectures
delivered at the University
College of Wales, Aberystwyth,
during the session 1975–76*

First published in the U.S.A. 1977
© 1977 by David Holbrook

Printed and bound in Great Britain
MCMLXXVII

With Gratitude
to all the students who have taken part in my seminars
at King's College, Jesus College, and Downing College,
Cambridge: in Australia and America, at Dartington,
and elsewhere.

When "the banishment from all regions of human thought of what we call spirit and spontaneity" is complete, when the last Celtic fringe of imagination has been swamped, how can the values dedicated to the preservation of morals and culture be counted upon to survive?

E. W. F. Tomlin, *Living and Knowing*, 1955, p. 194

Contents

Editorial Note

"We have been a little insane about the truth. We have had an obession," wrote Wallace Stevens. Our obsession with the mechanical truths of empirical science has led poets into the blind alley of nihilism, and away from what Klee called "the realities of art which help to lift life out of its mediocrity . . . add spirit to the seen, and make secret visions visible". Now the scientists themselves have begun to discover that in Stevens' words, "It is not only that the imagination adheres to reality, but, also, that reality adheres to the imagination and that the interdependence is essential." This book argues for a vision relevant to our new knowledge—one which must inevitably lead to a new, creative wholeness in poetry.

A.S.

1

Poetry Has Lost
Confidence in Itself

My theme in this book is that poetry has lost confidence in itself, and that this is part of a widespread failure of human creativity. Here I propose to make some literary critical analyses of poems, many of them contemporary, and to relate my findings to certain philosophical problems. The failure of confidence in poetry is not a consequence of a failure of philosophy as an academic discipline. It is one aspect of a widespread failure of the personal philosophy of people at large, of day-to-day attitudes to existence in our civilization. As Roger Poole declares, we each have a right to "philosophical space" of our own (*Towards Deep Subjectivity*, 1972). But our philosophical tradition has persuaded us to accept a point of view which contrasts strikingly with that of "Continental" philosophy; a view that only a highly specialized kind of person has the authority to engage in "philosophy", and that it is essentially a preoccupation with the analysis of terms, of logic, and is in any case not a preoccupation with the problems of the meaning of life, or the nature of man. By some perversity of logic, it would seem to follow that a philosophy which takes creativity, humanity, and life itself into account, has to deny that it is "philosophy". From correspondence with F. R. Leavis, for example, I gather that he is "anti-philosopher"—yet what he writes is often philosophy, even if not recognized or admitted as such. The contradiction reveals the fear that many people have of philosophy, because it seems to threaten them with meaninglessness, to make them feel that they cannot explore meaning and values with any confidence in the relevance of what they are doing.

At the same time, the world view of the natural scientist makes

11

it seem futile for us to explore the problems of life, in contemplating our experience. The world simply "is", is matter in motion, and happened by chance. Yet this is nonsense, too. This feeling that the world has no meaning, and that we cannot philosophize about it comes to us from an absurdity: that is, from an absurd extrapolation from empirical science to a general philosophy of man and existence. For certain purposes scientists adopt reductionism: they reduce the world for specialist purposes to a dimension in which it is seen only in terms of the topography of atoms, of mathematical entities, and confine their study to "primary qualities": the distance between things or their weight. "Secondary" qualities, of colour, texture, "display",[1] messiness, and the rest, are discounted, though we never can discount them in our own daily life. Without realizing how fallacious this is, some extend their reduction into a general philosophy, *mechanism*, which holds that everything is only "colliding atoms", to be known only by the laws of physics. Everything that surrounds us and with which we deal in everyday life thus comes to seem unreal—and because science is the one unquestioned authority of our time it seems that the world *is* that of "objective" science. In this we forget even ourselves—puzzled, joyful, passionate, tragic individuals—and leave man as he really is—who sees the world—out of the picture. Throughout the universe, life, which transcends physics and chemistry and cannot be explained by reduction, is excluded from recognition. From the arid model of the universe constructed on Newtonian-Galilean-Cartesian principles, science excludes all that belongs to meaning, creativity, and "life". As Marjorie Grene says,

> In the main tradition of modern naturalism, man must appear either as wholly alien to nature, like Galileo's "living creature", or as reduced to meaninglessness, simply one more expression of the laws of matter in motion.
>
> (*Approaches to a Philosophical Biology*, p. 31)

This, of course, is the dimension to which man has come to be reduced, in the characteristic present-day film, play, and novel—and in the popular mind, which declares that "everything is relative".

> The achievements of man: art, religion, legal and political institutions, science itself, *can* have no significance in a naturalistic one-

12

level world, where there *is*, on principle, nothing but particles in a four-dimensional space-time continuum. Admittedly, if mechanism were true—if the book of the universe spread out before us were Galilean—we should have to resign ourselves to this dismal fact: the only appropriate philosophy would be one of absurdism or of despair (*ibid.*, p. 31).

In a recent investigation among students at the University of Nottingham, a woman was said to have had, from time to time, a sense of meaning in existence, but to have dismissed this from her mind, because she could not reconcile it with her "scientific beliefs". It seemed to her that "since science tells us" that the universe and ourselves are but "matter in motion", there can be nothing but futility in any feelings of "at-one-ness" with the universe, or in our sense of mystery in the life that surrounds us.[2] There is no point in belief, because science has stripped the world of meaning, and, indeed, of the possibility of meaning.

In the modern arts, there has been a widespread resignation to what seem to be the "facts" or "truths" of existence, as promoted by popular scientific works like Desmond Morris's *Naked Ape*. As we often discover, these views harden into dogmas which are regarded by some as unquestionable, even when many scientists do not share them. In many people's minds man is "no more than" a mechanism whose efforts are endlessly doomed to futility because of his nothingness. And while this view is merely fashionable in the culture of film and novel, it also has serious philosophical backing in the work of the "old" existentialists such as Jean-Paul Sartre. (The links between Sartre's view of human nature, mechanistic concepts of human existence, and perversion and brutality in culture are made clear by Gabriel Marcel in his *Philosophy of Existence*, 1948).[3]

Where there is a feeling that no meaning can be achieved by symbolizing, a tendency takes over, to substitute for genuine culture an indulgence in sensationalism which gives, at least, a temporary feeling of being alive, and a temporary sense of pseudo-meaningfulness.[4] In the modern arts there is therefore a tendency to resort to the stimulation of "instincts", by pornography, violence, and a parallel wilful cultivation of derangement, despair, nihilism and absurdity. The "instinctual" content, it should be said, is largely mental, but promotes a dangerous mental rage full of negative potential. While much of this is offered as being a "criticism of society", it rather complements the empty materialism and hedonism of an acquisitive society itself, and its spiritual emptiness. But it also tends to inculcate an underlying principle of egoistical nihilism—the right to have any experience at whatever cost to others, or even to oneself, in desperate fear of nothingness. It is strange that the existential insistence on "choosing man", as Sartre has expressed it, should come, in culture at large, to such destructive barbarism—and several writers now have indicated their alarm: Theodore Roszak in *Where the Wasteland Ends* (1972); Phillip Rieff in *Fellow Teachers* (1975) and the authors in *The Black Rainbow*, edited by Peter Abbs (1975).

This decline into cultural sensationalism marks, essentially, a failure of confidence in the imaginative powers of the mind. And this may be linked with that difference already referred to, between the "Continental" tradition in philosophy, and the British. In Continental philosophy, the Leibnitzean tradition prevails, in which the mind has an active quality in perceiving the world. But in the English tradition, the mind is essentially receptive—the Lockean *tabula rasa*. It receives impressions: in the parallel psychology "stimuli" promote "impulses" along pathways, through synapses and loops, and so on. Anyone can hear this kind of mechanistic thinking about the human mind, on popular scientific or philosophical radio programmes on the "brain", in discussions of computers and cybernetics, and in much psychology given to students (often with a Behaviourist background). Apart from the staggering naïvety of the models behind such ways of talking, the effect of these passive views of the mind is that we lose sight of the *intentional*, and of the creative dynamics of consciousness.[5] The "I can" element in human nature is eliminated, and this contributes to that implicit nihilism in our attitudes to human nature discussed by Viktor Frankl in the Alpbach Seminar, (*Beyond Reductionism*, 1969), under the title "Nothing But. . . ."

Certainly, the effect is to destroy the poetic. The poet may know in his bones, and even declare with all the passion at his command, that the arid views of man and the world which prevail in our civilization do not represent the true nature of things. But he will feel that, in asserting as much, he has no support from "science", and little from criticism and the arts. Meanwhile on the

14

stage and screen, continually, man is portrayed as a brute whose primary reality is his passivity in the face of "forces" determining his conduct from without, and other impersonal "forces" operating from within. These views seem to be well based in animal ethology, or in the metapsychology of Freud, while there seems to be nothing in philosophy to overthrow these extrapolations from natural science, which seem to deny man's capacities to transcend himself, in the name of the "real".

Yet in the areas of serious scientific thought there is, in fact, a great deal, to suggest the need for a radical reconsideration of the prevalent view. The reductionist attitude is not shared for example by the animal ethologist Professor W. H. Thorpe, whose *Animal Nature and Human Nature* (1974) concludes by declaring "we are the supreme bearers of thought in the universe" and that man is "essentially a religious animal". The implicit reduction of man to his brute dimensions in Desmond Morris's work (and in the publicity campaign that made his book a best seller) has been rejected by a scientist and a philosopher in *Naked Ape or Homo Sapiens*, by Dr Bernard Towers and the late John Lewis, (1969), who find the book scientifically inadequate and harmful. In the work of those biologists who are discussed by Professor Marjorie Grene, there is still a totally different insistence: "Nature must be understood once more as the multifarious scene . . . of a vast variety of forms, energies and events, living and non-living, sentient and non-sentient, of processes alive, active, and striving. . . ."

But considerable effort will be needed, as Marjorie Grene makes plain elsewhere, in her Introduction to *The Knower and the Known*, to escape from what is virtually a state of paralysis of spirit, which almost amounts to a disease. Discussing both the characteristic conditions of certain patients, and the attitudes to life of our society, Abraham Maslow says, "reduction to the concrete is a loss of future" (*Towards a Psychology of Being*, 1968). This may be taken to indicate the effects upon us of the prevalent positivist-mechanistic view of existence: and the world-view of a barbarous culture. Both deny intentionality and can cripple our attempts to create meaning.

The problems are certainly so deep that they cannot be cured simply by writing more poetry. The poet himself cannot escape the feeling that poetry itself is not "real", a view from which not even

15

a W. B. Yeats could escape, as we shall see. F. R. Leavis discusses the question in *New Bearings in English Poetry* (1932):

> Victorian poetry admits that the real world is alien, recalcitrant, and unpoetical, and that no protest is worth making except the protest of withdrawal (p. 15).

But Leavis seems to imply that the successful poets were those who accepted the recalcitrance, and admitted it with courage. In this century, poetry certainly seems to have come closer to "real life", and there is not the same kind of attempt to escape into the twilight world of Victorian legends, or the charming weekend existence of the Scholar Gipsy. But poetry has still not managed confidently to assert human creativity against the world of "objectivity", of positivism, and the dead universe of the inheritance of Galileo and Newton. This is because poetry, and the whole literary critical tradition upon which new creativity depends, have not yet tackled the underlying philosophical issues, but have rather remained numbed by them. However, what is happening now is that by the admission of man's qualities as *animal symbolicum* to the universe assembled by human thought about existence, the primary realities now appear to be consciousness and imagination themselves. Poetry, in the newly emerging world-view, need not feel dwarfed or excluded, but appears, rather, as the most fundamental reality of all, since it belongs to that mysterious capacity of the human being, emerging from matter as if matter needed to become conscious of itself, to perceive a world which can only be known by the powers of symbolization and representation, in persons, whose capacity for perception exists in a body, and is bound up with their inner life.

In many movements in the subjective disciplines today, we have the impulse to restore the sense that *"sentio ergo sum"* rather than *"cogito ergo sum"*: to restore to man as a full reality the subjective life of his emotions, and, with those, his creativity and his visions. So, a long legacy of hostility to the poetic is being overcome.

Marjorie Grene, has described "the perspective of modern objectivism" thus:

> the "mathematical language", the instrument of an impersonal reason, is seen as the sole medium of truth and light, so poetry has

16

come to be mere tale-telling, at best invention and entertainment, at worst obscurity and untruth. And it is not only poetry in the narrow sense, the craft of making verses, that is here exiled from reality, but the whole work of the imagination: myth and metaphor, dream and prophecy. In the bare mathematical bones of nature there is truth; all else is illusion: yet that "all else" includes the very roots of our being, and we forget them at our peril.
(*Approaches to a Philosophical Biology*, p. 51)

Professor Grene points out that this exclusion of the "primary life world" excludes also the passionate roots of the scientist's impulse itself. She quotes Portmann, who is "not an artist or writer envious of the achievements of science and technology", but a scientist speaking of his own passion:

I myself work every day . . . at the advancement of knowledge, and it is out of my own inner impulse that I have chosen this work . . . out of the very passion for research, I emphasize the inevitable narrowness of every image of man that is formed through natural science alone, that does not draw its power from all the sources of man's being.
(*Nationalzeitung*, Basel, 16 February 1964 quoted by Marjorie Grene, *Approaches*, p. 53–4)

While such scientists may re-assert the "sources of man's being", those in the Arts still feel that poetry and other such expressions of the "inner impulse" seem no more than "old clothes upon old sticks to scare a bird". They may feel that "God is dead", and the universe bleak, so that the individual must conceive of himself as a mere organic functioning body-self which is no more than a bag of bones doomed to eventual decline and death, in a universe consisting of moving atoms controlled by the laws of physics and chemistry, changing only by chance and necessity, dominated by the laws of Evolution and the Second Law of Thermodynamics. The universe seems itself dominated by "being-unto-death", and thermodynamic decay. What can the human soul do against this great doomed eddy? What *Dasein*, what sense of *being there*, can we assert against this cosmic nothingness?

If we try in our minds to overcome such feelings, we may feel daunted by the predominant idea of what "philosophy" is, and one first task is to realize what a tyrannical hold certain ideas have over us: that it is our paradigms that are at fault. In a paper on

17

the French philosopher, Maurice Merleau-Ponty, Roger Poole has said:

> [he] represents a quite new style of thought for us, we who have been bludgeoned into silence by the Oxford and Cambridge Positivists. He is a freeing influence . . . he represents the final break with our narrow Cartesian Rationalism, and shows us how to embark on the study of those immense and complex problems of meaning, language . . . signs, inter-subjectivity which face us, the problems which we have recently come to recognise as authentically our own.[6]

We need to reach a point of vantage from which we give meanings to the world, rather than let the world shove its meanings down on us (see below p. 155).

But how do we escape into the new perspectives? Today, solutions to this whole problem fortunately are coming from developments in philosophy, among phenomenologists and the new existentialists; they are coming from psychologists working in the field of animal and human behaviour; from psychotherapy, and from the philosophers of science, who are examining the involvement of the scientist in his exploration of the world. The mechanistic view of man—the Newtonian ideal which Blake so hated, and which turned scientific procedure into "a mystic chant over an unintelligible universe"[7]—is being challenged. Marjorie Grene, for example asks:

> . . . why should we so resign ourselves? In loyalty to the "facts"? But the naturalistic interpretation of man is itself in palpable contradiction of the "facts" of our experience, even of living nature other than man, let alone of the massive human fact of consciousness of the inner lives we do in fact lead. It seems intellectually justifiable therefore, to try to revise our thinking about nature in such a way as to assimilate harmoniously to our basic view of things those aspects of our experience, so close to our deepest hopes and needs, which Galilean science must either deny or exile to some limbo of paradox and anomaly (op. cit., p. 31).

Here I shall try to show that the arguments of the philosophical biologists are relevant to the problems we may find at the heart of poems which demonstrate a failure of creativity. In Marjorie Grene's work, we may, in the field of poetry, begin to see how it is that philosophical biology and its wider context of philosophical anthropology can save us. Discussing Portmann, she points out that

18

he sees that in human existence, "the whole biological development of a typical mammal has been rewritten in our case in a new
key":

> The whole structure of the embryo, the whole rhythm of growth,
> is directed, from first to last, to the emergence of a culture-dwelling
> animal—an animal not bound within a predetermined ecological
> niche like the tern or the stag or the dragonfly or even the chimp-
> anzee, but, in its very tissues and organs and aptitudes, born to be
> *open to its world*, to accept responsibility, to make its own the
> traditions of a historical past and to remake them into an unfore-
> seeable future.
>
> (*Approaches*, p. 48)

Here is a man as, biologically, the *animal symbolicum*, as he is
seen in the work of Ernst Cassirer and Susanne Langer.[8] And
this is man as the poet sees him—or *should* see him, if only he can
have the confidence of his convictions. The poet is willy-nilly
involved in this philosophical struggle, and, indeed, it is bringing
his own liberation as a special manifestation of the symbol-using
animal.

Marjorie Grene goes on to discuss Portmann's insistence on giving heed to *both* aspects of our lives, *both* the world established
by our intellect—the "limited but lucid sphere governed by the
operations of the intellect—and that means, in our culture, by the
operations of science and technology"—*and* the "primary life
world" out of which this lucidity emerges. This life world not only
includes the "surface of experience, the colours, the rhythms of
movement",

> but it also includes our feelings, our desires, our dreams, the
> creative aspirations of artists, the visions of saints and prophets,
> even the delusions of the insane. . . . (*ibid*., p. 50).

This is why today it is urgent for those in the Humanities to pay
attention to the subjective disciplines, to psychoanalysis, to the
new Existentialism, to phenomenology and philosophical biology.
If we do revise our thinking, we find two things happening, parallel
to one another. First, with Portmann, we recognize that "centricity" of any living creature. That is not to recognize consciousness or even sentience in it: but it is to see that any live creature
(even a plant, perhaps) has a literally subjective centre, and oper-

19

ates from its inwardness, through its boundaries, to the world—as no inanimate system does. This, "centricity", and developments of it variously called "positionality" or *Weltbeziehung durch Innerlichkeit* ("relation to the environment through inwardness") by other observers, cannot be found by empirical methods: cannot be found by positivism: and so, as science studies living things it must come to recognize that it must devise new disciplines, and open up new perspectives. As it does this, in turn, science dispels its own bleak "matter in motion" world, and begins to show us a world in which life is at home, and manifests its mysteries, in a benign context, in which autonomy and centricity are facts, and in which poetry can exist.

For the world of this new biology is also a world in which we exist, as higher beings, with consciousness, and in our additional dimension of cultural existence. If we take into account both the fact that man is the *animal symbolicum* and also develops his inner fantasies from body-life (as psychoanalysis tells us), then we are on the way to putting man back into his body, a body which has meanings: we are on the way, that is, to healing Cartesian dualism. So, we are able to include in our model of man-in-the-universe all those aspects of experience which Galileo and others in the scientific revolution drove out, to live in that limbo of paradox and anomaly.

Moreover, the change involves a special kind of relationship to time: a protension towards the future. Here the growing awareness of creative dynamics in psychoanalysis is relevant. Abraham Maslow says that therapists often realize that in dealing with a patient, they are "grappling with and systematizing the dynamic role of the future in the presently existing personality, e.g., growth and becoming necessarily point towards the future; so do the concepts of potentiality and hoping, and of wishing and imagining" (Maslow, *Towards a Psychology of Being*, 1968). Even threat and apprehension, says Maslow, point to the future (no future = no neurosis): "Self-actualization is meaningless without reference to a currently active future: life can be a *Gestalt* in time."

No theory of psychology, says Maslow, will ever be complete which does not centrally incorporate the concept that man is *his future within him, dynamically active at this present moment*. "The future can be treated as a-historical in Kurt Lewin's sense."

Also we must realize that only the future is *in principle* unknown and unknowable, which means that all habits, defenses and coping mechanisms are doubtful and ambiguous since they are based on past experience. Only the flexibly creative person can really manage *future*, only the one who can face novelty with confidence and without fear. *I am convinced that much of what we now call psychology is the study of the tricks we use to avoid the anxiety of absolute novelty by making believe the future will be like the past.*

(Maslow, p. 16, my italics)

It is not insignificant here that some of Maslow's phrases sound like phrases from *Four Quartets*. The one poet (and he was a believer) who has dealt with problems of the present and past, time and creativity, is T. S. Eliot—and I find that in my own teaching I come back, time and time again, to those poems, as the culmination of attention to contemporary poetry. And yet, because Eliot was a believer, (but not only because I do not and cannot share his belief) there seems to me a kind of stalemate in this—for I cannot believe that we can give meaning to the universe, the self, or time, in his way. We are left—at least most of us are left—with the need to give meaning to the world without God. And we are also aware that even with God, Eliot somehow fails in the end to express confidence in human creativity, though there can be no doubt of his creative achievement out of perplexity as a poet.[9]

The seminars from which my explorations of certain poems below developed were an attempt to relate the problems of the failure of creativity in our era to these philosophical issues. Anyone who engages in such work becomes aware that he is up against not only "science" and "philosophy" but the whole implicit nihilism of the educational system, as it at present largely operates. Even as we struggle to see the problem, the students with whom we work are drilled in "the study of the tricks we use to avoid the anxiety of absolute novelty by making believe the future will be like the past". I am thinking especially of young student teachers who are going into "creative" occupations in which openness to the becoming of the child is the essence of the work —but who are trained by the "objective" psychology they absorb, based on scraps of Behaviourism or Freudian metapsychology, to lose sight of creative time, and even to adopt attitudes which are hostile to becoming. This is nonetheless true of those who study "English", imprisoned in the examination system, encouraged to see poems and novels as "facts", trained to analyse and discuss poetry without passion, feeling or even interest, while not only the private agonies behind the works may be ignored, but their very creative power itself—even if the agonies belong to "becoming", and the creative quest is the only reason for the work's existence or place in the syllabus.[10] This happens, moreover, in a system in which, as Frankl says,

> the nature of our education, heavily weighed as it is on the side of materialism, has left us with an exaggerated respect for the findings of the so-called exact sciences. We accept without question the picture of the world presented by physics. But how real, for example, is the entropy with which physics threatens us—how real is the universal doom, or this cosmic catastrophe which physics predicts, and in the light of which all the efforts of ourselves and our posterity seem to dwindle to nought? Are we not rather taught by "inner experience", by ordinary living unbiassed by theories, that our natural pleasure in a beautiful sunset is in a way "more real" than, say, astronomical calculations of the time when the earth will crash into the sun? Can anything be given to us more directly than our personal experience, our own deep feeling of our humanity as responsibility?
>
> "The most certain science is conscience", someone once remarked, and no theory of the physiological nature of life, nor the assertion that joy is a strictly organized dance of molecules or atoms or electrons within the grey matter of the brain, has ever been so compelling or convincing. Similarly, a man who is enjoying supreme artistic pleasure or the happiness of love never doubts for a moment that his life is meaningful.
>
> (*The Doctor and the Soul*, p. 39)

It ought to be (as I am sure it was to the Impressionist painters) that a man who is writing or reading poetry "never doubts that his life is meaningful". But today nearly all our art is given not only to such doubts, but to actually declaring life meaningless: and we are bound to teach such works! We have been taught to doubt and we teach doubt. As Blake said,

> If the Sun & Moon should doubt,
> They'd immediately Go out.

—and more darkly (when it comes to education):

22

He who shall teach the child to Doubt
The rotting Grave shall ne'er get out . . .

Today, even in the creative act the poet finds himself engaged with such doubts, as we shall see—not least doubts thrust upon him by false claims of science to exclude values, meaning and creativity from the world, and to deny man's moral being and the intention—even his "centricity"—from his existence. Our first task is the recovery of the intentional. And this requires a new combination of attention to those forms of psychology which can find man-as-he-really-is, and of a disciplined attention to the dynamics of creative being in poetry, by attention to the meaning of poems. The discussions of poems that follow mostly emerge from seminars on poetry held in Cambridge and elsewhere from 1961 to 1974, and are related in one way or another to the urgent need to capture a confidence in the poetic dimensions of human creativity, not least in poetry itself.

NOTES

1. Darwin said he used to blush whenever he saw a peacock's tail as he could not explain this in terms of Evolutionary theory. Adolf Portmann sees "Selbstdarstellung" as the fundamental character of life, "life's showing itself on the surface". Yet of course such a quality cannot be found by a science which follows Galileo's rejection of secondary qualities. See Marjorie Grene's discussion of this question in Chapter One of *Approaches to A Philosophical Biology*, 1968. Adolf Portmann is the distinguished German biologist, author of *Animals as Social Beings*, 1961, and *New Paths in Biology*, 1964.
2. For a discussion of this question from a different point of view, but one also concerned to change our paradigms by "the liquidation of the concept of life as a process of blind autonomy intervening between matter and mind", see the chapter on "Nature" in *Living and Knowing*, by E. W. F. Tomlin, 1955.
3. The present author discusses these questions in a work in hand, *Education, Nihilism and Survival*.
4. See Rollo May, *Power and Innocence*, 1975.
5. See Erwin Straus, *The Primary World of Senses*, 1963.
6. "The Bond of Human Embodiment", a review of *The Prose of the World*, Maurice Merleau-Ponty, *Universities Quarterly*, Autumn 1974, p. 488.

7. A. N. Whitehead, quoted by Marjorie Grene in *The Knower and The Known*, 1966. q.v. p. 13.
8. See *An Essay on Man*, 1962; and *Philosophy in A New Key*, 1963.
9. See F. R. Leavis in *The Living Principle*, 1975, though I cannot feel as Leavis does (for example) about the lovely opening of *Little Gidding*. See my "F. R. Leavis and 'Creativity' ", *Universities Quarterly*, Winter 1975, p. 66. Although it may be true that Eliot implies that there can be no secure achievement of meaning in this life or through this life, this is not the effect of his best poetry, like the opening lines of *Little Gidding* which enact, and recreate in us, the anguish of the human striving for meaning, and our transient joy in the sense of meaning, which is itself a triumph of meaning in being-in-the-world.
10. And, as I find increasingly, instructed to swallow at A-level nihilistic works by Beckett or Sylvia Plath, *without giving their own opinions*— a quite evident form of conditioning in negative attitudes, even despair and nihilism.

2

Criticism Has Lost
Confidence in Itself

The disciplines I have called "philosophical anthropology" have thrown up insights which confirm one another, often in an uncanny way—for instance, many of the observations of "encounter" in F. J. J. Buytendijk and Helmuth Plessner confirm observations in the psychotherapeutic work of D. W. Winnicott and Melanie Klein. Moreover, emerging from these insights are fundamental ethical principles. So now no satisfactory discussion of the relationship between man and his culture can be conducted without reference to these. Once science accepts subjectivity—as manifest in the "centricity" of living creatures and the complex nature of human consciousness and culture—it must also find intersubjectivity: monkeys convey meanings to one another; lions have elaborate relational patterns; man is naturally sociable. And from the exploration of intersubjectivity it becomes apparent that human existence itself depends upon "encounter"—complex and close relationships especially in the formative years. The capacities of the human person to mature; to perceive the world and to act in it; to exert his freedom and fulfil potentialities; to be creative—all these have their roots in that complex of "being for" which we call love. These truths could be argued on the basis of the psychology of Sullivan, Winnicott or Rollo May; the philosophy of Martin Buber; and the phenomenology of Buytendijk and Plessner.[1]

But before we accept the new "facts" (so that we see a clear connection between love and our capacity to see and deal with the world) we must re-examine our concepts of what a human "fact" is. Buytendijk asks how we can study the specifically human phenomenon, meeting or encounter (*Begegnung*). He argues (in an address "Zur Phanomenologie der Begegnung", 1951, *Das Menschliche, Wege zu seinem Verständnis*, Stuttgart, Köhler, 1958, pp. 60–100, translated in part by Marjorie Grene in *Approaches to A Philosophical Biology*), that we cannot study encounter as a characteristic of human societies *and* retain the objectivist methodology, looking at it as something that belongs to spatio-temporally perceived objects. That may be the ambition of the sociologist: but encounter is a mode of "being-in-the-world" and can only be understood if we *live* encounters with others and approach the subject by participation as well as observation.

Buytendijk distinguishes between the way we encounter things and the way we *meet* other people. Things are simply there. The other person comes into view inviting encounter, as "a question expecting an answer". Things may offer themselves as instruments or as obstacles to our projects: or they may just *be*. Living things meet us by way of encounter: a snake or person are met in a wood in a different way from the rock or tree.

Yet (as the poet demonstrates) there is an analogue of true encounter in our perceptual awareness:

> In the concreteness of existence, every objective perception, in its indissoluble union with intentional movement, is produced only out of a *productive encounter* of man with his environment. . . . Man perceives, insofar as he at-tends, takes notice . . . and he perceives not first and foremost colours or sounds, nor things and objects, but surprises (*Auffälligkeiten*) like the railway crossing's being blocked, the piano's sounding out of tune, the appearance of a light in the dark, the coming of evening over the fields, a key's not fitting, an increase in prices. . . .
>
> (*Das Menschliche*, p. 70)

And at this point Buytendijk quotes Merleau-Ponty, "in order to perceive things, we have to live them" (*Phanomenologie de la Perception*, 1945, p. 376). Buytendijk is describing perception as a normal interaction between man and his world, and it is clear that he sees this as a creative intentional process—yet (as we shall see) it is just the *failure* of these elements in perception today which poets are describing, in such a way as to show that they have lost faith in them. So, we have reached a point at which the philo-

26

sophical biologist has had to take over from the traditional custodian of creative vision.

In this active life in the world things "show themselves, withdraw, approach, play games with us—and so are able to encounter us". Here Buytendijk opens up all that strange area of the not-yet-perceived, or half-perceived: all those mysteries with which poets have been traditionally concerned, and to which Merleau-Ponty gave the name "antepredicative" when he described perception as

> the original faith which binds us to a world as to our fatherland; perceived being is the antepredicative being toward which our whole existence is polarized. . . . The thing offers itself to perceptive communication like a familiar face whose expression we immediately understand.

(p. 372)

This "expression" in the face of things, Buytendijk calls "the language of things" and the reason why they speak to and encounter us. In a world in which the universe has become blank of face (as in the poetry of Sylvia Plath and Ted Hughes's *Crow* for example, or in E. M. Forster's Marabar Caves, or in Eliot's *Hollow Men*), and in which we cannot say anything over the universe except meaningless incantations, things obviously *cannot speak to us*, and there may be a radical disturbance of that faith which binds us to our world, our sense of belonging in it, our sense of its benign familiarity (such as Coleridge recreates at the end of *Frost at Midnight*).

Buytendijk then goes on to discuss the origins of encounter, in the child's first play activity—his playing with his mother's breast. Encounter is linked with *play*, and this (if we follow Winnicott) is the origin of symbolism and thus of culture.[2] It is also the origin of love-play: the movement of fondling, for example, which will be preserved in erotic encounter, seeks "surrender to the quality and *Gestalt* of the other (object or person)" (Grene, p. 166).

The loving encounter of person with person (*liebende Wirheit*) is something "surplus and above the 'natural' foundation of animal life": and here Buytendijk takes his emphasis from Ludwig Binswanger, the "new" existentialist psychotherapist, or Dasein-

27

analyst. Butyendijk's and Binswanger's attitudes to human existence differ radically from those of Heidegger and Sartre in the "old" existentialism. These could find no faith in encounter. The old existentialism portrayed a world which was threatening, while the lonely individual was flung into it, in ultimate contingency. He must try to choose and act in such a way as to "choose man" and define himself: but because he was ultimately to be swallowed up in death and nothingness, this attempt to transcend himself, even in the most aware moment of his "being unto death", was doomed to failure. Man must always fall tragically short of the world-creation and self-creation at which he aims, so the only courageous philosophy to adopt was one of isolation, alienation and despair.

> For Heidegger *Mitsein* is chiefly an aspect of forfeiture, of inauthentic existence. For Sartre, each *pour-soi* is forever alienated from every other.
>
> (Grene, p. 167)

In Sartre, there can be no "we", and "groups" are constructed indirectly through need, seriality and the *practico-inerte*. Love must end in sadism, masochism or indifference. The world of things presses upon us its nauseous thing-ness: the effect of "meeting" is that one experiences a reciprocal objectification of oneself under the gaze of the other that turns one into an object. There is no transcendence, and man is but a useless passion and waste matter.

This old existentialism, and all that has followed in our culture from its influence, leaves no room for the poet, nor any opportunity for successful creativity. Sartre himself has lost faith in his own: "For about ten years I have been a man who is waking up, cured of a long bitter-sweet madness, who cannot recall his old ways without laughing, *and who no longer has any idea what to do with his life*" (*Words*). The same fate overcomes many contemporary writers from Henry Miller to Samuel Beckett, who have nothing to say, in their essential nihilism, except that they are simply living out their time to the end. They are not striving toward their *Ninth* and *Tenth* symphonies, continually trying to assert a meaning, in terms of the *Dasein*, against nothingness. They will not die like Beethoven shaking a fist at the thunder. Theirs is the characteristic failure of creativity in our time.

Binswanger and the "new" existentialists start from Heidegger's

Daseinanalyse, with its emphasis on the need to find meaning in being-unto-death, but they add another dimension which Heidegger ignored. As Heidegger argues, man is a questioning being—the only being for whom Being is in question. But besides existence in Heidegger's sense as the singular being of the questioner, *Dasein*, there is (argues Binswanger), human being, as *liebende Wirheit*, "loving communion". This is to recognize *dual* being, a way of existing which "dispenses with puzzlement and fear", as Marjorie Grene puts it.

Before we can study man's individual and social existence we not only have to experience encounter: we have to take the risk of looking at the *Dasein* problem: *das Wagnis der Daseinerkenntnis*. We also have to encounter the real relationship between two individuals in mutual question and response. The relation between the "individual existent and questioner" and the "union of two persons in mutual understanding of the more than personal" is evident (as I have tried to show) in Gustav Mahler's dealings with love and death in *Das Lied von der Erde* and in the *Ninth Symphony*.[3] So, too, in his work is it evident that a perception of the world as benign and meaningful is bound up with the capacity to love.

The connection is pursued further in Buytendijk. The child's development of speech, and his body-meaning-expressions, like the smile, emerge from his earliest encounters with other beings, and are his first steps towards humanity: "the child enters into a relation of communion, a common being of man with man."

> On this ground of mutuality, and only on this ground, the life of the mind, with its impersonal, "objective" content, can take root.
>
> (Grene, p. 169)

Science and the Humanities, poetry and civilization itself, all depend upon these processes of encounter, of "having a presence in the being of the other" (Buber)[4] in which language and sign develop, and a "world"—a specifically human world—can be created:

> So the child comes to discover the presence of his fellow man, first in direct encounter, and then indirectly in signals, noises, events and all the cultural objects that surround him. His own world develops, in its differentiation and its inwardness, as the world, at

29

the same time, of other human beings: his awareness of "coexistence" and existence, of the being of others and of his being himself, develops as a unity.

(Grene, p. 171)

"The individual becomes aware of himself in unity with the other"
(Buytendijk, op. cit, p. 84). The failure in our culture, to find
liebende Wirheit, or, for that matter to find an adequate relationship between man and his world, marks a radical disturbance
of the natural creative processes in the development of human
potentialities: a failure of "life".

As we have seen, looking at the "old" existentialism in Sartre,
the stumbling block has been a failure to discover how "true minds
can meet". As Marjorie Grene points out, in philosophy, both
idealism and empiricism proved unable to deal with the problem,
while it was the unsurmounted obstacle in Husserl's phenomenology. Buytendijk tackles this problem by using the work of Merleau-Ponty closely, which enables him to investigate the embodied
nature of encounter, the "bodily presence of two to one another"
on which it depends: "I present myself to another in and through
the body which I both am and have. Encounter is *confrontation*"
(Grene, p. 175).

> When I "present myself" it is I, the whole person, my very nature,
> that opens out to confront another person in his world . . . "Through
> the body, the person presents himself in the body."
>
> (Grene, p. 16)

The argument here is very difficult to follow, especially (apparently)
since Buytendijk uses puns, as about "essence esses"—which may
be set against Heidegger's "nothing noths". But Buytendijk's
emphases are easily apprehended by the literary man when he
speaks of "when two freedoms meet", and says:

> One only needs to read a novel, say Dostoevsky's *The Idiot*, to be
> convinced of the way in which all human life is caught in a net of
> encounters, how many forms of bodily presentations can occur and
> how the slightest alteration of behaviour . . . gesture, words, syntax
> and tone of voice alters the character of an encounter. . . .
>
> (*Das Menschliche*, p. 92)

Yet it is through the infinite variety of such meetings, says Marjorie Grene, that one became human: "existence is actualized only

30

in communication" (Buytendijk). By such encounter "human beings come to full awareness of their existence in the world" (Grene).

My point here is that, in the most sensitive of all forms of gesture, of reciprocity, in poetry, we find a paralysis of this awareness of existence in the world—caused by a failure of confidence in encounter itself. Even the poet, who is, or should be, the embodiment of creative intercourse between mind and world, has felt himself overthrown by philosophies which have no room for these realities of reciprocity. Speech is full of ambivalence, as the passage from Buytendijk above about the novel emphasizes: but there should be no ambivalence about the primary fact of reciprocity in human existence. Through poetry and the imagination as forms of encounter human beings come to full awareness of their existence in the world.

Buytendijk underlines his emphasis by referring to Michelangelo's *Creation of Adam* which Marjorie Grene say represents the achievements of humanity through the body's taking on of a spiritual life:

> In the encounter in which the dreamlike, earthly nature of man is transformed from the determinateness and limitation of mere life to that of a living mind—to the free initiative of an indeterminate and unlimited transcendence—in this encounter God presents himself in the lightly touching movement of his hand. And at the same time man presents himself in his own hand, and its helplessness is transformed into a grasping toward the world and into bodily participation in creative power. But the existence (*Dasein*) of the man in the power of the hand, with its skill and concern, is already shared existence (*Mitsein*) for out of the dark shadows the first woman is watching this awakening, rapt as if in the expectation of her own existence in the humanity of care for others. Timeless, because beyond the world, is the encounter, eternally recurring in time, of man with the ground of his transcendence and the meeting of man and woman.
>
> (*Das Menschliche*, p. 93)

Alongside this marvellous comment we may place the quotation from Tagore which D. W. Winnicott puts at the head of his essay *The Location of Cultural Experience*: "On the seashore of endless worlds, children play." Both speak of "the continuity of life" through creativity. My fear, expressed here, is that the dead hand

31

of "objectivity" has, in our time, almost suppressed the creative morale on which continuity—continuity of any mode of meaningful existence worth having—depends.

In *New Bearings in English Poetry*, in 1932, F. R. Leavis discussed this wider question of meaning over the poetry of W. B. Yeats, and de la Mare. I note, in writing this book, that the same problem is still central to the question of the relevance of poetry to the modern world, and its survival, forty years later. De la Mare was quite explicit:

> "I have come to the end of things," [says a character in one of his stories, describing his state]. "For me, the spirit, the meaning—whatever you like to call it—has vanished, gone clean out of the world, out of what we call reality."
>
> (*The Connoisseur*, p. 142)

> And this character plays with the idea of enchanted spectacles that should give meaning back to the world. But the magic has ceased to work for Mr. de la Mare.
>
> (*New Bearings*, p. 55)

Leavis goes on to say that de la Mare with his faery poetry, "cloys", and with characteristic energy dismisses him. But he notes "curious traces of Hardy's influence":

> It is as if, in his straits, he had gone for help to the poet most unlike himself, strong where he is weak.

Hardy, says Leavis, "presents barely the fact [of utter loss] recognized by a mind more than commonly responsible and awake." I hope to examine elsewhere the assumptions underlying F. R. Leavis's values, and his commendation of "responsibility" and awakenedness. Here, I simply want to trace a little further, this theme of *meaninglessness*, and how poets deal with it. This is perhaps the most important theme in *New Bearings* and I take my clue here from it with gratitude.

Leavis goes on to say, quoting the end of *After a Journey*, "Hardy's solidity appears archaic . . . Hardy is a naïve poet of simple attitudes and outlook" (p. 54). In this, I believe, Leavis shows a strange underestimation of Hardy's strength—which may be compared with our view of the triumphant achievement of Mahler's "simplicity". Was Hardy able to achieve resignation to "utter loss" only because he was "simple" and "naïve"? Is *resigna-tion* all the poet can achieve?

F. R. Leavis, I believe, has persistently refused to encounter this problem openly. One may begin from the language of the poet, as Leavis insists we must, but this cannot be separated from its manifestation of the quality of the relationship between the writer and his world. One judges his *art*, but one also examines his *philosophy*—that is, his insight into the human condition. By philosophy I mean the kind of sense of existence which could (say) be examined on the lines of the existentialist philosophy such as I have discussed above in Buytendijk or Merleau-Ponty. This kind of exploration of man as a being-in-the-world is what "philosophy" is: it is not necessarily what Wittgenstein reduced it to. This is not to vindicate carelessness in definition or argument: it is to point to a need to engage with problems of being, and not dodge them, or leave them to the "philosopher", who refuses to accept the task.

In any intellectual discourse or work of cultural criticism, it is legitimate not only to discuss the symbolism ("the words on the page") but also the implicit philosophical anthropology, or "model" of human nature—the philosophical biology, say, behind a poem. What picture does it give of man as being-in-the-world? If we are to make adequate discriminations, these aspects of the philosophical anthropology in a work of art must be examined for their truth, even if the work is fantasy, since even then it is the dramatization of dynamic in "inner reality" (de Sade's Fantasies, for example, are a vicious travesty of human truth, not least in the light of psycho-analysis).[5]

This need to examine the philosophical anthropology of a work is not, however, to be confused with the examination and judge-ment *of the life-experience of the poet*, which is not a legitimate task for the critic.

Leavis himself has rejected the interpretation of literature in Freudian terms, because he believes it has a reductive effect on the art, by explaining away the artist's creative impulse in terms of the personal life. Dickens's work he asserts is not to be explained in terms of his grim experience as a child working in a blacking factory, as Edmund Wilson would have it. But Leavis does some-thing of the same, when he says

Eliot's poetry hasn't a rich human experience behind it. It reveals rather a restriction; it comes, indeed, out of a decided poverty.

(*English Literature and the University in Our Time*, p. xx)

or when he says

So inferior a mind and spirit as Browning's could not provide the impulse needed to bring back into poetry the adult intelligence.

(*New Bearings in English Poetry*, p. xx)

Throughout Leavis and the *Scrutiny* movement one finds attacks being made, not on ideas, or on the quality of works of art, or concepts of humanness—but on *persons* and their lives. The effect of these attacks on individuals has been to evoke sympathy for the victims, even among those who would have agreed with an impersonal attack on the art or the ideas.

The objection to such attacks on *persons* is itself philosophical: it is impossible to know the facts. There *are* facts available but these are cultural entities: the language of the poems, the intellectual arguments. The life experience is not available to us; how then can we condemn it? And in dealing with the quality of a person's mind and spirit, who are we to judge *that*? (And what shall we do about Villon, Verlaine and Baudelaire?). Many have been alienated from Leavis's causes because of his assumption of a God-like right to declare that a poet's "mind and spirit" are "inferior". The critic may only declare the poetry or art, and/or the philosophical attitudes to life, "inferior", or "fine" or whatever. He has no authority to judge personal qualities, and certainly no authority to judge a life: when Leavis does so, we react with dismay because, while he is so right (often) about the work, he displays only cruelty and meanness to the person—thereby seriously damaging the central principle of his own work, that the close study of literature is a refining and civilizing force, itself a version of *liebende Wirheit*.

Perversely, Leavis will use his analysis of poetry as an index of a man's "character" or moral quality: but yet he refuses to use it as the embodiment of his *Weltanschauung*, and examines this philosophically. Yet where he discusses Hardy, for instance, he makes it plain that the question of *belief* was the central one for Hardy:

Hardy is a naïve poet of simple attitudes and outlook. The attitudes and outlook were the product of what Mr. I. A. Richards in *Science*

34

and Poetry (see particularly Sections V, and VII) calls the "neutral-ization of nature". Hardy's greatness lies in the integrity with which he accepted the conclusion, enforced, he believed, by science, that nature is indifferent to human values, in the completeness of his recognition, and in the purity and adequacy of his response. . . . Hardy's great poetry is a triumph of character. . . . (*ibid.*, pp. 57–59.)

As I shall try to show, there is nothing naïve about Hardy's greatest poems: nor do they show merely the triumph of "character". His is a creative triumph, a triumph of being-in-the-world, and this is a triumph of philosophical engagement with the human predicament.

Leavis's attitude, as so often, when he commends "character" or "mind" is here patronizing, failing to see both the personal agony, and the way in which an artist can find a position whereby he gives meaning to his world, rather than allowing himself to be overcome by its blankness. It is not that Hardy (with unrelenting "character") accepts, with fatalistic realism, the "truth" that nature is indifferent to human values: it is that he accepts the differences between "things" and "animals" on the one hand, and man, on the other, who is the creature capable of questioning his existence: but then *also* determines to triumph over his temporality and mortality, because he feels he must exist in a more meaningful way than the rocks or the animals around him. Leavis seems to place an emphasis on stoicism, and to commend a passive suffering in the face of nature's "neutrality"—when the emphasis should rather be placed with Hardy on the creative acts of perception and the will to meaning, to overcome "neutrality". Leavis tends to end up only with "character", because he cannot escape from the personal, having denied himself "philosophy".[6] Commendation of character cannot indicate the essential strength, of existential authenticity, which Hardy achieves, as artist, by the philosophy created in his art and which, of course, only exists *in* the art.

It may be worth saying, by way of interpolation here, that Hardy's worst faults as a writer lie in the way he strips his characters in the novels of their existential freedom. In the great poems, the protagonist asserts his freedom against the worst that death can do: in the face of the fact that "nothing noths" he asserts that "essence esses". But in the novels he gives way to a fatalism. If it were this fatalism which gave "character" to his poems, they would not be as successful as they are as art. In *Tess of the d'Urbervilles*, for instance, it is clear early on that Hardy contrives the failure of the "right" Significant Other to meet Tess, as a comment on the dreadful elements of chance in existence. At the beginning, when she is still a virgin, Tess is dancing with the other girls and Angel only passes briefly by: he never even dances with her. The Victorian melodrama-type villain, Alec d'Urberville, by contrast, is placed squarely in her way. The result, declares Hardy, will be chaos in her life. But, of course, we see clearly that it is not "chance" which has brought about this chaotic situation for Tess, but Hardy's will—in the sense that he will evidently not allow Tess to have any capacity to choose and act successfully from her own volition. She *must* be a victim of the "gods", or a malevolent fate, of forces beyond herself: and this is predetermined, and does not grow out of her life-situation. This difficulty afflicts us over many Hardy novels: he destroys interest by making it plain from the beginning that there is no escape from this "destiny". But we are only interested in characters in a drama if they have freedom to choose. Our interest in action in any work of art is an interest in how man defines himself existentially. Unless a character has such freedom, obviously there can be no achievement of the *Dasein*: the character cannot create an ineradicable assertion of having meaningfully existed, because his life-patterns have been virtually taken over and allowed to be determined by forces outside himself, and so he is robbed of the capacity for such definition.

But this is how Hardy seems to have felt about his own life: he felt reduced to inauthenticity by no act of his own. We know this from his poems, and from the accounts we have of his disastrous marriage. There had been the meaningful moments he experienced with Emma as a girl. But throughout forty years this most meaningful love-relationship had been destroyed by mental illness—by the "Interloper":

> Nay; it's not the pale Form your imaginings raise,
> That waits on us all at a destined time,
> It's not the Fourth Figure the Furnace showed;
> O that it were such a shape sublime

In these latter days!
It is that under which best lives corrode;
Would, would it could not be there!

(*The Interloper*)

Being neither death, nor the glimpse of Christ in the furnace, madness is simply a menace to all meaning, corroding even the hope of fulfilment or joy: "save one, mirthless, / Who ought not to be there. . . ."

This feeling of this alien "figure" haunting normal life and destroying potentialities in it generates in Hardy a bitter paranoia, which appears in several poems: *Honeymoon Time at an Inn*, for instance, and *In a London Flat*. Again, this involves a certain ironic attitude to Time: "under which best lives corrode": "Time's Laughing Stocks" is the title of one of the sections of his *Collected Poems*. And it even seemed to him at times as if consciousness was a curse:

A time there was—as one may guess
And as, indeed, earth's testimonies tell—
Before the birth of consciousness,
When all went well

None suffered sickness, love, or loss,
None knew regret, starved hope, or heart-burnings;
None cared whatever crash or cross
Brought wrack to things . . .

But the disease of feeling germed,
And primal rightness took the tinct of wrong;
Ere nescience shall be reaffirmed
How long, how long?

(*Before Life and After*)

Here we have, even in Hardy, a "longing for non-being".[7]

Because of this agony, he sought to show how—bitterly—lives could become the butts of malignant chance. This paranoid view is made quite clear at the end of Chapter Five in *Tess*—and the paragraph makes it clear why his novels are so often unsatisfactory:

In the ill-judged execution of the well-judged plan of things the call seldom produces the comer, the man to love rarely coincides with the hour for loving. Nature does not often say "See!" to her poor

37

creature at a time when seeing can lead to happy doing; or reply "Here!" to a body's cry of "Where?" till the hide-and-seek has become an irksome, outworn game. We may wonder whether at the acme and summit of human progress these anachronisms will be corrected by a finer intuition, a closer interaction of the social machinery than that which now jolts us round and along; but such completeness is not to be prophesied, or even conceived as possible. Enough that in the present case, as in millions, it was not the two halves of a perfect whole that confronted each other at the perfect moment; a missing counterpart wandered independently about the earth waiting in cross obtuseness till the late time came. Out of which maladroit delay sprang anxieties, disappointments, shocks, catastrophes, and passing-strange destinies. . . .

One feels moved to answer, "only because you made it so!". Why should Angel be implicitly blamed for *"crassly"* wandering about the earth, and not relating to Tess? How else was he to know? What is the connection between this, and the impossible (and recognized as impossible) yearning for perfect union, which it yet seems could be made possible by some better intuition, or some better social arrangement? The answer is clearly that Hardy felt himself imprisoned in an imperfect marriage, while, it seemed, somewhere there wandered a perfect partner (the bodily elements of sexual maladjustment seem clearly to surface here—"the comer", "coincides", "happy doing", "body's cry", "closer interaction", "perfect whole"). He would not have written like that had his own marriage been happy; in the end in the poems he found the perfect partner answering to his call, in the disembodied ghost of the girl whom he had loved forty years before.

We may, I believe, postulate that Hardy's fatalism about "destiny", when it mars his work, arises from some complex relational problem which caused some deep maladjustment in sexual love that proved intractable. His misery was the experience of failure of relationship through the effects of mental illness, beyond the powers of intelligence and love. His creative triumph is the struggle to overcome this bleakness, in philosophical terms. We get a glimpse in *Tess* of the magnificence of his struggle against psychic suffering:

The only exercise that Tess took at this time was after dark; and it was then, when out in the woods, that she seemed less solitary.

> She knew how to hit to a hair's breadth that moment of evening when the light and the darkness are so evenly balanced that the constraint of day and the suspense of night neutralize each other, leaving absolute mental liberty. It is then that the plight of being alive becomes attentuated to its least possible dimensions. She had no fear of the shadows; her sole idea seemed to be to shun mankind—or rather that cold accretion called the world, which, so terrible in the mass, is so unformidable, even pitiable, in its units.

This passage, at the end of Chapter Fourteen, conveys a personal feeling of trying to assuage deep sorrow, and a sense of guilt which prompts philosophical meditations:

> A wet day was the expression of irremediable grief at her weakness in the mind of some vague ethical being whom she could not class definitely as the God of her childhood, and could not comprehend as any other.

In such passages, we can see that Hardy felt a deeply troubled sense of the relationship between self and world (with all its moral complexities) which he could not solve. He idealizes a perfect relationship between Tess and nature at first, and her love of Angel develops out of this. Hardy clearly yearned for such a creative sense of benign encounter with the earth, as in the work of milking, that should reflect his own love. But irony and bitterness take over often, as with that reference to how, by attending to certain movements in nature, it is possible to reduce the "plight of being alive" to tolerable dimension, "for the world is only a psychological phenomenon", and "what they seemed" (i.e. the natural processes) "they were". Even Tess is capable of those processes of perception by which natural processes may be imbued—in her case, however, this serves only to torment her with her own guilt and dread:

> At times her whimsical fancy would intensify natural processes around her till they seemed part of her own story. . . . The midnight airs and gusts, moaning amongst the tightly-wrapped buds and bark of the winter twigs, were formulae of bitter reproach.

Hardy seems to have believed that science enforced nihilistic conclusions upon us. In our time Michael Polanyi and Marjorie Grene have made it plain that he was right, insofar as science clings to its inheritance from Descartes and Newton:

39

For the Cartesian-Newtonian world was, in the last analysis, a world
without life. That simple fact had, and still has, disastrous consequences for the conception both of the object of knowledge and of
the subject who knew it. These consequences lie so deep in our
habits of thought that the recovery from them is slow and difficult.
                              (*The Knower and the Known*, p. 14)

It was hardly "naïve" or "simple" in Hardy to register and oppose
this predicament, especially when one considers the anguish he
suffered because of the failure of his marriage. In his greater poems
he wrung the possibilities of meaning out of that "world without
life" imposed upon our consciousness by scientists. Because of the
undisputed authority of science in our world scientists are believed
still to be "those best qualified to judge" the nature of the world
and human existence in it, though a general philosophy cannot be
based on scientific data and methodology, as scientific criteria
should make clear. Yet the common belief in Hardy's time, as in
ours, was that science can tell us what is "true" as no other
discipline can, and so other means of arriving at truth (like the
whole tradition from Ancient Greek Philosophy) are not reliable
sources of such knowledge. Yet, as Husserl and Polanyi have both
said, the findings of science answer none of our serious questions
at all, though we do not notice this, and suppose they do.

If there is anything "naïve" about Hardy, it is in his too un-
questioning acceptance of scientific "explanations". Tess herself,
for example, surely embodies Hardy's own feelings about the
universe: " '. . . I do know that our souls can be made to go outside our bodies when we are alive. . . . A very easy way to feel 'em
go,' continued Tess, 'is to lie on the grass at night and look
straight up at some bright star; and, by fixing your mind upon
it, you will soon find that you are hundreds and hundreds o' miles
away from your body, which you don't seem to want at all' "
(Papermac edn, p. 158). This is a description of what Maslow
calls the "peak moment" of feeling that life has a transcendent
meaning. Who is to say such feelings are not "true" (and not
astronomically significant therefore unreal) when what matters to
us is such a feeling of transcendence? Such experiences are more
real in Frankl's sense than the universe of astronomy.

Hardy seems to sympathize with Angel who criticizes his
father's Christianity by declaring that "it might have resulted far

better for mankind if Greece had been the source of the religion of modern civilization and not Palestine" (p. 199). Yet by his remarks about geocentricity in the same passage Hardy seems to be equating Greek civilization with the natural scientistic view:

> Latterly he had seen only Life, felt only the great passionate pulse of existence, unwarped, uncontorted, untrammelled by those creeds which futilely attempt to check what Wisdom would be content to regulate.

It is one thing to reject Christianity in favour of scientific "freedom" and to believe in the wisdom of reason: but it is another to embrace a "Life" as presented by Science as "unwarped" and "uncontorted", which yet offers the bias of excluding everything that makes that life worth living. Taking the scientific world-view as one that (since it was undistorted) *must* be swallowed because it is "real", Hardy could only explain the miseries of happenstance by a "destiny" which seemed inherent in the celestial game of billiards. But yet (as is clear in the passage quoted) he also wanted to embrace the "great passionate pulse of existence" untrammelled: so, under the blows of fate which fell on him as he embraced this "Life", he almost came to feel that entities in this scientific universe were persecuting him. So, he combines Greek tragic "destiny" with scientific "chance", as a philosophical "explanation" of how things were for him.

We can see the connection, if we read Part I of Edmund Husserl's *The Crisis of European Sciences* (1970):

> Scientific, objective truth is exclusively a matter of establishing what the world, the physical as well as the spiritual world, is in fact. But can the world, and human existence in it, truthfully have a meaning if the sciences recognize as true only what is objectively established in this fashion, and if history has nothing more to teach us than that all the shapes of the spiritual world, all the conditions of life, ideals, norms upon which man relies, form and dissolve themselves like fleeting waves, that it always was and ever will be so, that again and again reason must turn into nonsense, and well-being into misery? Can we console ourselves with that? Can we live in this world, where historical occurrence is nothing but an unending concatenation of illusory progress and bitter disappointment? (pp. 6–7).

Obviously Hardy would have understood the language here. But his fundamental error was to accept as "Life" a view of the world which Husserl finds totally inadequate. Husserl requires us to return to the *telos* of Greek philosophy, in its search for the whole truth—a very different solution from Hardy's invocation of the Greek explanation of the woes of existence in terms of the manipulations of whimsical gods.

Yet Hardy also believed that love could change the whole pivot of a man's life: when Angel Clare eventually declares his love to her, Hardy says:

> something had occurred which changed the pivot of the universe for their two natures . . . based upon a more stubborn and restless tendency than a whole heap of so-called practicalities. A veil had been whisked aside; the tract of each one's outlook was to have a new horizon thenceforward—for a short time or a long.

The new dimension transcends time: it is beyond practical considerations. In *Tess* Hardy could not, however, allow this new quality between his lovers to triumph—it must be overcome by the futility imposed upon it by change and necessity. Only in his later poems did he find a love which could triumph over the universe as "science" presented it to him. And he could hardly have achieved the philosophical transformation which with the help of Husserl, Polanyi, Marjorie Grene and others we are still trying painfully to bring about.

But Hardy is not "naïve" or "conservative" as Leavis so scathingly says. Of Pound Leavis says "he has no creative theme". Hardy *did* have a creative theme, which was to try to overcome the "neutralization of nature", in the name of what he knew to be capable of changing the pivot of the universe in man's experience. We can see this clearly in *At Castle Boterel* and *After a Journey* (see below, pp. 207–16).

Where are there greater achievements of this philosophical kind? Leavis writes as if he is invoking, confidently and with authority, some relationship expressed somewhere, between man and the universe, which is not "naïve" or "simple" like that of Hardy. Where is there a more accomplished solution to this problem? According to Leavis, T. S. Eliot failed just in this attempt to find an adequate sense of relationship between man and "reality". Lawrence never solved the problem, though he was engaged with it, in relation to the problem of love:

42

He felt as if he were walking again in a far world, not Cossethay, a far world, the fragile reality.

A swift change had taken place on the earth for him, as if a new creation were fulfilled, in which he had real existence. Things had all been stark, unreal, barren, mere nullities before. Now they were actualities that he could handle.

He was nothing. But with her, he would be real.

(The Rainbow)

But where, in Lawrence, is there an achieved sense of having triumphed, in terms of this personal and relational reality, over the universe presented (as by Dr Frankstone to Ursula Brangwen) by science? Men who have worked all their lives roughly speaking in the aura of *Scrutiny*, like Professor E. W. F. Tomlin, are still struggling painfully to explore the possibilities of overcoming the legacy of European science, torn as it is now by the crisis Husserl delineated.

Mahler's problem, his anguish, and his achievement, are also close to Hardy's: was he naïve and simple, too, in the light of our alert *Scrutiny* intellectual life?[8] Was Leavis's view based on his discussions with Cambridge scientists? It seems doubtful: but if he had such a view of existence, why did he not declare it in *New Bearings*, as a touchstone? I believe he *had* no such more adequate concept, and that his implicit invocation of such a non-naïve, non-simple, more adequate approach to the problem of existence is bluff. Only in his recent work has Leavis himself begun painfully to grope towards a philosophical basis for criticism as in his attention to Marjorie Grene and Buytendijk: but his criticism still fails to have faith in itself as a philosophizing act, squarely engaged with the problem of the meaning of existence. Until now, he seems to have taken it as axiomatic that there is a "reality" to which the best poetry is resigned.

The same question arises earlier in *New Bearings in English Poetry* when Leavis is discussing Yeats. Here, he sees Yeats' position as "a response to the general characteristics of the age". In Victorian times and among the Pre-Raphaelites, "the real world is alien, recalcitrant and unpoetical. . . ." (p. 15). Some felt that "the only protest worth making was the protest of withdrawal". But there was another aspect of Victorian England. We may associate it with a predominance of religion—but it was also a

43

period of the emergence of Huxleyean "objectivity", of the dead Godless universe to which Marjorie Grene refers. Does the rejection of "religion", however, inevitably mean one must embrace meaninglessness?

In our time, as I have tried to argue elsewhere, as in the philosophical anthropology of Martin Buber, so long as we stop short of "revelation", we are beginning to see that it is possible to be "religious" without having a specific belief. That is, it is possible to allow the mystery of the world, to admit man's spiritual needs, to accept the primacy of culture and man's need to symbolize, to acknowledge the unanswered questions of why this universe—and life—came into being at all, to accept the need to work on problems of meaning through exercising one's rights to philosophize and be poetic—without moving into mysticism, or into devotional belief, or needing to find or restore God or gods, and yet to share a degree of the "spiritual dimension" with those who *do* have a faith. We can restore man's *moral being* to our view of the world, in defiance of science which has falsely excluded it, without needing to base the human moral dynamic or our recognition of values, on any transcendental realm, or on absolute values defined by God. The new kind of stance is clear from my quotation from Lewis Mumford below, p. 128. (But is one discusses the problem with scientists, alas, mistaking one's position, they leap over into a discussion of God or mysticism to avoid it.)

In Yeats, as Leavis makes plain, the alternative to scientific rationalism and objectivity seemed to be the construction of an arbitrary and self-made mythology, even an occultism, by which defiantly to assert the realm of the mysterious and irrational. This is a feature of our time lying behind developments in the region between cultural decadence and commercial exploitations of anxiety and spiritual sickness. The "occult" today is both a perverse expression of the need for meaning, and a form of exploitation of hate and superstition.

"I am very religious," says Mr. Yeats in his *Autobiographies*, "and deprived by Huxley and Tyndall, whom I detested, of the simple-minded religion of my childhood, I had made a new religion, almost an infallible church of poetic tradition, of a fardel of stories, and of personages, and of emotions, inseparable from their first expression, passed on from generation to generation by poets and painters

44

with some help from philosophers and theologians. I wished for a world where I could discover this tradition perpetually. . . . I had even created a dogma: because those imaginary people are created out of the deepest instinct of man, to be his measure and his norm, whatever I can imagine those mouths speaking may be the nearest I can go to truth."

(*Autobiographies*, pp. 142–3, quoted in *New Bearings*, p. 30)

Yeats hated Victorian science with a "monkish hate" and hated *The Doll's House* because it was but "Carolus Duran, Bastien Lepage, Huxley and Tyndall all over again". Yeats yearned for a kind of withdrawal into retreat, and for "invisible gates" that would "open as they would for Blake and Swedenborg". It is only when he escapes from such yearnings that he achieves a voice for which Leavis can commend him:

> The new verse has no incantation, no dreamy hypnotic rhythm; it belongs to the actual, waking world. . . . It is spare, hard and sinewy and in tone sardonic . . . expressing . . . bitterness and disillusion. . . . (p. 42).

But here we touch on the whole central issue of new bearings and lost bearings. *New bearings are not to be found in bitterness and disillusion:* nor in being simply "awake", or in the "actual world", "sardonic" or resigned. Surely, there are questions begged by the word "actual"?

There is something else, to which we need to be awake. *Yeats was right*—right to insist on the primary need in man to pursue meaning, through vision and imagination. It is this emphasis which is being made in our time, in books as various as Theodore Roszak's, Susanne Langer's and Roger Poole's: and by the new existentialism. Moreover, while the demolition of religious belief by Huxley and Tyndall may have been based on a sense of what was "true" and "real", we are now moving into an era in which the "truths and realities" of physical science seem no longer truths and realities at all but ghostly chimeras which have led us into a new obscurantism. But the answer is neither sardonic bitterness, nor a resort to irrationality or morally inverted obscurities: it is rather to find creative being.

The Newtonian ideal, as Whitehead said in the quotation above, has turned scientific procedure into a mystic chant over as unintelligible universe. The Galilean exclusion of all other than mathematical bones has excluded from what we regard as truth "the very roots of our being". But if we think about "knowing" the world, it is evidently very different from this. As Polanyi argues, there is no knowing without tacit roots deep within us. We know that knowing is like the kind of exploration the poet makes: it is absurd for the poet to feel daunted by those who reduce the world to the thin mathematical entities of Cartesian models. As Marjorie Grene argues, there are no "clear and distinct ideas", even in science, while "knowledge is never finished, never at rest in 'manifest truth' ".

> We are always beyond ourselves in the venture of knowing, the task of finding and giving as best we can significance to our world, the world which is always beyond us at the horizon, but whose concrescence, whose interpretation, whose meaning we are. Knowledge is an achievement, but like every living achievement a stage in history, neither an end nor simply a beginning, but a "stage on life's way". The ideal of wholly explicit, wholly certified truth, ignoring this insight, falsifies at once the nature of the knower and the known, of mind and world.
>
> (*The Knower and the Known*, p. 91)

Thus, the feeling among poets and critics that imaginative meanings cannot be upheld against the dominance of the "scientific world-picture" arises from a failure to recognize in positivism and "objectivity" a falsification of the ways in which our minds work, of the nature of knowledge and of the nature of being.

Today the subjective disciplines of philosophical anthropology—no less rational or arduous than "objective science"—are insisting on the urgent and primary need to take account of the meanings we give the world by our intentional perception as the *primary* realities of existence. Even science itself is but such a way of describing the world. There is no bleak "scientific" reality demanding mere "acceptance", nor is the "actual waking world" a reality to which we must resign ourselves, in sinewy or unsinewy sardonic disillusion. Even the stoic resignation which seems in F. R. Leavis's criticism to have been (at least till now) the hallmark of creative "character" may be no more than a mark of submissiveness to a false idea, to a crippling, but inauthentic extrapolation of scientific procedures into a general philosophy. As Marjorie Grene says, there

46

is only one process: that is ourselves trying to make sense of things, trying to find significance in what else would be chaos, and this requires us to overcome within ourselves our Cartesian fear of the category of life and our Newtonian simplemindedness about the nature of the nature we strive to know. This is not a matter of "character" nor even of "creativity" alone: it is a philosophical task, not least for the poet, of opening our minds to a new and richer ontology.

NOTES

1. See, for example, H. Guntrip on Sullivan and Winnicott in *Personality Structure and Human Interaction* (1961): Rollo May in *Love and Will*; Martin Buber's "Distance and Relation" in *The Knowledge of Man*, M. Friedman (1965).
2. See "The Location of Culture" in *Playing and Reality*, 1971. It will be clear to readers of Winnicott how Buytendijk's work runs parallel to the former's theories of play and perception.
3. See my *Gustav Mahler and the Courage to Be*, 1975.
4. See the last paragraph in "Distance and Relation", in *The Knowledge of Man*.
5. See, for example W. R. D. Fairbairn's examination of schizoid falsifications in *Psychoanalytic Studies of the Personality*, 1952, ch. 1. Fairbairn himself is notable for his insistence that dreams are dramatizations of endopsychic entities and dynamics.
6. A judgement he himself makes of E. M. Forster, of course, invoking Lawrence.
7. The impulse is brought out beautifully by the sombre setting by Benjamin Britten in the Hardy sequence *Winter Words*. The phrase "longing for non-being" is from Saul Bellow, see below p. 156.
8. E. W. F. Tomlin (writing of Samuel Butler) says "A man of acute intelligence is too intelligent to exhibit that element of naïvety, almost of *insouciance*, characteristic of great men." *Living and Knowing*, p. 168.

3

Paralysis as "Space is Nearer": Robert Lowell's *For the Union Dead*

Robert Lowell's poem *For the Union Dead* is a useful example with which to begin, to try to show the spiritual paralysis that has overtaken the poet in English today, a paralysis which is that of our consciousness at large. Of course Lowell is an American: but he is also of New England, and his predicament is at one with a historical problem which affects all of us, who have respect for the past, for the "air / Of sparse sincere rebellion", whether in New England, or at the Martyr's Memorial in Geneva, or in the church at Little Gidding. Lowell's poem is about a historical monument in Boston: but it is also about creativity, as well as about choice and action—about "authenticity", and how we find it, not least through poetry.

"They gave up everything to serve the state" is presumably the Latin motto on the monument itself: RELINQUUNT OMNIA SERVARE REM PUBLICAM. "Public affairs"—what is one's relationship to public affairs, to the needs of society, or human culture? This is one question posed by the poem—and Lowell cannot answer it. He cannot answer it because he cannot find a vision to guide him, or values upon which he can rely. All he can find is empty space—and the symbolism of space is central in the poem. It takes the political and social questions to the heart of today's spiritual vacancy, and to the empty space in ourselves, where intentional vision should inform our souls.

The grounds of Lowell's exploration of this emptiness is his evocation at the opening of the poem of his boyhood vision. The

48

old aquarium is snow-bound—but it has also suffered neglect and dilapidation. This symbolizes a number of things—the fading of the old cod-fishing community (celebrated so energetically in his poetry by Charles Olson): the lack of first-hand public interest in animal life and biology: but, at a more radical level, it symbolizes a new aridness: a "desert of snow" surrounds the old aquarium, which once stood for a warmth of unity in the community, and the tanks, which once held a world of life, are "dry":

> The old South Boston Aquarium stands
> in a Sahara of snow now. Its broken windows are boarded.
> The bronze weathervane cod has lost half its scales.
> The airy tanks are dry.

The boarded windows suggest a blindness, to those meanings in the world that belong to intentional perception, like that of a child lost in reverie.

> Once my nose crawled like a snail on the glass;
> my hand tingled
> to burst the bubbles
> drifting from the noses of the cowed, compliant fish.

His nose itself almost belongs to the "dark downward and vegetating kingdom": his hand tingles with life and expectancy—wants to reach out into that world to burst the bubbles: but to burst them out of joy, joy in childish experiment, moving forward excitedly into the world and future time. The boy child has some contempt for the fish, which have been penned in the aquarium, and he feels a superiority to them in his own freedom, and his imaginative preoccupation with this mysterious world of life:

> My hand draws back. I often sigh still
> for the dark downward and vegetating kingdom
> of the fish and reptile.

The poet draws back his hand, because, as an adult, he cannot achieve this kind of fascination with the mysterious world of the intangible: the old traditions are gone; the aquarium cod have gone: the touch with life has gone. Today, he looks into a different tank, a different kettle of fish:

49

> One morning last March,
> I pressed against the new barbed and galvanized
>
> fence on the Boston Common. Behind their cage,
> yellow dinosaur steamshovels were grunting
> as they cropped up tons of mush and grass
> to gouge their underworld garage.
>
> Parking spaces luxuriate like civic
> sandpiles in the heart of Boston . . .

The language becomes that of the modern world, with its feet in journalism: "barbed", "galvanized", "dinosaur" (in Disneyland there are big life-size plastic dinosaurs), "underworld". In contrast to the vegetating kingdom we have "parking spaces" which *luxuriate* like *civic sandpiles*. Our luxury is useless, sterile space (later, as we shall see, it *slides by on grease*, by comparison with the compliant movement of the fish in the tanks): the plethora of space for *parking* in the *underworld* is as arid as the heaps of sand dumped all over the place to make the concrete. The crops of mush, the sahara of snow, the sandpiles surround this space with heaps of material being moved around, pointlessly—while the *civic* authority that gouges them has lost its sense of community functions and ideals in a mere adjustment of the sterile environment.

> A girdle of orange, Puritan-pumpkin colored girders
> braces the tingling Statehouse,
>
> shaking over the excavations . . .

The only connection between this civic power and the Puritan tradition is in the colour of the paint used to prevent rust on the girders, which just happens to be the colour of pumpkins. The little boy's hand tingled with expectancy and the intentional: here the old Statehouse tingles with the expectancy of being undermined, of collapsing into the excavations. It will not, of course; but instead of standing on firm ground symbolizing historical continuity, it is itself almost swallowed, by rapid but pointless change, fallen into the "new space", the new emptiness.

Lowell might be supposed merely to be "setting the scene" for his attention to the monument: but he is also setting a spiritual scene: the monument exists only by a kind of ignorant tolerance, in the heart of a new and barbaric emptiness (we may compare Venice, overcome by pollution from Mestre, or Roman sites under investigation in England, hurriedly excavated before being buried under a mass of concrete).

> . . . as it faces Colonel Shaw
> and his bell-cheeked Negro infantry
> on St. Gaudens' shaking Civil War relief,
> propped by a plank splint against the garage's earthquake

["St. Gaudens" of course is the name of the architect.]

The monument is a symbol, but is at the moment "propped" by a "plank" against the earthworks: so many of our symbols are in this predicament, merely temporarily sustained. The Statehouse is shaking under the onslaughts of the machine, and so is the bas relief. But Lowell depicts these all the same as the products of persons: "Colonel Shaw", the "bell-cheeked Negro infantry", "St. Gaudens".

> Two months after marching through Boston,
> half the regiment was dead;
> at the dedication,
> William James could almost hear the bronze Negroes breathe . . .

We go back to an earlier period, which contrasts sharply with the present, where the new dinosaurs are blindly at work. The men in the Civil War do not fall into a moral void: they march off to die. Then they are flung in a ditch. (My tenses indicate a perplexity about time.) When the monument is unveiled, a distinguished intellectual, a psychologist, says he is made to feel they breathe again, so life-like is the bronze. But a deep irony underlines the poem: the bas-relief is not shaking with life, but with death. The actual bronze soldiers are not alive, and never were: they are metal. The negro soldiers they represent were already long dead at the dedication. Yet by a strange ambiguity, they seem more alive symbolized in the sculpture, because of their act of courage, than the emptiness round about it. The symbol of their (dead) courage is alive: the symbolic (live) space of barbarism is empty and dead.

What is still alive in the monument is their decisive choice, to act in that way: and this disturbs the society of today:

> Their monument sticks like a fishbone
> in the city's throat.
> Its Colonel is as lean
> as a compass needle.

He points, like a compass needle, to an exact moral direction: the monument celebrates a life of sparse dedication, which is only irritating to the sensual barbarism of today's affluent America.

> He has an angry wrenlike vigilance,
> a greyhound's gentle tautness:
> he seems to wince at pleasure,
> and suffocate for privacy.

> He is out of bounds now . . .

The statue is perhaps marked "OUT OF BOUNDS"; but it is the symbolized qualities of man as a moral being which are out of bounds: beyond the bounds of the contemporary sensibility, and "beyond the pale" where present-day society is concerned. What price "angry wrenlike vigilance" and "gentle tautness" when even the foundations of civic community values are being shaken— simply to provide space, for the cars that slide by in "savage servility"? Those who judge literature in terms of politics and class would perhaps regard Lowell's attitude as "elitist": he cherishes the values of a traditional, aristocratic ruling class. Yet his concern—for the loss of meaning—is universal.

For his use of Colonel Shaw is no more than (say) Shakespeare's use of kings or lords, to investigate aspects of human nature and the values by which men exist and can go on surviving. Such *wrenlike vigilance* and *gentle tautness* could be found among negroes (as they are in *Uncle Tom's Cabin*) or poor folk (as they are in *Huckleberry Finn*), or working-class people (as they are in Dickens): the point is that there are important moral qualities which are lost to view in our society altogether, between the steam-shovel barbarism of economic growth and expansion, and the thought about man of those who merely accept a parallel materialism—to whom such moral qualities are as much out of bounds. Who today, in London's culture, or the climate of our predominant

52

"enlightenment", would have any respect for the "privacy" for which Colonel Shaw seems to suffocate?

Yet often, such vigilance had its penalties: the cost was often death: DULCE ET DECORUM EST:

> He rejoices in man's lovely,
> peculiar power to choose life and die—
> when he leads his black soldiers to death,
> he cannot bend his back.

This is both a comment on the statue, which perhaps exaggerates the unbending fearlessness: but it is also a comment on the subject of the sculpture: the word "cannot" suggests a limitation, a stiff-necked, unbending quality in the colonel, which meant that he went to his death in inflexible determination. Yet who could deny the high value, in such rejoicing in man's capacity, if he chooses, to die for a purpose: this is his "peculiar power"—and it is or can be morally "lovely". But, now we have had Hiroshima, and are faced with new and immense moral emptiness—dare we continue to speak of this "lovely, peculiar power . . ."? In those days, it was possible to seem more "alive" by choosing death: morally, it can be more authentic to choose "life" and die. But at the same time, we cannot speak of such qualities without dread: "lovely", and "to choose life and die" are phrases full of irony— while the word "peculiar" means more than "strange": it means more specifically "belonging to man because of his will and his consciousness—his moral dimension—which distinguishes him from the beasts."[1]

Once, these peculiar qualities were part of a predominant civilization:

> On a thousand small town New England greens,
> the old white churches hold their air
> of sparse, sincere rebellion; frayed flags
> quilt the graveyards of the Grand Army of the Republic

Today, the relics of that civilization are wearing thin:

> The stone statues of the abstract Union Soldier
> grow slimmer and younger each year—
> wasp-waisted, they doze over muskets
> and muse through their sideburns . . .

53

—again, we have the juxtaposition of living man and dead arte-
fact. But the apparent way in which the soldiers seem to become
younger is in fact a process of erosion. Their apparent musing and
dozing is in fact the static, bowed posture of dead stone, wearing
away in the rain. Their meaning is being worn away, too.

Those who choose to die, like Shaw, sought no monuments·
they only wanted the ditch:

> Where his son's body was thrown
> and lost with his "niggers".

Today: "The ditch is nearer". The statues and monuments seem
remote from us: the reality behind them is the ditch full of dead
bodies. But the poet is looking into a vast ditch, being dug under
the Statehouse and its monument—and this space seems to the
poet like the great spaces of our wars—whole cities devastated,
whole areas become a vast crater:

> The ditch is nearer.
> There are no statues for the last war here;
> On Boylston Street, a commercial photograph
> shows Hiroshima boiling
>
> Over a Mosler Safe, the "Rock of Ages"
> that survived the blast.

The great desert of atomic fission, obliterating hundreds of thou-
sands of people, cannot be symbolized—as Colonel Shaw's battle
can be. Symbolism is itself devastated: the hideous act of mass
extermination is trivialized by being used as an advertisement, to
sell safes—in which to keep your money. Someone's money "survived" that holocaust: this has its own symbolism. But even religious faith and its meanings are cheapened by the use of a
hymn-tune as the name of this safe.

All these trivializations belong to a moral decline, a collapse of
"tautness" and "vigilance" in the dimension of meaning, of that
complex in which choice and action are taken. This is why the poet
goes on to say "space is nearer": what we have lost is each man's
"philosophical space" in the general decay of meanings and moral
values:

> Space is nearer.
> When I crouch to my television set,
> the drained faces of Negro school-children rise like balloons.

Leaving his position gazing into the big empty space of the car-park (so different from the boy peering into the aquarium tank) he sits "crouching" at his television set. The attitude contrasts with the musing postures of the Union Soldier, and the wrenlike vigilance of Colonel Shaw; it is man's subservience to technology, and to the emptiness of the literalism (and bubbles) of the media. At the same time all the idealism of the negro soldiers and the North in the Civil War, the "bubble" of their pursuit of equality and freedom, is reduced to the "balloons" of the faces of disadvantaged negro children on TV, the screen itself a bubble.

Colonel Shaw continues—in death, in the monument—to ride the bubble of his vision and hope: he hopes for the great "break" whereby all men shall become free and equal.

> Colonel Shaw
> is riding on his bubble,
> he waits
> for the bléssed break.

But it hasn't come: it is as if the impulse represented by the Civil War has become "drained", has led to the savage servility, the ditch, the new meaningless space:

> The Aquarium is gone. Everywhere,
> giant finned cars nose forward like fish;
> a savage servility
> slides by on grease.

The word "nose" links the end of the poem with the beginning, and is a word which symbolizes intentionality: the boy's nose pressed against the glass was expressing (like his "tingling" hand) a bodily urge to move forward into his world—into a world he was both making his own, and which was full of dark mystery. But the way the car's nose is blunt and insolent rather than a searching into a dark mysterious world.

The cars nosing forward like fish do not release fascinating bubbles. They simply fill the parking spaces. They are not mysterious, but servile—they do what they are told (and this "cowed, compliant" quality was the worst aspect of the fish in the tanks). The boy wanted to free the fish from their imprisonment—yearning for a world which was the "dark downward and vegetating kingdom" of Creation. But this, too, is a symbol of the creative unconscious—that which underlies the problems of act and choice. The adult poet cannot feel anything but impotent contempt, for the "giant finned cars" which slide by on grease: they go easily, and they "nose forward"—but they are locked in a world which has lost its capacities for vigilance and tautness—and for meaning, value and imagination.

The poem is full of images of space; of emptying and filling space. At the deepest level, these are images of the *Dasein* problem—of nothingness sweeping everything away ("the ditch is nearer . . . space is nearer . . ."), and of the problem of asserting "being there" against it.

The child was much more able to look forward to a sense of "being there" in his interaction with the fish, the attention to natural science, the fishing industry, the New England community, Boston, America and her history. All these have decayed—the tanks are dry, the scales have gone, the windows are boarded up, the earth dug away under the State house and the monument—for space, for more and more space, for nothing but "parking" a savage servility, that "noses forward" but cannot convey a sense of meaningful existence: nor can religion (which is reduced to the level of old hymns advertising "safes"—which can yield no other security), nor can political choice and action: nor can bravery, nor ideals (which dissolve into the bubble of the television set)—*but nor can poetry, nor can creative art.* For the quotation from William James, and all the irony in the descriptions of the statues and monuments, convey a deep doubtfulness about the value of poetry itself: as Ezra Pound puts it:

> The "age demanded" chiefly a mould in plaster,
> Made with no loss of time,
> A prose kinema, not, not assuredly alabaster
> Or the "sculpture" of rhyme.
>
> (*Hugh Selwyn Mauberley, Selected Poems,* 1928)

And once a poet feels like this, he cannot move from the spot where, trembling, he is transfixed by the dead space that threatens to envelop him and the world. Yet it has to be said, however, that Lowell has wrung out of this paralysis a marvellously poised and insightful poem, and to express such suffering is itself the first step towards a new freedom. But there remains the problem of moving forward from that transfixed paralysis, in the face of the new empty spaces of man's loss of meaning and potentia.

NOTE

1. Falstaff, of course, raises such questions around the concept of "Honour" in *Henry IV, Part I*!

4

The Lack of a Creative Theme:
Ezra Pound's *Stone mouths*
biting empty air and
Eliot's *Hollow Men*

In Robert Lowell's poem I have tried to indicate a certain kind of stasis, or paralysis, which I believe to be characteristic of modern poetry. Of course, Lowell has taken part in certain radical political movements in recent years. But what I am concerned with is not the poet's choices in the area of politics or his participation in events. I am concerned with the confidence with which he does his own job, whether he can feel that the power of imagination can alter the world, and make new worlds. Perhaps it is significant that Sylvia Plath expressed her debt to Robert Lowell: in the end her failure of confidence in the imagination led to suicide. There is a kind of "resignation" to the terrible facts of existence which leads to Ted Hughes's kind of nihilism, which I propose to examine below. Such failures of confidence, I believe, originate in the "failure to find a creative theme", in the whole tradition of modern poetry.

The phrase is Leavis's, and he uses it of Ezra Pound. This leads me to a dilemma which I would like to record. Every now and then I feel that I must introduce my students to Pound: yet every time I do so I end up with a feeling of sterility. I try to approach him by way of *Hugh Selwyn Mauberley*, because this poem expressed with concentration, wit and economy the failure of creativity in our century. In this, and other poems by Pound, one tastes the

58

petrification of creative powers, and the futility of trying to exercise the poetic impulse in our time, in phrases like this:

> Beneath half-watt rays,
> The eyes turn topaz . . .

> 'I was
> And no more exist;
> Here drifted
> An hedonist.'

> . . . his final
> Exclusion from the world of letters.

> Mouths biting empty air,
> The still stone dogs . . .

Yet (and I have the same problem with T. S. Eliot), one is left with a deep feeling of dissatisfaction. Leavis records, in detail and at great length, his own dissatisfactions over *Four Quartets*, in *The Living Principle* (1975). In the end the marvellous texture of the verse serves only to convey an inability in the man to believe in creativity, in human capacities to find meaning (although, in one's experience, the poet's words echo in one's mind, and give meanings, even to experiences in which one wished to find meaning, and found none).

Of course, Ezra Pound in *H.S.M.* is trying to chronicle a particular episode, the fin de siècle malaise, the profound trauma of the 1914–18 war, its vast destruction of youth, and the catastrophic effects upon consciousness. There is a sense in which we have not yet recovered from that catastrophe, which itself belonged to the same loss of faith, of belief in God, of the sense of what might be set against nothingness: all, indeed, that Nietzsche foresaw:

> disillusions as never told in the old days,
> hysterias, trench confessions,
> laughter out of dead bellies.

> There died in a myriad,
> And of the best, among them,
> For an old bitch gone in the teeth,
> For a botched civilization,

Charm, smiling at the good mouth,
Quick eyes gone under earth's lid,

For two gross of broken statues,
For a few thousand battered books.

As Leavis says, "It is significant that the pressure seems to derive
(we are reminded of Mr Yeats) from a recognition of bankruptcy,
of a devoted life summed up in futility!" (*New Bearings*, p. 138).
Leavis seems to take the poem as the expression of Pound's own
life:

> Mauberley is in the first place (the description suggests itself
> readily) the summing up of an individual life. It also has representa-
> tive value, reflecting as it does the miscellaneousness of modern
> culture, the absence of direction, of an alphabet of forms or of any
> one predominant idiom; the uncongeniality of the modern world to
> the artist; and his dubious status there . . . One might, at the risk
> of impertinence, call it quintessential autobiography, taking care,
> however, to add that it has the impersonality of great poetry: its
> technical perfection means a complete detachment and control
> (p. 139).

"Detachment" and "control" are, of course, words of positive
commendation in Leavis's criticism. Yet he is often severe on any
preoccupation with "form", at the expense of a content which
manifests "life". But surely Pound's "technical perfection", his
"complete detachment and control", are bound up with a failure
to find any way out of the sterility he registers?

Let me say at once that I endorse completely everything Leavis
goes on to say about *Mauberley*: "the whole is great poetry, at
once traditional and original." But isn't it (like Eliot's) great poetry
wrung out of the impossibility, not only of saying anything creative, but of finding a creative relationship with experience, finding
a creative perception? What we have to say is, I believe, that
Pound registers the failure of the old bearings: but he doesn't
really offer any new bearings—except by the indirectly creative
quality of his capacity to be "as the seventeenth-century poets
were, serious and light at the same time, sardonic and poignant,
flippant and intense", (p. 193)—in recording creative failure. But,
again, may we not challenge that commendation of the "sardonic",

60

and suggest perhaps that behind this there is a schizoid emptiness and a failure of personal philosophy?

In *Hugh Selwyn Mauberley* Pound is, as Leavis says, detached and "controlled". In some later fragments a personal note comes through which I find moving—moving because it speaks yet more directly of sterility and failure, even of the schnizoid predicament itself. Before we look at *Mauberley* in detail, it will perhaps help to look at *Canto CXVI* (*Drafts and Fragments*, p. 25)

> Came Neptunus
> > his mind leaping
> > > like dolphins,
> These concepts the human mind has attained.
> To make Cosmos—
> To achieve the possible—

At times we find in Pound a powerful recognition of the immense powers of consciousness, to make worlds, to imagine and attain what may be possible but which has not yet been brought into being.

In this poem he speaks as if he has paid a severe price for having such vision:

> I have brought the great ball of crystal;
> > who can lift it?
> Can you enter the great acorn of light?
> > But the beauty is not the madness
> Tho' my errors and wrecks lie about me.

Pound—suffering from a schizoid illness—is not one of those like Laing, who erect a cult of schizophrenia: he recognizes, like D. W. Winnicott, that the art cannot, either, bring health:

> "Have made a mass of laws"
> > (mucchio di leggi)
> Litterae nihil sanantes
> > Justinian's,
> a tangle of works unfinished.

Justinian appointed a commission of jurists to draw up a complete body of law: Pound compares himself to the Great Emperor of Constantinople who is remembered only for that: but despite the "laws" (and his *ABC of Reading*) Pound leaves only "a tangle of works unfinished".

And I am not a demigod,
I cannot make it cohere.
If love be not in the house there is nothing.
The voice of famine unheard.

(p. 26)

The rhythm here resembles that of Sylvia Plath's direct account of madness—and her account of the mouth-hole, "crying the locations" of the love-starved Regressed Libidinal Ego, the unborn infant self:

> The mouth-hole crying their locations
> Drunk as a foetus
> I suck at the paps of darkness.
> (*The Colossus,* p. 87)

Pound's *Canto* itself is full of disparate references brought together (Disney, Linnaeus, Jules Laforgue), but related to the quest for a transcending vision, a search for *il Paradiso*:

> a nice quiet paradise
>   over the shambles,
> And some climbing
>   before the take-off,
> to "see again",
> the verb is "see", not "walk on"
> i.e. it coheres all right
>   even if my notes do not cohere.

Some creative impulse unites all his striving, he sees that, and the impulse is to envisage, not to be actually in a paradise. The word "cohere" echoes the cry of Herakles at his dying moment in Pound's marvellous translation of *The Women of Trachis*:

> SPLENDOUR,
>   IT ALL COHERES . . .

Pound's striving is to overcome that schizoid terror recorded by Eliot: "I can connect / Nothing with nothing." Pound says

> Many errors,
>   a little rightness,
> to excuse this hell
>   and my paradiso.

62

And as to why they go wrong
thinking of rightness
And as to who will copy this palimpsest?
al poco giorno
ed al gran cerchio d'ombra

—somewhere between the small daytime hours and the great circle of the shadows is the answer to the problem of the meaning of life. Perhaps it is in the mosaic wall-images at Torcello: perhaps it is at Tigullio.[1] It is this gold thread that Pound declares he has always sought. His has been the perplexity of the schizoid who does not have a firm sense of meaning and values:

To confess wrong without losing rightness;
Charity I have had sometimes,
I cannot make it flow thru.

I find this a poignant admission, that Pound, with his inclination towards the fascistic, the solutions of hate—hating "usury", hating Jews—knew that he could only occasionally find love, and could not make it "flow through"—but that his impulse was to bring back "splendour", while all he could offer was a rushlight:

A little light, like a rushlight
to lead back to splendour.
(p. 27)

How different in this modest, diffident feeling Pound from the one who attacks *neschek* the serpent, the defiler, the crawling evil, slime, Τόξος, Fafnir the worm, Syphilis of the state, entering and corrupting all things—this is, the Pound who projects the dark emptiness in himself as hate, trying to expunge it as a blackness in others, and in the body politic.

Τόξος hic mali medium est
Here is the core of evil, the burning hell without let-up,
The canker corrupting all things, Fafnir the worm,
Syphilis of the State, of all kingdoms,
Wart of the common-weal,
Wenn-maker, corrupter of all things.
Darkness the defiler,
Twin evil of envy,
Snake of the seven heads, Hydra, entering all things . . .
(p. 28)

This sense of a split-off evil entity of force in the world is itself schizoid, and it is at this level of feelings about the identity in relation to the world that I wish to examine Pound's sterility, and his sterile influence on English poetry.

Of course, one needs to recognize that Pound said, "Of course I'm no more Mauberley than Eliot is Prufrock." He also said, "The worst muddle they get into [commentators on the poem] is in failing to see that Mauberley buries Ezra Pound in the first poem . . . gets rid of all his troublesome energies." But at the moment of embarking on the poem one has a strange feeling of double vision, of not being able to get the persona and poet into focus. Donald Davie says that Pound cannot be the "apprehensive and diffident Mauberley" because "Pound . . . alone among his associates and contemporaries had Browning's (and Chaucer's) zestful appetite for the multifarious variety of human personality and human activity" (*Ezra Pound: Poetry as Sculpture*, p. 318). But *is* that the impression one gets from Pound? One may admit the richness and poignancy of many of his poems, especially the translations: but nothing surely robustly Chaucerian? I believe (in *Canto CXVI*) Pound makes it quite clear he knew his own limitations here: "I cannot make it flow thru. . . ." (*Drafts and Fragments*, p. 27).

I believe this is what the motto of *Hugh Selwyn Mauberley* means: " 'VOCAT AESTUS IN UMBRAM' " (*Nemesianus*, IV). 'From the shade, summer calls . . .': an image of the desire to express ripeness, but a recognition that he cannot make it "cohere", being overcome by the shade—both of a philistine civilization, and his own schizoid coldness:

> And I am not a demigod
> I cannot make it cohere.
> If love be not in the house there is nothing.
> (p. 26)

This is from where we should begin in *Mauberley*: from a sterile character, a sterile persona in front of that character, and a sterile philosophy of existence, lacking in "Love's warm sunshine"[2] lacking *aestus*.

Yet, since Pound has achieved important poems, it is also true that

i.e. it coheres all right
even if my notes do not cohere . . .

So, the poem is about this dilemma, this dichotomy, this ambiguity. "Notes"—well, why take a phrase from M. Aurelius Olympius Nemesianus, a Roman poet at the court of the Emperor M. Aurelius Carus, who was struck dead by lightning in 283 B.C.? It implies, merely, that in desperation over the absence of love compacts and confidence, Pound feels he must rely on the most distant fragments of pedagogic references, on the one hand, and the "Mauberley persona" on the other. Yet this may be dismissed by us as a "distracting nuisance" (Davie, 1961, p. 101) so that *"Hugh Selwyn Mauberley* falls to pieces".

So, the sequence opens with a monumental ode to the poet himself, *E. P. Ode Pour L'election de son Sepulcre,* which expresses that ambiguity we find in *Drafts and Fragments*: "a tangle of words unfinished". Am I an "adjunct to the Muses' diadem"—or not? Villon passed, he tells us, from men's sight in *"L'an trentésme de son eage".* It was Ronsard who wrote an ode *Pour L'Election de son Sepulcre*—and he is certainly remembered.

> For three years, out of key with his time,
> He strove to resuscitate the dead art
> Of poetry: to maintain 'the sublime'
> In the old sense. Wrong from the start . . .

His concern, as Leavis says, has been "art", but behind this concern (as we feel from the word "resuscitate") is a deeper desire to create a *living* art, not merely to make "aesthetic discrimination".

Who is disagreeing with whom in the next lines?

> No, hardly, but seeing he had been born
> In a half-savage country, out of date.

It is as if Pound was never able to solve this problem, that his striving to maintain the sublime was "out of date", that he feels he must put "sublime" in inverted commas. We have tended to take him at his "word": but the truth is that the Impressionists didn't feel they were wrong or out-of-date, or that the "sublime" was inexpressible in a society which shewed its half-savagery by laughing at them. Charles Ives didn't feel it (and what is *The*

Hausatonic at Stockbridge but sublime?). Mahler didn't feel it. Hardy and Bonnard didn't feel it. The Henry James of *Portrait of A Lady* didn't feel it. So, what is missing from the poem is a really *convinced* recognition of the preciousness and thinness of Pound's art, and of the Villerant-like limitations of Pound, whatever Donald Davie says, as compared even with Yeats.

Yet, as soon as one has said as much, of course, as so often with Pound, the next two lines do give us something like that:

> But resolutely on wringing lilies from the acorn;
> Capaneus; trout for factitious bait . . .

The resolution deserved oaks perhaps, but it preciously strives after lilies: he is struck by lightning when scaling the walls like Capaneus, one of the seven heroes who marched against Thebes: he catches real trout, but with false flies, made by artifice like Yeats's golden nightingale.

The motto is taken from a writer who was at the court of a king who was struck by lightning: Capaneus was executed by Zeus in the same way. In this poem there is, I believe, an undercurrent of feeling that Pound himself has been in some way "stricken by the gods", and that the failure to make reparation is associated with this—that this failure to bring oaks out of acorns, to try instead to wring lilies from them, the use of false bait to catch real trout— the failure of confidence in creativity (like the confidence won by Yeats at the end of *Among School Children*) is related to that schizoid, blighted, condition.

But the beauty is not the madness Pound says in *Canto CXVI*: "Many errors, / a little rightness . . ." is all he feels able to achieve; and I believe all these are references to his schizoid problem, which was that of developing sufficient integration to be able to use symbols in a fully creative way, and yet feeling from time to time that he can't "make it" (as Sylvia Plath felt from time to time, as she expresses in her poem about stillborn poems, or in *The Wishing Box* about the dreadful failure of her imaginative powers). This, to a poet, feels like being struck dead by the gods: yet, at the same time he goes on, like Ulysses, seduced by the sirens of poetry, hypnotized by the story of Troy, facing perils, experiencing fragmented stalemate:

"Ἴδμεν γάρ τοι πάνθ',ός' ἐνὶ Τροίη"[3]
Caught in the unstopped ear;
Giving the rocks small lee-way
The chopped seas held him, therefore, that year.
His true Penelope was Flaubert,
He fished by obstinate isles;
Observed the elegance of Circe's hair
Rather than the mottoes on sundials.

Penelope was true to Ulysses: it is Flaubert who is true to him, and whom he seeks as "saint and martyr" of the artistic conscience (as Leavis puts it). But the obstinacy goes with "resolute" earlier: he has been flying his artificial baits in remote and difficult cultures, but yet has been seduced by the woman who turns men into pigs, while they exclaim over the elegance of her hair. The obstinacy and sensuality go unnoticed by both Leavis and Donald Davie: yet these, surely, are the troublesome energies "buried" in this first poem? And because they, libidinal impulses of aggression, *are* buried, the rest of *Hugh Selwyn Mauberley* moves towards sterility—so that, as Donald Davie notes, it is the "sleek head" of Venus Anadyomene which rises from the sea, not the breasts or loins. In the last line there is another reference to Villon: "the unfastidious blackguard" as Leavis remarks "whose 'wasted' life produced such a rich harvest of poetry" (a challenge surely to the *Scrutiny* moral atmosphere about which we would have liked more from Leavis—he having dismissed the author of *Fern Hill*, for example, as a "drunken lout"). The schizoid individual can generate beauty: but the problem always arises of bringing the mind-spun structures into relationship with "whole being".

Between "observed the elegance", "Circe's hair", and "the mottoes on sundials" we have a perplexity expressed in Pound, as to how to relate "art" to one's sensual (and sexual) life. How does the poet relate cliché admonitions of mutability to the dreaming state of being seduced—by libidinal woman, or sensual poetry? All this points to a sphere beyond the quotidian and the mundane and to the realms of *being* and *intentionality*: so, we have inverted commas:

Unaffected by "the march of events" . . .

—but there is a languid and bewildered air, belonging to that failure of confidence in the resolute, wringing work that writing is—a languidness that comes perhaps from Jules Laforgue, who conveys a similar perplexity and bewilderment:

> Quand j'organise une descente en Moi,
> J'en conviens, je trouve là, attablé
> Une societé un peu bien mêlée
> Et que je n'ai point vue à mes octrois . . .[4]

How can one relate the imagos of one's inner world to everyday existence?

Of course, Section II of Pound's poem is more immediately sympathetic, and we can give whole-hearted assent: indeed, it is the most penetrating and damning negative analysis of our society and its attitude to the Arts:

> The age demanded an image
> Of its accelerated grimace,
> Something for the modern stage . . .

—"accelerated" is the perfect word, and gathers force with the technological momentum—of cinematic technique, television faces everywhere, the car chase, the increased sophistication of film technology (how much the television advertisement with its need to exploit expensive time, and to make an IMPACT, has contributed to the phrase!) "Grimace", too, is a perfect word for the schizoid mask itself—the sex-symbol, the blank face of the humiliated human, the repeated images in Warhol's not-art, the Lichtenstein use of strip-cartoon, the accelerated athletics of pornography (not least on the "modern stage"). And, significantly, the "age demanded" itself comes to be put in inverted commas: today, with the decline even of editorial responsibility, and the triumph of exploitation, who decides, what the "age demands"? Opinion polls? Those who have created the "atmosphere" in which our culture can be persistently and deliberately debased?

One wonders what Pound, who could write

> Dance and make people blush,
> Dance the dance of the phallus
>   and tell anecdotes of Cybele!
> Speak of the indecorous conduct of the Gods! . . .
> Ruffle the skirts of prudes,
>   Speak of their knees and ankles . . .
>
>   (*Salutation the Second*)

68

would think of certain obscenities in today's entertainment in London.

> Not, at any rate, an Attic grace . . .
> Not, not certainly, the obscure reveries
> Of the inward gaze . . .
> Better mendacities . . .

This is a poem one might offer in a course to awaken students to the urgency of today's cultural problems. As Davie points out, there are continual shifts in tone, and here we have Hugh Selwyn Mauberley speaking, directing "his" intelligent irony against Pound himself—who spent so much of his time offering "the classics in paraphrase", not least his own version of the *Odyssey*. But "mendacities"—the justness is perhaps made clear by referring to Mr Anthony Burgess's latest novel, in which a life of Napoleon is written to the shape of Beethoven's *Eroica*, combined with fragments from a project bringing together (God save us) Jane Austen and the Marquis de Sade. This kind of destructiveness is a target of Pound's poem, because he can see that it undermines all possibility of getting beyond aestheticism, towards true creativity. As Davie says, he implies very plainly that English culture is riddled with commercialism and false values (though we may not agree that the message of the poem as a whole is acceptable as meaning that "no English artist is likely to do better than Mauberley's did").

Whatever one does about the Mauberley-Pound-persona problem, it is certain that in these lines Pound gives us an irony, and a felt poetry of negative emotion, that takes us to the heart of sterility of symbolism in our time:

> chiefly a mould in plaster
> The "age demanded"
> Made with no loss of time . . .

One thinks perhaps of children's sets for making model dogs, or of similar "art" sets (painting by numbers) for adults: or the alsatians and little girls holding their skirts which one can buy in kitsch shops: who "demands" such travesties of "sculpture"? In attachment to such "instant" sculpture, as compared with the sculpture at the "popular" level made by the mediaeval stone-mason, or the carver of miserichords, we "attach ourselves to the concrete", and *lose the future*. That is, we are not prepared to "go with" a Barbara Hepworth into a new unique form and creative experience: "we" (popular taste, that is) want an instant "copy"—and though we ask for this to be done "without loss of time", we forfeit creative time, by "demanding" the mass-produced travesties commerce thrusts upon us. This is the triumph of literalism. "Minimal" art removes all effort and creative time—and with these, symbolism and imagination, so that all that remains is a schizoid "concrete thinking", incapable of engaging with meaning.

In III Pound concentrates on the actual destruction of the symbol, at the deepest level of being. This section has perhaps had more influence on the Cambridge English school, and English poetry since, than any other major poem apart from *The Waste Land*. But from my point of view, there is something perverse in the emphasis, something missing. Leavis applauds the reaction against Victorianism, because during that period poetry had widely "ceased to interest the intelligent". But if we look at a Preface which Pound wrote to the *Poems* of Lionel Johnson we find some revealing emphases. At one point, for instance, Pound speaks of how Johnson's language "would never have deigned to be the common speech":

> It was part of his fear of life, a fear that he was not afraid of, but which he openly acknowledged [Nihilism]:
>> I shall be calm soon, with the calm death brings.
>> The skies are grey there without any star.
>
> (p. XVI)

The previous lines are:

> of life I am afraid.
> Where silent things, and unimpassioned things,
> Where things of nought, and things decaying, are:

But further down the page Pound says:

> I dare say our fashion is no more permanent than his fashion, but we are done with imaginative reason—at least for our time. Poetry is concerned with statement, not with arguments and conversions (p. XVII).

Pound begins this discussion by quoting Lionel Johnson's belief that poetry was *not* "a rendering of one's own time in the terms of one's own time", but "a using of the lineal term in the purest sense of that lineage. . . ."

Johnson was "not in accord with our present doctrines and ambitions":

> His language is a bookish dialect, or rather it is not a dialect, it is a curial speech, and our own is a natural speech, the language as spoken. We desire the words of poetry to follow the natural order. We would write nothing that we might not say actually in life—under emotion. Johnson's verse is full of inversions, but no one has written purer Imagisme than he has, in the line
>
> Clear lie the fields, and fade into the blue air.
>
> It has a beauty like the Chinese. . . .
>
> (p. vii)

Johnson wrote Latin, and "set himself the task of bringing into English all that he could of the finest of Latinity. He wrote an English that had grown out of Latin. He, at his worst, approached the Miltonian quagmire. . . ." In reading this Preface we begin to gain many insights into Pound and his influence on Leavis. This volume was published in 1914. Miltonian poetry is a "quagmire":[5] academic language with its inversion as poetry is rejected, in favour of natural speech and directness; the use of a language remote from natural speech (though Pound here seems to approve) is seen to go with a fear of life (with "Nihilism" in the background).

On the other hand, Johnson is respected "in part for his hardness, in part for his hatred of amateurishness".

> The impression of Lionel Johnson's verse is that of small slabs of ivory, firmly combined and contrived. There is a constant feeling of neatness, a sense of inherited order. Above all he respected his art. . . . (p ix).

It wasn't the vehicle of opinion, or doctrinaire: "It was the art of good writing. The last is a rare thing in England."

> One thinks that he had read and admired Gautier, or that at least, he had derived similar ambitions from some traditional source. One thinks that his poems are in short hard sentences. The reality is that they are full of definite statement. For better or worse they are doctrinal and nearly always dogmatic. He had the blessed habit of knowing his own mind, and this was rare among writers of his decade (p. viii).

71

Pound's interest, then, is in a certain kind of disciplined attention to "art", to a non-amateurish capacity to put together
sentences like small slabs of ivory, firmly contrived and combined
form. That is "art". But, of course, there is something else required—which is that quality Pound could not fail to see in Hardy.
And now follows as astonishing comment:

> The "nineties" have chiefly gone out because of their muzziness, be-
> cause of a softness derived, I think, not from books but from Impres-
> sionist painting. They riot with half decayed fruit (p. viii).

What I find interesting in this is that Pound should find "soft-
ness" and "muzziness" as an influence coming from Impressionist
painting, when one's impression of that creative outburst is its
capacity for new definition: and, moreover, not the definitions of
passive slavish recording of things, but a kind of involved definition
in which the world is coloured by the being-in-the-world who sees
it.[6] But the last remark is strange: for one does not associate the
nineties with ripeness or over-ripeness—though one may smell
decay in it. There seem no grounds for tracing this back to the
Impressionists—except perhaps for Van Gogh's ear and Gaugin's
syphilis. There was never a creative moment less given to morbidity, rottenness, decay or indulgence in decay. And it is utterly distinct from the Pre-Raphaelites' paintings of Lizzie Siddal as
Ophelia, or the muzziness of the poetry of William Morris and
Rossetti.

These strange remarks of Pound's illuminate, I believe, a whole
stream in contemporary letters: a preoccupation with discipline
in the handling of language, and a concern for the soundness of
the creative symbol—but combined with *a fear of creative
dynamics, of passion, even of intentional vision.* Strange as it may
seem, Pound is as afraid of life, as nihilistic as Lionel Johnson, in
his pedagogy. He seems able only to be able to find passion, joy
and tragedy, in some distant piece from Li Po or Villon. He often
resorts to defence against feeling in irony and the shifts of tone
and persona: "I cannot make it flow thru." The same problem, of
course, afflicts Eliot, and it is the schizoid one, involving a schizoid
sense of superiority to normal existence.[7]

Thus, in section III, one may agree with the castigation of our
culture: but there is something missing. There is no admission

72

of those possibilities which can transcend our situation, even our endemic disease of language. Since Pound's poem there have been Vaughan Williams, Messaien, Aaron Copland, Bonnard, Britten, Henry Moore, Solzhenitsyn, and D. H. Lawrence: *Hugh Selwyn Mauberley* presses upon us a conviction that creativity could not exist in our time, but surely this is not true?

> The tea-rose tea-gown, etc
> Supplants the mousseline of Cos,
> The pianola 'replaces'
> Sappho's barbitos.

Like the phallus dance he asks his poems to perform, it must be said, Pound's Dionysiac libidinal propensities are mental ones. The idolization of Pan and the body-life of the Bacchanalia (like those occasionally found in C. S. Lewis as in the Narnia Books) are merely bookish. One cannot imagine the author ever, in fact, engaged in an orgy; and one certainly can't imagine Pound being anything but horrified by the naked dancing and simulated copulation (or real copulation) on the stage and screen today.

So what does he mean? Cos was famous for its "Light transparent dresses called 'Coae vestes' ": Sappho's female society would listen to stringed instruments called barbitos. But the playing of instruments in Vienna under Mahler was raised to a pitch of quality unthinkable to the Greeks, while there is no shortage in the modern world of diaphanous *coae vestes* in truly beautiful balletic works, even though surburban house-wives may wear conventional tea-gowns and grow stereotyped tea-roses. (*Some* new cultivated roses are lovely!) There *is* a debasement abroad in our time, of quality and meaning at the level of the middle-brow. But it has not wholly replaced or supplanted all creative symbolism. We may take the contrast between mechanical sound and creative immediacy (involving what Stravinsky called "the risk" in live music) in pianolas/barbitos. But there is also in Pound an unreal idolization of the classical world, to devalue our world unfairly by contrast:

> Christ follows Dionysus,
> Phallic and ambrosial
> Made way for macerations;
> Caliban casts out Ariel.

73

Again, Pound's Dionysian yearning is mental. Nietzsche tried to define the necessary combination of the Dionysiac and Apollonian required to restore wholeness to man, and it is no use simply bewailing the loss of the Dionysiac. What we need is a subtle combination of the libidinal with the numinous. The rise of Christendom cannot really be seen as the substitution of asceticism for good living (if, say, we think of Chaucer's Frankleyn)—though the image of Caliban casting out Ariel is more telling, about our age. Yet even here it might be more exact to write of Caliban casting out Prospero.

> All things are a flowing
> Sage Heracleitus says;
> But a tawdry cheapness
> Shall outlast our days . . .

The poem, says F. R. Leavis, is not only "tragically serious but solemn": "The second and third poems introduce the modern world of mass-production and levelling-down, a world that has destroyed the traditions and is hostile, not only to the artist, but to all distinction of spirit" (p. 145).

That fits in very well with the thesis of *Culture and Environment*: but the philosophical anthropology of III is surely not very profound? The poem lapses into invective, for instance, over "a tawdry cheapness". What has this to do with Heracleitus, (who incidentally believed knowledge to be based on perception by the senses)? The use of a reference to classical philosophy here is journalistic: "Heracleitus said everything was in a state of flux— well, he ought to see our world." It isn't as intelligent a use of such invocations as Yeats's "Plato thought Nature but a spume that played. . . ."

And what is wrong with "tawdry cheapness" in this context? And how does our tawdry cheapness differ from that of popular taste in Ancient Greece or whatever? It is difficult (I find in teaching) to find exactly how to interpret Pound's irony here—and some students find it simply snobbish, as if Pound were saying "for one who has tasted the exactitude of classical writers, it is painful to go into Woolworth's". Is he criticizing modern commerce, or Christianity (has it offered no beauty since the mysteries were celebrated at Samothrace)? What is the relationship between

74

debasement of standards and the love of the pristine qualities of the Early Christian Church?

What gives the poem some unity is its juxtaposition of symbols, empty on the one hand, and alive on the other. Its important central theme is the *loss of meaning in symbols*:

> Faun's flesh is not to us,
> Nor the saint's vision.
> We have the Press for wafer;
> Franchise for circumcision

At the time of an election, we are only too aware of the relevance of Pound's irony:

> All men, in law, are equals.
> Free of Pisistratus,
> We choose a knave or an eunuch
> To rule over us.

Pisistratus was a tyrant who achieved power by despicable tricks: a model, one might think, for the fascists Pound later admired.

But, one's intelligence persistently asks, are these the only alternatives? Is it true that to recognize that men are equal in law must inevitably be followed by rule by knaves or fools? Are democracy, the Press, franchise equality, inevitably bound up with the loss of vision, and the decline of being? How do we associate the commercialization of the idea of beauty and goodness (TO KALON) with the difference between Samothrace and Christianity (and must all Christian beauty be reject after Samothrace?—is there no Christian comparable in [say] Bruckner or Messaien?)

If Leavis is right about poetry and intelligence the poem should provoke us to ask such questions, just as—by Davie's account— Pound's poetry should send us to the British Museum. But to ask them is to expose the narrow pedagogic prejudice behind Pound's position, vis à vis the decay of meaning. The "phallic" is looking at old erotic prints or sculptures: the yearning for circumcision is nostalgia for that kind of sense of mystery—with no thought of its superstitious cruelty. (If Pound were to visit present-day circumcision of a child of eight in Turkey he would have felt very differently, and would have seen it as barbarous. So, too, he might, had he been brought to realize by studying life in Africa that female circumcision actually seems to represent an unconscious attack on woman, by denying her sexual pleasure as a penalty for her creativity, of which man is envious.[8])

I am bringing up to the judgement of Pound's poem a philosophical anthropology which is itself tremendously concerned about the decline of symbolism—because this is a primary human need. What this philosophical anthropology would see by contrast is a democratization of the capacity for using symbolism, and a rich experience of creativity. But Pound does not express a desire for this in his poem. For him, *Caliban, a tawdry cheapness, the substitution of the Press for wafer and the failure of politics are an inevitable consequence of populism, of democracy*. On the other hand, mousseline, Sappho's barbitos, TO KALON, and the saint's vision are associated with minority groups, with mystery cults, and his own kind of intellectual sophistication. His target is not commercial debasement, but *democracy*—and there is a sneer in the irony focussing on that word "free' in "Free of Pisistratus . . ." —so much so that one almost expects inverted commas round it. But who does not want to be free of a Pisistratus—even at the cost of having some fools and knaves in government as the price to be paid for democracy?

Pound's antithetical opposition between all that he cultivates from the past that is meaningful, and a universal "tinniness" of contemporary England is, in fact itself sterile—examined in the light of philosophical anthropology—*because it is not based on the recognition that there is a thwarted craving for symbolic creativity, for meaning, in all men*. Yet the failure of our civilization lies in not providing for such hunger for meaning at all levels. It does not lie in "bad taste", in the failure of mass culture to come up to scratch, by contrast with Sapphic orgies or Dionysiac rituals. The sterility of our failure to penetrate into the universal human need which this civilization thwarts by its triviality is a sterility which not only affected the "Culture and Environment" movement: *it infected the poetry of negative emotions*, which has inclined it to be defeatist. To give allegiance to Pound's art may be to forfeit intentionality and hope, and to connive, albeit complainingly, in the decline of meaning—even, at times, to hasten that decline. To take a clear example from another poet, I believe that the "HURRY UP PLEASE IT'S TIME" passage from the *Waste Land*, by its gross and malice-laden caricature of the sensual destructiveness of "the people", has this kind of effect—an effect we can place, I believe, if we compare it with a story by D. H. Lawrence such as *Odour of Chrysanthemums*, or a passage in a novel by Solzhenitsyn, in which "people" are treated with a sense of the essential dignity of which they are capable: their capacity for self-transcendence.

The double-exposure effect of Pound's persona and the uneasy confusion of Mauberley with the Self is dispelled in Section IV. I find this poem deeply moving, more so than anything else in Pound, and I have no doubt the deep emotions are "his". The poem may be, as Donald Davie tells us "a learned imitation of the measures of the late-Greek pastoral poet Bion": but the "form" here (as in David Jones' *In Parenthesis*) serves to keep under control almost uncontrollable feelings, the inexpressible traumatic shock. The reiterations ("some . . . some . . . some", "home to . . . home to" . . . "as never before . . . as never before") echo the immense "wastage": one seems to see processions of "Young blood and high blood/Fair cheeks, and fine bodies" on their way to the cemetery's field of crosses.

And in V there is genuine passion in the bitterness and rhythm:

> For an old bitch gone in the teeth . . .
> For a few thousand battered books . . .

Here the passion of the pedagogue for his "civilization" is seen for what it is—but *was* the 1914–18 war fought for that? There are those who think it was fought, in part, over the division of Africa, and over the conflicting interests of European industrialisms. At a deeper level, however, it can be said to have been a catastrophe, of a conflict between "objectivity" and old deluded ideas of a stand on values: the mass industrialization of war, as in the Maxim gun, met ideas of valour and conquest appropriate to the age of the sword and horse. By no means a "defence" of civilized values, it was a clash of archaic values with the new barbarism—a catastrophe of consciousness.

At any rate, that cataclysm, from which the English sensibility has never recovered, lies behind the inability to believe in anything, and the impulse to compare with the fragmentary and vacant *now* the clear Apollyonic of the past

O bright Apollo

τίν’ ἄνδρα, τίν’ ἥρωα, τίνα θεὸν,[9]

What god, man, or hero
Shall I place a tin wreath upon!

—the tin wreath of Horatio Bottomley journalism becomes a tin hat, and the phrase "putting a tin lid on it", lies beneath the contempt expressed here, and the poignant lament for symbols gone trashy.

The rest of the sequence is full of images of impotence, whose meanings can be studied with the help of Donald Davie's brilliant analysis. It is a historical sketch of a whole period: the Pre-Raphaelites painting Miss Siddal; Fitzgerald; Dowson and Johnson; Max Beerbohm (perhaps); Arnold Bennett; the modern woman; the patron. As Donald Davie shows, how intense at times is the concentrated communication of sterility.

> "Daphne with her thighs in bark
> Stretches toward me her leafy hands"—
> Subjectively. In the stuffed-satin drawing-room.
> I await the Lady Valentine's commands.

Mauberley's way of dressing does not "stimulate" in her a "durable passion". With sophisticated concentration Pound conveys to us that she is the poet's mistress as well as patron, but her attentions have purposes quite distinct from those of genuine intelligent understanding or taste. He is doubtful of the value of her "well-gowned" approbation, but not of her vocation. ("Well-gowned" and "stuffed-satin" have the effect Pope achieves in his line, "To rest, the cushion and soft dean invite".)
Poetry takes on a mere role as socialite fashion:

> Poetry, her burden of ideas,
> The edge, uncertain, but a means of blending
> With other strata
> Where the lower and the higher have ending,
> A hook to catch the Lady Jane's attention,
> A modulation toward the theatre,
> Also, in the case of revolution,
> A possible friend and comforter.

She wants to put one up over a rival society lady, perhaps to get on to the stage, and, if social trouble breaks out, she'll be helped to find a sanctuary by her intellectual protegés, like HSM himself.

As Davie shows, the first stanza conveys the sterility of a poetry sustained by such patronage:

> The quotation marks are Pound's acknowledgement that the first two lines are an adaptation from *Le Chateau du Souvenir* by Gautier. But the borrowing is made utterly Poundian by the deflating word "subjectively", which meets the reader as he swings around the line-ending, thus achieving the maximum surprise and shock. In the Greek legend the river-nymph Daphne was saved from ravishment by the amorous god Apollo, when her father, the river deity, transformed her on the instant into a laurel tree.

Mauberley is no Apollo, but a poet attending to the whims of a patroness from whom he hopes to receive the laurel-wreath. But in reality she represents "no body or principle of taste as could permit the poet to value her approval. It would require nothing less than a divine miracle to metamorphose her in this way, from a false patroness to a true one!" (Davie, p. 323).

But, again, there is a deeper symbolism: the god-transmuted thighs in bark, the hands leafy with growth, or with tributes to creativity, stretch toward him—but only in a *memory* of Gautier, and behind that a memory of classical mythology, only in his own ironic translation and borrowing, only to Mauberley the aesthete from a "stuffed-satin" woman, trying to hook some other woman's attention, in her low and calculating way, rather than serve genuine art. Eliot's complaint seems relevant: "I have measured out my life with coffee spoons."—How can poetry survive in this world? How can it survive in the world of low journalism and advertisement copy-writing?

> Conduct, on the other hand, the soul
> "Which the highest cultures have nourished"
> To Fleet St. where
> Dr. Johnson flourished
>
> Beside this thoroughfare
> The sale of half-hose has
> Long since superseded the cultivation
> Of Pierian roses.

79

Advertising and commerce, the sale of half-hose, have increasingly eroded the last trace of editorial responsibility and journalistic integrity, such as Dr Johnson represented (who could be both journalist, as writer of the proceedings of Parliament, and a great critic). The Pierian roses of poetry are drowned in the Fleet Dyke itself, in the general mess of language.

Envoi, as Davie suggests, is addressed to London by Pound himself: "Siftings on siftings in oblivion. . . ."

The poem henceforth tends towards two themes: careful, obsessional, attention to form in "sculpture", and self-defeat. Pound compares fine craft-work of the past continually with his persona's inability

> Colourless . . .
> . . . lacking the skill
> To forge Achaia . . .
>
> Drifted . . . drifted precipitate
> Asking time to be rid of . . .
> Of his bewilderment . . .
>
> To be certain . . . certain . . .

Can this be about "Mauberley"? Isn't it about the Pound who "cannot make it flow thru"? Isn't it about the obsession with form of which he speaks (of himself) so poignantly in *Canto XCVI*? It is the same voice.

> Mouths biting empty air,
> The still stone dogs,
> Caught in metamorphosis, were
> Left him as epilogues.

Such images in the poem, in fact, are characteristically schizoid,[10] and may be compared with those of Sylvia Plath—of "anaesthesis", of the failure of perception expressed in abstract, diagnostic, Latinate (almost medical) language

> He had passed, inconscient, full gaze,
> The wide-banded irides
> And Botticellian sprays implied
> In their disastasis;
> Which anaesthesis, noted a year late,
> And weighed, revealed his great affect.

The petrified dogs are his epilogue because they suffer meta-morphosis just as they are biting—the oral impulse becomes petri-fied, biting empty air, as it seeks its engagement with the object. A hunger for both love and meaning is, as it were, struck in the mouth. And as in the *Canto* discussed above, the failure is linked with the fact that love is "not in the house": the motto to the poems is this:

"Qu'est ce qu'ils savent de l'amour, et qu'est ce qu'ils pouvent comprendre?
S'ils ne comprennent pas la poésie, s'ils ne sentent pas la musique, qu'est ce qu'ils peuvent comprendre de cette passion en comparaison avec laquel la rose est grossière et le parfum violettes un tonnerre?"

(CAID ALI)

Yet this is doublebarbed, for the poem is dry and loveless—and the aesthetic obsessions of "Mauberley" are no pathway here to the finer vibrations of love, which are so finely superior to the coarse ones of the rose and violet.

In *The Age Demanded* the language becomes that of textbooks of aesthetics, or committee language.

> Incapable of the least utterance or composition,
> Emendation, conservation of the "better tradition",
> Refinement of medium, elimination of superfluities,
> August attraction or concentration.
> Nothing, in brief, but maudlin confession,
> Irresponse to human aggression.

"Mauberley" is here trapped in his own posture towards the world. Impressions burst in upon his aesthetic preoccupations with "the glow of porcelain":

> The coral isle, the lion-coloured sand
> Burst in upon the porcelain reverie:
> Impetuous troubling
> Of his imagery . . .
>
> Invitation, mere invitation of perceptivity
> Gradually led him to the isolation
> Which these presents place . . .

"these presents"—the language is almost that of a legal document. There are "phantasmal sea-urges", but in his abstraction he is in a state of accidie:

> Strengthened . . .
> > his desire for survival,
> But in the most strenuous moods,
> Became an Olympian *apathein*
> In the presence of selected perceptions.

Apathein means "a state of not suffering"—but also here, surely, "of not feeling". In the next poem, as Donald Davie points out, there are references to Flaubert's *Salammbô*, "metaphors from the physical world for the state of abstracted passivity" which is now Mauberley's condition: the oar stuck in sand on the beach marks the grave of one who drifted into nothingness a hedonist:

> "I was
> And I no more exist;
> Here drifted
> An hedonist"

Elbenor's inscription read "a man of no fortune and with a name to come": both the epitaph for Mauberley (? and Pound) and that invoked from Homer raise the *Dasein* problem.

What shall we set against our existlessness? Can it be the "Medaillon" of the last poem? Who is speaking it? Davie believes it must be Mauberley, the medallist of poetry. But in its "rhythmical inertness" don't we experience Pound's own failure of confidence—in his kind of art, the Flaubertian doctrine of *"le mot juste"*, the programmes of the Imagists, to which Davie refers?

> All his scrupulous research for *le mot juste* to describe the braids of hair only transforms the hair with all its organic expressiveness into the inertness of metal. Venus Anadyomene, the mythological expression of how sexual and other vitality is renewed, hardens under Mauberley's hand into the glazed frontispiece to a book on Comparative Religion . . . Mauberley's deficiencies as a writer are identical with his deficiences as a human being (p. 329).

Davie sees the woman here as the same whose challenge earlier Mauberley could only evade. *"Everything that is hard, metallic and ominous in Mauberley's description of her as an image in a poem symbolizes his fear of her as a person, and his inability to meet her with any sort of human response."* So, the petrifaction sets in, out of a fear of the "flowing through" of love (as in Laing's patients).

Let us not, however, talk of "deficiencies as a human being", and land ourselves in discussions of personality, but rather talk of attitudes to life, of capacities to perceive and relate. And let us bring to bear on this, at the conclusion of *Hugh Selwyn Mauberley* ("life and contacts") the assertion from philosophical anthropology that our capacity to perceive in a meaningful way, to act freely and responsibly, is bound up with our capacities to "find the significant other"—to love. In *Drafts and Fragments* Pound clearly bewails the failure of love in his perception and art.

The human being in *Medallion* is turned, with the most concentrated aesthetic attention, into a *thing*—a thing of studied beauty —carved or sculptured by a steely kind of perceptivity: glazed, petrified by the dim light, turned into stone, spun,

> The face-oval beneath the glaze,
> Bright in its suave bounding-line, as,
> Beneath half-watt rays.
> The eyes turn topaz.

And the final image is of the woman dying: her eyes are not only turned up, but turned to (beautiful) stone. The art is as dead to meaning as is "comparative religion": the poet writes about her, of art even, artistically: but he cannot "make it flow thru", except where "a little light . . . coheres".

Hugh Selwyn Mauberley is thus a poem about the failure of creative perception, of love, of finding the significant other, of finding humanness. The human being is turned into *artifice* at the end, out of a flight from life, akin to Lionel Johnson's itself, out of fear. And (as we know from that self-confession, out of a dead belly, in the *Canto* CXVI) this creative death of which Pound writes is not only the death and petrification of the persona *Hugh Selwyn Mauberley*, but also of the Pound in double focus with him, schizoid and unable to find his whole humanness. Where does Pound write a poem which has a creative theme as much in touch with life as the Hardy of *After a Journey* which he so much admired? Nowhere, though there are glimpses, at a distance, in some translations (e.g. *Liu Ch'e*).

Moreover, with all its poignancy, *Hugh Selwyn Mauberley* is also a penetrating registration of the failure of creativity—of confidence in man's creative power to give meaning to his world—throughout English poetry this century. And it is also an example of the paralysis, in itself.

How shall we diagnose the problem further, to make a cure possible? Here I need more than Leavis's comment "Pound had no creative theme"—though that comes nearest to my feeling. I need something still more penetrating than the concluding paragraphs of Professor Donald Davie's excellent essay on *Hugh Selwyn Mauberley* in *The Modern Age* Volume of the *Pelican Guide to English Literature*. Davie's conclusion is that:

> the most chastening reflection for a British reader is that Pound implies very plainly that in a culture so riddled with commercialism and false values as English culture is (or was, in 1920), no English artist is likely to do any better than Mauberley did (p. 329).

It will be realized that I am as aware as Professor Davie of the way in which commercialism has corrupted symbolism. The parenthesis is odd—for surely between 1950 and 1974 we have witnessed a destruction of culture by commercialism that makes the 1920s seem rich and secure by contrast—an observation I make after thumbing through the *Calendar of Modern Letters*, 1925–7. We could produce nothing like that today, with its richness of creative content; its strong recognition of values ("This book is dead . . ."—the opening sentence of a review by E. M. Forster). The Editorial tone of *The Calendar* expresses a confidence that there is an audience there to *take* that tone. Of course, it could be argued that the failure of the *Calendar* demonstrated that there was no such public: but this, again, may be wrong—it was perhaps simply that Wishart, (whose money it had been behind *The Calendar*) had decided to go in for Left-wing political publishing. Because of the social and economic catastrophes of the time intellectuals felt some other battle needed fighting than the cultural one. But the depth of creative failure I feel to be there in Ezra Pound is a deeper matter than commercialism or the existence of a public: a deeper matter even than that suggested by George Steiner's emphasis on "contexts".

Certainly, the triumph of *Scrutiny* showed that there was a public: and the present-day use of *Scrutiny* all over the world shows that there still *is* a public. The audience for Pound must have been very considerable indeed: even in *The Times*, even in the lesser newspaper *The Times* has become, Ezra Pound had nearly a whole page for his obituary. There is still a context. The problem is rather an inner problem of *conviction*, and this is a problem of philosophy, of attitudes to life.

For comparison, we may take into account the work of the Impressionists and Post-Impressionists, who began by showing as young men in the *Salon des Refusés*. Their audience now runs into millions, and its response is an understanding, attentive one, as I know from my own son who, at eighteen, is already even more deeply aware of what they stand for than anyone in my generation. Nothing commercialism can do can eradicate this creative impact, and the continual growth of new receptivities.

Or we may take Mahler, who has "come into his own" during the last decade, and is now really listened to and understood: indeed commercialism has in fact helped this creative discovery, by producing cheap discs, and making stereophonic radio possible.

The paintings of the French painters, and the music of Mahler, have offered, and will continue to offer an immense amount of "intentionality" by their symbolism, throwing benignity and meaning over the world, and infusing it deeply with humanness and gratitude.

And this is true at a time when all around us "Caliban casts out Ariel", while consciousness is being severely damaged by cultural nihilism. Art need not fail in our time. The transformation of English musical taste over the last two decades is an immense gain—not paralleled, alas, in the sphere of poetry. The failure of poetry to sustain a belief in itself and in the poetic faculties is an inward problem (as, indeed, Davie shows it to be in his critical study up to that concluding paragraph!). Commercialism is destructive: but the failure lies within poetry itself, that it remains an underling, and that it cannot rise from its defeat by all the forces lampooned in Pound's poem.

We would like to bring poetry to bear on the crisis of our culture, and, indeed, this is what I am trying to do in this book. We can invoke Hardy as poet, and Yeats, Edward Thomas, Rosenberg and others, like Hopkins. But our most serious problem is that the two figures who dominate the literature of the last hundred years—Pound and Eliot—have tended to transfix us in a certain sterility of inner failure of belief in human creativity. The one important exception is D. H. Lawrence—who as Donald Davie says, makes comments as penetrating as those of Pound on the state of English culture in his *Letters*. But even Lawrence ended up as a writer—as Kate Millett argues—generating "demented fantasies". Though this is not the place to argue it, there is a disturbing sense in my mind that Lawrence's fantasy assaults on woman in his later works, in which she is put to death by a stone dagger, itself represents a symbolic attack, in desperation, on the creative power itself, in vengeance for not having provided the meaning in existence for which he hungered. Despite Leavis's commendations, I believe that in the end, we cannot use Lawrence as a guide to "life", not least in the sphere of sexuality: he turned to hate, and lost confidence in creativity, too.

But where the powerful influence of Pound is concerned we need to explore not his social and economic politics, but pass a little further into the *concept of man* behind *Hugh Selwyn Mauberley*, to try to detect in the background a philosophical anthropology—a feeling about human life that belongs to the paralysis I have tried to point to symbolized by the "still stone dogs . . . biting empty air".

As Donald Davie and F. R. Leavis help us to see, Pound's poetry is continually sending us off to encyclopedias and dictionaries of quotations. In *How to Teach Reading: A Primer for Ezra Pound* Leavis made it clear that Pound's sense of what a civilized man should have read was eclectic, superficial, and based on a characteristic American anxiety about covering the whole of civilization, and knowing what it was "right" to know. Donald Davie takes a more charitable view:

> For Pound these names represent experiences which should be familiar to any educated man, and he is arguing, in particular, that neither we nor the Americans can see our own cultural traditions in proper perspective except in the context of achievements in other languages or by other cultures. He would be happy if these lines sent us to the Victoria and Albert Museum, the British Museum, and the National Gallery to look at late Roman or Italian Renaissance coins, and at Italian paintings. . . . (p. 317).

But, Davie adds, "He has never ceased to be the pedagogue"—and that illuminates a great deal. For the lines of enquiry he sets us off upon do not, somehow, take us along the most creative paths. They take us to artefacts which may be used to expose by contrast the "accelerated grimace" of our age: but not always to art that restores our vision and intentionality. The art he sends us to is not often alive in such a way as to expose our own culture by contrast as dead: it is itself often dead—in its refined cultivation, and in the fact that we can know it only in paraphrase anyway: and *intellectually*. His guide-lines tend to lead to a precious, esoteric, recondite, cultivated art, very much akin to the mosaics and golden birds of Yeats's *Byzantium*, art for the aesthete, rather than for a man tormented by the problems of "life" among the mackerel-crowded seas, or by the way the sap has been dried out of his veins by engagement with the actual problems of generation, values, community life and politics, as Yeats was.[11]

Here, I believe, we need to puzzle over Donald Davie's sentence. "Mauberley's deficiencies as a writer are identical with his deficiencies as a human being." If Mauberley is so confused with Pound himself, what attitudes does Pound take to these deficiencies? Or are they his too? Mauberley, Davie says, "is no fool . . . he is a man of principle, as well as a man of true poetic ability. The judgement is all the more damning: his principles and his abilities go *for nothing because they are not informed by any vitality*." But, as Davie says earlier

> the device appears to work only if the persona is sufficiently differentiated from the poet himself—otherwise the irony lapses, and the reader overlooks the presence of the persona. It thus happens with Pound's Mauberley, it seems to me to happen, too, with Eliot's Gerontion (p. 323).

If we ignore the persona of Hugh Selwyn Mauberley, and read the poem as being by Pound himself (and the structure permits of this, or, at least, isn't satisfactory enough to prevent it) then doesn't it appear that it is Pound who doesn't have the "vitality" either? And this lack of vitality is not only a matter of "character", but of his sense of the relationship between culture and the man (as Leavis saw in his *How to Teach Reading*)?

Pound *has* influenced English poetry enormously: yet Hugh-

Selwyn-Mauberley-Pound and his abilities *"go for nothing"*. When we follow Pound's trails, how is it we are not led to the immense creative achievements (say) of Renoir, Monet, Manet, Degas, Van Gogh, Berthe Morisot? Why Bennett, Dowson, Beerbohm, Mallarmé? Why not Baudelaire? Why Flaubert (though Pound is also ironic about Flaubert)? Why not more to the Chinese poetry that Mahler found so seminal—or, indeed, why not Mahler? If Henry Lawes, why not Dowland, Purcell, or Blow? Why Pater rather than Dickens?

Of course, in *Hugh Selwyn Mauberley* Pound was recording a particular impotence, a particular decadence and stalemate: and he is caught between cultivation and barbarism. But by the influence of this ironic poem he confines the debate disastrously by limiting the alternatives, between sterile aestheticism and sterile vulgarity. A solitary visit to the *Jeu de Paume* should have demonstrated a way in which man's vision can redeem his world, filling it with mystery, meaning and human gratitude for existence— such as poetry could have followed, without seeing the choice as between Caliban and "the mottoes on sundials", or the hollow lifeless paralysis expressed in *Medallion*.

Donald Davie occasionally skirts this problem, but never seems to find it. His attention is directed at how Pound's poetry transcends "techniques"—to give an astonishing sense of freedom. It is no good telling us that what looks like or seems to be *vers libre* (like the poem on the '14–'18 war) in fact has an immense technical skill behind it: what comes to us is an impression of a free if exact rhythm—as in many of the translations in *Cathay* from the Chinese. What is more important is the quickening sense of a creative exploration of experience. And so, it is understandable to me that Pound found Hardy so worthy of praise—and an occasion for "painful self-assessment".

Davie finds it "surprising", because "Hardy, with his insularity and his clumsiness (sometimes calculated, often not) is so much the last poet one would have expected Pound to admire", Davie commends Pound for patronizing Hardy (when he said "Now *there is* the harvest of having written twenty novels first" —*Letters*, p. 386): "this tribute to him gives us a new respect for Pound's generosity and open-mindedness, the genuine catholicity of his taste. Yet there is no blinking the fact that it makes nonsense of many of Pound's other professions, at this date as well as earlier."

So be it: but, as I hope to show below, Hardy in his greatest poems is neither "insular" or "clumsy": his "technique" can really be called "technique" in Donald Davie's way—it is language at the tip of the senses and the intelligence—and governed by a profound tragic sense. Po Chü-I and Li-Po would have no difficulty about understanding Hardy's *Vestigea Veteris Flammae*—and not because of any similarities of "technique" or "form", but because of the philosophical anthropology which the poem, phenomenologically, communicates. This is why

> 20 novels form as good a gradus ad Parnassum as does metrical exercise, I dare say they form a better *if the gods have granted* light by that route. Hardy is Gautier's successor as Swinburne could not be.
>
> (Pound, *Guide to Kulchur*, Chapter 52, quoted by Donald Davie, p. 150)

Also,

> a craft that occupies itself with imitating Gerard Hopkins or in any other metrical experiment is a craft misdirected . . . we engage in technical exercise *faute de mieux*, a necessary defensive activity (*ibid.*).

Donald Davie speaks of a *"volte face"* when Pound discussed modernist intricacy and technical sophistication in favour of a limpidity he considered "totalitarian" in his pages on Hardy.

But yet, I believe, in the best of Pound's writing, despite all his attention to technique, he *is* close to Hardy's limpidity. When I turn to Pound, unburdened with the pedagogic attention to technique that Donald Davie loads me with, I find it, immediate and fresh, in poems like *Francesca, Commission, The Study in Aesthetics, Liu Ch'e, Song of the Bowmen of Shu, The River-Merchant's Wife: A Letter, Ballad of the Mulberry Road,* and even *Moeurs Contemporaires*. Some of these poems I have included in anthologies for English teaching, quite sure that they will be apprehended directly by unsophisticated, uneducated readers.

As Donald Davie says, Pound played "a militant and decisive part in the crucial literary and artistic battles then being fought

out on the English scene . . . in particular . . . as at once mentor
and sponsor of the youthful T. S. Eliot." In *Hugh Selwyn Mauberley* . . . he "explicitly attempts to portray and diagnose the state
of British (not at all of American) culture at the historical
moment which, for instance, D. H. Lawrence in *Women in Love*
similarly took to be for England a tragically momentous turning-
point". If, as I have suggested, this poem fails to find a creative
theme, "every subsequent British poet at all serious about his
vocation . . ." who has "found it necessary to come to terms with
this work" has tended to be influenced by a model whose deep
petrification of posture to the world is only come at after considerable effort of deciphering, and whose invocation of artefacts
still yields no essential intentionality in the realm of being.

Leavis says that "It was possible for the poets of the Romantic
period to believe that the interests animating their poetry were
the forces moving the world, or that might move it." The Victorian
poets couldn't believe this. But the Impressionists obviously *did*
happily believe it, as did Mahler, Bonnard and D. H. Lawrence
at best. "All that we can fairly ask of the poet is that he shall
show himself to have been fully alive in our own time." But where,
in the tremendously influential writers of this century, does one find
a vision "in advance of itself"—as one finds it in (say) the concluding bars of *Das Lied Von Der Erde*, or in Hardy's most deeply
tragic poems?

This is the question we can now ask, on the grounds of phenomenology. As Roger Poole says, Merleau-Ponty makes it plain that
his philosophy "is a part of a web of cultural assertions, denials,
advances, retreats, in which our own gestures are intermingled,
to which we can give a meaning because we too are embodied
subjects, freely choosing. . . ." From the discussion emerges, says
Poole, "the central thought-dimension which differentiates all
phenomenological thinking . . . the concept of intentionality . . .
which assumes the creative presence of human freedom in perception and thought. Intentionality, crudely spelled out, is the
presence of freedom in meaning-conferring in the perceiving subject. The subject as observed by the phenomenologist confers
meaning upon the world, and, in doing so, implicitly asserts his
freedom. . . ." (*Universities Quarterly*, Autumn 1974, p. 498).

It is this concept of embodied, intentional man, creating as he sees, exerting his freedom by giving meaning to his world that Ezra Pound cannot find or believe in:

> I cannot make it cohere.
> If love be not in the house it is nothing.
> The voice of famine unheard[12]

—in those three terrifying statements we have a confession of the creative failure in poetry, during the whole period which Pound has influenced.

And of course he was a great influence on Eliot, who is a powerful influence himself in turn. Here I shall only discuss Eliot briefly, to suggest that he too suffers from the same syndrome, symbolized by those "stone dogs . . . biting empty air", and impelled by a dread of relationship, of woman, and of creativity. As Leavis has argued, what he expresses most powerfully is a failure to believe in human creativity. A characteristic concentration of images in his work is to be found in *The Hollow Men*:

> This is the dead land
> This is cactus land
> Here the stone images
> Are raised, here they receive
> The supplication of a dead man's hand
> Under the twinkle of a fading star.
> (*The Hollow Men, Collected Poems*, p. 88)

—the voice of the hungry, unborn self in the schizoid, which we are only just learning to hear.

Here is the universe of the Second Law of Thermodynamics ("fading", "twinkling") and the dead hand of man as a bag of bones, begging the dead images to save man, all making meaningless incantations.

> It's like this
> In death's other kingdom
> Waking alone
> At the hour when we are
> Trembling with tenderness
> Lips that would kiss
> Form prayers to broken stone . . .

Throughout Eliot's work there are images of love which has failed—failed in encounter, and failed in meaning. Instead, the lips, frustrated of tender encounter, turn to worship broken stone. Perception, in consequence, fails: "There are no eyes here . . ." And so there is a failure of perception

> Between the idea
> And the reality
> Between the motion
> And the act
> Falls the shadow . . .

> Between the conception
> And the creation
> Between the emotion
> And the response
> Falls the shadow . . .

> Between the potency
> And the existence . . .

The world ends, not with a bang, but a whimper, because of the schizoid reduction of life: "Our dried voices . . . Are quiet and meaningless" in a world in which there is

> Shape without form, shadow without colour,
> Paralysed force, gesture without motion . . .

Eliot's poems are taken as the delineation of a civilization which has lost its meaning, a "hollow valley". This is not only a civilization which has debased its symbols, into broken stones: it is one in which consciousness itself has lost its capacities to give meaning to existence: speech has failed:

> We grope together
> And avoid speech
> Gathered on this beach of the tumid river . . .

Ritual, any "motion" extended to restore meaning, seems like madness in a desert:

> *Here we go round the prickly pear*
> *Prickly pear prickly pear . . .*

Behind the stone fragments he erects, although it is carefully masked, there is a fragmented Self, behind the disguises:

Let me also wear
Such deliberate disguises
Rat's coat, crowskin, crossed staves
In a field
Behaving as the wind behaves
No nearer . . .

Behind this image of a scare-crow, a hollow man, is Yeats's "old clothes upon old sticks to scare a bird", and, as in Yeats, the bird is death: the final meeting is the encounter with nothingness, and to behave as the wind behaves is to escape from that embodiment which involves death, that belongs to "being-unto-death".

Eliot's central creative theme is the sterility of his own relationship with the other and the world. He translates this into a criticism of our civilization, and its spiritual and cultural emptiness and fragmentation. His criticism may be just, but he yet allows no roots to grow out of this stony rubbish. There is a reference to the need to "put my lands in order", and we can share in *Four Quartets* Eliot's creative quest to do so, in poetry of great artistic quality. But in the end, as at the end of *The Waste Land*, there is only incantation: almost a kind of magic, in hope that "when the fire and the rose are one", "all manner of things shall be well"—despite the creative elements in the poems, this remains a *pious* hope. The radical failure of relationship between self and other, between the experiencing I and the world is not solved, despite the poignant beauty of its rendering, as in the opening lines of *Little Gidding*.[13]

In *The Waste Land* there is perhaps the most evident expression of the failure of *liebende Wirheit* in Eliot's life:

'You gave me hyacinths first a year ago;
'They called me the hyacinth girl.'
—Yet when we came back, late, from the Hyacinth garden,
Your arms full, and your hair wet, I could not
Speak, and my eyes failed, I was neither
Living nor dead, and I knew nothing,
Looking into the heart of light, the silence.
Oed' und leer das Meer.

Of course, Eliot pushes this back—into fragmentary echoes of *Tristan and Isolde*, into fertility myth, into the impersonal figures of some classical landscape (as in *La Figlia Che Piange*). But it has that unmistakeable rhythm of some remembered ecstasy, which is there also in *La Figlia*: it is a reminiscence of the "awful daring of a moment's surrender". The word "late" suggests having been lost in passion: her arms are full of flowers, but this and the wet hair suggest sexual consummation. For the protagonist to be unable to speak suggests the depths of his passion: but the rest suggests a *total loss of meaning and a failure of perception, as a result of sexual union*:

> my eyes failed, I was neither
> Living nor dead, and I knew nothing,
> Looking into the heart of light, the silence . . .

The sea is wide and empty: the line from the Wagner opera may have been supplied by Pound. But the lines convey not only the feeling of loss of self, or a kind of death, such as may be experienced in sexual communion: but they also convey how such an experience seems to the schizoid individual a glimpse into nothingness, silence, and the total loss of all sense of being in existence.

After "give", we have "sympathize"—and then "control" which in its context seems more like "choose and act":

> The boat responded
> Gaily, to the hand . . .
> your heart would have responded
> Gaily, when invited . . .

But even this is in a past tense, rather than an imperative one. Yet although one might have expected sympathy after that daring moment of surrender in the hyacinth garden, this is not what follows. Throughout *The Waste Land* what one has is bitterness— the kind of bitterness Hardy inflicts on Tess: someone whose own relationship with "the other" and the world has come to be empty is condemning the attempts of others to solve the same problem.

Eliot, that is, does not see his neurasthenic rich woman (compared with Cleopatra) as seeking meaning by the same opulence and sensuality, albeit turning (in a more ersatz age) arid and empty. He caricatures and condemns her, with a sermonizing intrusion:

> I think we are in rats' alley
> Where the dead men lost their bones . . .

There *is* sympathy in the fine verse of the earlier passage in the grand style, because the desperation in the sensuality is conveyed so subtly and ambivalently:

> The glitter of her jewels rose to meet it. . . .

The opposition between *freshened* and *fattened*: the tension between *synthetic, unguent* and *drowned* in their texture and felt movement belong to real poetry, and the predicament is *ours*, with our withered stumps of time.

But with working class people, we have only caricature: Mr Eliot is taking off his daily help. There is none of the dignity in ordinary people's lives we find in *Odour of Chrysanthemums*, and the speech is the speech of the stage cockney type. The savage passage is unsympathetic, and inhuman (imagine it in, say, a contemporary anti-abortion pamphlet and how facile it would appear there, in relation to the real anguish of the problem such as we recognize it today).

So, too, is the portrayal of the meaningless act of seduction, to which Eliot seeks to give classical status by the introduction of Tiresias. The "young man carbuncular" merely conveys Eliot's distaste, and the attitude of schizoid superiority from which he describes the scene, with cruel fun.

"Her drying combinations touched by the sun's last rays. . . ." The characters are low, and are guyed: "One of the low on whom assurance sits. . . ." The man is hated, much as Leonard Bast is hated in E. M. Forster's *Howard's End*: and the hatred arises from fear, as does the contempt for ordinary people. This contempt for all that is ordinary in Eliot may be compared with that of Heidegger: and it arises from the same problem, a fear of not leading a meaningful existence ("A life-time burning in every moment") by being dragged down to the level of an inauthentic *Mitsein*, by *Das Mensch*, by *masse mensch*.

Ostensibly, the horror of this seduction lies in the indifference: but the caricature is unsympathetic in its caricature, because it falsifies experience: "Hardly aware of her departed lover. . . ." Was there ever a woman who was seduced for the first time, who became immediately hardly aware? Or who thought of her defloration like that: " 'Well now that's done and I'm glad it's over' "? The episode is, in fact, a gross travesty of the most insignificant sexual act: all sexual acts however trivial, have for the protagonists an element of the search for love, and the search for meaning.

The theme of *The Waste Land* is this, the spiritual sterility of London, symbolized by the emptiness of promiscuous sexuality at large there. Yet even in our time, when promiscuity is flagrant, one may find in this manifestation elements of the quest for the release of potentialities, while in the life of any individual sex never has this automatic quality:

> Smooths her hair with automatic hand
> And puts a record on the gramophone.

To support a contention that this is a falsification, one need only turn to any book of case-histories.

The scene is one to which Eliot displays much hostility because he is afraid, and so (I believe) we must interpret it as the primal scene—the disturbing vibration arising from fear and compulsion. Why should the fact that *some* people—the loitering heirs of city directors, typists, bank clerks, rich demi-mondaine ladies—are superficial in their sexual relations, even displaying "the broken finger-nails of dirty hands", so disturb Eliot that he sees it as an index of the spiritual sterility of the whole civilization? Or, more exactly, what is the difference between them and Anthony and Cleopatra, and Elizabeth and Leicester? It is that their encounters lack grandeur and style? It can't be that they are unmarried! But would mere style, with silver oars and a chorus of Rhinemaidens, save the meaning of that deathly sexuality?

The answer is, of course, that Eliot does not know, and can never say, what it could be that could save them, or save our civilization. In the face of the fear we are shown in a handful of dust—our nothingness. We may come in under the shadow of the red rock of the church, or try to put our lands in order by invoking fragments of European culture. But what satisfies us least in *The Waste Land* are the invocations of a "give", "sympathize" and "control" which are only given in terms of opportunities missed. The central protagonist, who hides under so many masks—Tiresias, Phlebas, the drowned king whose eyes turn into pearls, the Fisher King, the Hanged Man—*is* drowned: he is nothing but a bag of bones, picked by the sea-currents of an indifferent universe. A schizoid madness afflicts him, even as he comes near to the source of his problems: but even there

> Dry bones can harm no-one

> How have we existed?
> By this, and this only, have we existed . . .

—by "The awful daring of a moment's surrender / Which an age of prudence can never retract". That moment in the Hyacinth Garden was one of those moments, then, which enabled the protagonist to feel he existed, but at the end of it the sea was wide and empty. Sympathy? "We have heard the key turned in the lock, and turn once only." Control: "Your heart would have responded . . . beating obediently. . . ." What is left, if these are the potentialities—which seem, by the way they are put, to have escaped us, irretrievably? What is lost are our meanings: but Eliot never discovers how genuinely creative meanings could be created, from the moments of communion that he gestures towards.

Rather, the poet attempts to ensnare the reader in his sense of ever-lost opportunities:

> We who were living ar now dying
> With a little patience . . .

If we have reached the point of (as it were) burying our mortality (that is, accepting being-unto-death) and seeking to transcend it by a sense of continuity (as Mahler did), then it will be dug up again, and spoiled:

> 'Oh keep the Dog far hence, that's friend to men,
> 'Or with his nails he'll dig it up again . . .

He seeks to enlist us in his own feeling that nothing we achieve in the sphere of creative symbolism can ever be relied upon: " 'You! hypocrite lecteur!—mon semblable,—mon frère' " In his analysis in *The Living Principle* F. R. Leavis seems to be struggling with a seductive quality, even in the finest of Eliot's poetry in *Four Quartets*, which threatens to lure us into a feeling that we can never triumph in this world, over the failure of meaning, that there is no escape from the dead land in which we have our existence.

Eliot's horror of existence is bound up with fear of woman, which again we may interpret as a fear of sensitive-creative elements in the self. This is perhaps indicated by the holograph version of the original lines from *The Burial of the Dead*:

> We knew we had passed the farthest northern islands
> So no-one spoke again. We ate slept drank
> Hot coffee, and kept watch, and no-one dared
> To look into another's face, or speak
> In the horror of the illimitable scream
> Of a whole world about us. One night
> On watch, I thought I saw in the five cross-trees
> Three women leaning forward, with white hair
> Streaming behind, who sang above the wind
> A song that charmed my senses, while I was
> Frightened beyond fear, horrified past horror, calm
> (Nothing was real) . . .

(TLS, 7 November 1968)

The original quotation from Conrad at the front of the draft of *The Waste Land* ended with the words "The horror! The horror!"—and Pound persuaded Eliot to drop it. What Eliot conveys is that being-in-the-world itself is a horror, and in the image of the three women we can see the link between the "significant other" or Woman and the world-as-object, in Eliot's inner life: the nightmare image of woman fiddling whisper music on her black hair, and the bats with baby faces in the violet light belong to the same horror, of being frightened beyond fear: "Looking into the heart of light, the silence"—and finding only emptiness. It is against this emptiness that his fragments are shored. His heaps of broken images, like Sylvia Plath's house of the self, are but constructions made of bits of male doing, to set against ruin. Eliot can find no creative "female element being"[14] by which the sterility of self and world is to be overcome, except for that moment glimpsed in *Marina*:

> Let me
> Resign my life for this life, my speech for that unspoken,
> The awakened, lips parted, the hope, the new ships . . .
> My daughter . . .

But this real feeling of creative transcendence is seldom found in T. S. Eliot, nor in the tradition he has influenced so powerfully, together with his mentor, *il miglior fabbro*.[15] These two most power-ful influences in twentieth-century poetry have no creative theme, because, despite their achievements, they cannot, because of their schizoid problems, find a confident sense of being able to love the world, and to give it meaning. This capacity, according to philo-sophical anthropology, derives from the perceptual dynamics aris-ing from *liebende Wirheit*, those encounters by which "from man to man the heavenly bread of self-being is passed" (Buber), to inform being-in-the-world. In love of this kind they have no confi-dence, and so they never find a conviction that poetry can give meaning to the world. Though, again, one has to add that, para-doxically, their efforts to do so, in great anguish, at least express that human meaning which is forever bound up in man's attempts to find it, even if he fails. His mere awareness of his own predica-ment has the meaning which belongs to the inevitable pains of being conscious and aware of before and after.

NOTES

1. I cannot find out where Tigullio is, not even from the author of a number of guides to Italy: nor what its significance is, of course. Torcello is of course the ancient religious site near Venice.
2. "Oh Love's warm sunshine—are you gone forever?" *Das Lied Von Der Erde.*
3. Pronounced HIDMEN GAR TOI PANTH HOS ENI TROIE, meaning "such things as we saw in Troy".
4. *OCTROIS*, customs posts, as outside a town, to collect local taxes.
5. The wheel has come full circle. On my desk lies a notice from the English Faculty at Cambridge on Prelims: *"In particular it should be noted that the complete works of Milton are included within the scope of this paper."*
6. Compare Hardy's image of the "air blue gown" in *The Voice* with Claude Monet's "Femme a l'Ombrelle" 1886 (Musée du Louvre, Paris), as poetic definitions of this kind. For the energy and qualities of creative perception behind such disciplines see Jean Renoir, *Renoir, My Father,* 1962.
7. Also found, for example, in Heidegger. Perhaps the Impressionists were "muzzy" for Pound because they were eminently *not* schizoid, but normal and full of human warmth.
8. See Lomas, Peter, "Dread of envy as an aetiological factor in puer-

peral breakdown", *British Journal of Medical Psychology*, 1960, 33, 105, and *Symbolic Wounds* by Bruno Bettleheim, 1956.

9. Pronounced TIN ANDRA TIN HEROA TINA THEON meaning "what a man, what a hero, what a god! "

10. See the discussion of petrification in R. D. Laing's *The Divided Self*, 1960.

11. A relevant character in fiction is the aesthetic Gilbert Osmond in *The Portrait of A Lady* who was also capable of cold calculation and hate.

12. Cf.   The head-stone quiet, jostled by nothing.
        Only the mouth-hole piped out,
        Importunate cricket

        In a quarry of silence.
                    Sylvia Plath, Poem for A Birthday,
                                The Colossus, p. 87

13. My paragraphs here were written before I read F. R. Leavis's *The Living Principle* and I have left them as they were. There is a great deal more to say here.

14. I say nothing of the excised expressions of hatred: "the good old female smell" and other lapses, revealed in the facsimile.

15. I find Donald Davie's remarks illuminating on the character with whom Pound seems to identify, Walter Villerant, in some "imaginary letters" to *The Little Review*, dandified, effete, mannered, self-regarding: see Davie, 1965, pp. 91–101, and p. 66 above.

5

From "Vitalism" to a Dead Crow: Ted Hughes's Failure of Confidence

Writing in *Children's Literature in Education* on *Myth and Education*, in March 1970, Ted Hughes said:

> We can't ignore that when we read a story, and enter it in a completely imaginative way, the story works on all parts of our nature, and it's impossible to know finally what the influences are.
> . . . if you are to think of imaginative literature as an educational tool you are finally up against the fact that imaginative literature is therapeutic and does have a magical effect on people's minds and their ultimate behaviour. This is the appeal of great works of imaginative literature to us as adults, that they are hospitals where we heal, where our imaginations are healed, that when they are evil works they are also battlefields where we get injured. . . .

Hughes believes, evidently, that literature has an effect on attitudes to life and behaviour at the deepest level. And he believes that there can be a damaging effect, from literature, on our souls. What is the effect of his own work, leading to *Crow*?

There is no doubt about the success of *Crow* as a publishing venture. And for this Hughes may thank Al Alvarez, who had a clear idea about how poetry *must* develop—towards more nihilism, unbalance and hate:

> The movement of the modern arts has been to press deeper and deeper into the subterranean world of psychic isolation, to live out in the arts the personal extremism of breakdown, paranoia, and depression. . . . The modern artist seems to create his sickness in his

work, giving himself over to it for the sake of the range and intensity of his art. He cultivates not his own garden, but his psychosis, or at the very least his psychopathic tendencies.

(Encounter, 1965)

If we study Alvarez's tone and manner, it is obvious that he is excited about the cultivation in the artist of what he calls an "internal fascism", and while he can see the emptiness and aestheticism of some of the new postures, it is clear that he endorses the way in which "intellectual energy becomes a way of promoting hopelessness", in the Arts today. That is, to cut a long critical story short, Alvarez acclaims such deranged tendencies as those of Sylvia Plath, towards suicide, insofar as such a negative dynamic produced what he believes to be good poetry. And so he has no qualms about development in the arts which could help man to move further towards a situation in which it might well prove impossible for him to survive, because he has lost the will to survive.

Writing on Ted Hughes, Alvarez applauded the powerful violence he unleashed in himself:

> Even an Englishman like Ted Hughes, who starts out as a nature poet and whose work contains more animals than the London zoo, lavishes all that loving, sharp detail on his menagerie only for whatever corresponding sense of unpredictable violence he finds in himself. He writes as a nature poet gone blind. . . .

I believe the effect of this kind of advocacy has been disastrous on Ted Hughes's development, and I believe this is of philosophical importance, in our examination of poetic developments in our time, because it urges the poet towards false solutions of hate, and destroys belief in poetry.

The problem of finding philosophical bearings, an adequate sense of being-in-the-world, is painfully evident in the career of Ted Hughes. He has been said to be the "vitalist" among our new poets: but what kind of vitalism is his? The *Observer* said that his poems in *Hawk in the Rain* and *Lupercal* were "the most psychologically profound, original and exciting work to appear since *Four Quartets*": the judgement was repeated later in *Vogue*, and he has since been awarded the Queen's Medal for poetry. Can we imagine him reading *Crow*, and especially *Song of a Phallus*, to

102

Her Majesty in Buckingham Palace? The mere assumption that there is nothing wrong in such a situation is itself part of our sickness. Suppose all this endorsement is being given to "evil works" by which we are "injured"? In order to avoid this question (as in *The Art of Sylvia Plath*) we are often urged towards a new aestheticism: but we must not shirk it.

The word "vitalist" suggests to us that Ted Hughes is telling us something philosophically profound about life, about the creatures, about Nature, in his art. There is a kind of natural philosophizing, it is true, in Hughes's work, as is evident in such a well-known poem as *Thrushes* (in *Lupercal*). At first the language has texture and movement: it is a genuine response to the natural savagery of the bird:

> Terrifying are the attent sleek thrushes on the lawn,
> More coiled steel than living . . .
> . . . Nothing but bounce and stab
> And a ravening second.

But as the poem proceeds the particular perception gives way to vague philosophizing—the poet ceases to observe and emphathize with the birds, and a kind of moralizing predominates over the poetic organization. A philosophical biology predominates, and this really belongs to a certain orthodoxy of unmodified natural scientism, a kind of mechanism. I will print it as prose:

> Is it their single-mind-sized skulls, or a trained body, or genius, or a nestful of brats gives their days this bullet and automatic Purpose? Mozart's brain had it, and the shark's mouth that hungers down the blood-smell even to a leak of its own side and devouring of itself: efficiently which strikes too streamlined for any doubt to pluck at it or obstruction deflect.

The language is clumsy and awkward: the philosophy is even more lame. When animals become involved in certain patterns of response, it is true, they behave with a kind of single-mindedness —and from our point of view they therefore seem to be without "doubt". By contrast men are full of doubts, because their acts are modified by consciousness. In the rest of the poem (and in *Crow* later) this view is to be used to man's disadvantage—the fact that man lives in a "world", while the animal lives more

103

immediately in its "realm" (see Martin Buber, "Distance and Relation" in *The Knowledge of Man*, ed. Maurice Friedmann).

But, it is not really true of animals, whose behaviour is not "bullet and automatic" except in certain limited circumstances, and then perhaps only as seen from our point of view (as with the attack of the shark). Closer attention finds such behaviour to be part of highly complex processes, to which such names as "positionality" have been given—the autonomous moving about of the creature in its world, making its choices (even a bacterium). If we read philosophical biologists, moreover, we find what they say about birds (say) is more interesting than what Hughes says. He is using "bird savagery" to moralize about man's behaviour, and his use of nature is not particularly observant, insightful, or original. His philosophy, in fact, is based on a wilful travesty of the facts, and rooted in his own "violence".

The poem begins by trying to draw our attention to something dreadful, the ruthless way a bird feeds—which we take for granted, without really looking at it. But if the poet is to open our eyes, he must offer us something as least as perceptive and intelligent as (say) Professor W. H. Thorpe F.R.S. or the observers quoted in Marjorie Grene's *Approaches to A Philosophical Biology*. Hughes's subsequent thoughts are too vague: his anthropomorphism too wild—how is Mozart's *brain* "like" the thrush's "bullet and automatic" purpose? The workings of a man's creative powers symbolizing are hardly comparable with the response of a bird to a noise in the earth. Did the (redundant) word "automatic" come only from "bullet" which suggested "gun"? What is implied by the word "efficient"? What is the point of the tone in "a nestful of brats"? If we ask such questions, do we not see that the poem tends to evoke a crude analogy between human and animal experience? The texture of the first stanzas which evoke a sense of amazement at the behaviour of the birds (cf. "attent, sleek") dissolves into a portentous generalizing which compares unfavourably with scientific writing, and is used in fact for purposes which are unscientific, anti-Humanities, since they are concerned to falsify the truth, to establish a philosophy of existence on a spurious sense of "animal" strength, which one (awkwardly) shares with other creatures of nature.

By any account, any comparison between animals and man must

104

recognize the differences in levels of being. But a clue to the perverse nature of Hughes's "vitalism" is given when, later, in this poem, the comparison between bird and man is used for the disparagement of consciousness. By contrast with the direct actions of the thrush, Man is not simple, clear and "efficient". He is overcome with self-delusion; consciousness is his enemy:

> With man it is otherwise. Heroisms on horseback,
> Outstripping his desk-diary at a broad desk,
> Carving at a tiny ivory ornament
> For years: his act worships itself—

The inadequacy of the thought is revealed by the clumsy inadequacy of the verse. If we read this with the senses alert, as to movement and image, do we not become confused? We are at one moment taking a jump on horseback over the desk, only to find that the "outstripping" is a dead metaphor (not the "o'erleap" we expected, echoing *Macbeth* perhaps, in relation to "ambition")—to do here with a diary book. That man's acts worship themselves—how can this be true of a cavalry soldier—or a carver—or a business man? How does this differ from "Mozart's brain", or the thrushes?

The poetry has the air of being based on a philosophy of nature: but its effectiveness depends upon our *not* invoking genuine philosophical biology. The poem invites us, indeed, to suspend our intelligence, and to accept its "wisdom" which is of that "naked ape" kind, and we are not to bring to bear on it anything from true science, or even thought. It assumes a philosophical anthropology; but what study of man would actually sustain it? Yet, in its implicit disparagement of consciousness, it tends to strip the world of meaning.

So, in conclusion, it can only plunge into a flood of somewhat theatrical pity for man in his useless passion:

> Though he bends to be blent in the prayer, how loud and above
>   what
> Furious spaces of fire do the distracting devils
> Orgy and hosannah, under what wilderness
> Of black silent waters weep.

There is a vague general philosophical statement in the poem: that thrushes prey without being inhibited by consciousness, that sharks operate by terrible efficiency, man by contrast is confused by delusions, and so the poem ends in a kind of hwyll about this.

But Hughes reveals his impulse to strip the world of significant consciousness, by one significant phrase: "Mozart's brain". Was not Mozart's brain not at one with a human (highly civilized) consciousness? To Hughes, it seems here to act by itself, as if it was an animal in his head. The brain, in Hughes's thinking, is seen as a mechanism, like the instinctual operation of the feeding thrushes. This in fact (as Erwin Straus points out in his *The Primary World of Senses*) is a kind of anthropomorphism, making the "brain" into an alien kind of creature in one's head. Because Man is bedevilled by this "apparatus" his consciousness is a burden, making for bewilderment and "inefficiency". So, in the end Hughes's "vitalism" turns out to be the usual general pessimistic philosophy spun out of reductionism and mechanism which sees man (even Mozart) as the "product" of instinctual and organic forces and implicitly denies even the passion behind science itself, let alone poetry.

In the light of philosophical biology, such a view is absurd. Not only is animal life much more complex than what is implied. While some animal reactions are "efficient", the animal cannot exert such adaptation and free will, or show as much intentionality as man can, and this shows to man's *advantage*. Man can in fact be *more* "efficient", because he can adjust to varying circumstances, and be both more responsible and flexible. Man can accommodate himself to circumstances, because of his culture and because he has a sense of meaning by which he can transcend his mere existence—as animals cannot. He does not live in his immediate world like a fruit in its skin, as Buber argues, but lives in the "mansions" of his consciousness, in which his range is endless, while he knows both before and after.

Once we reach this point of view, this recognition of the boundless powers of consciousness and intentionality that make man a creature of a higher level of being, we can see that Ted Hughes's "vitalism" is a naïve adulation of "natural" animal life, by contrast with which he wishes to see human consciousness as an impediment. Civilization by this view is an enemy to man, and so it is not surprising that Ted Hughes has spoken of the end of

106

civilization. By his essential rejection of the civilizing powers of consciousness, and so of the *poetic*, he is contributing to the possibility.

It is not only that an intellectual orthodoxy has been imposed on the poetic material, but rather that the poet has not had the confidence to develop his own poetic insights out of his engagement with the original experience. In the face of "objective" science (pseudo-science, really) he abrogates his function as poet: he does not tell us *as a poet* about animals and the world. This may be linked with a parallel journalistic carelessness with language: which is clear over such phrases as "bullet . . . automatic" above. Both the "vitalist philosophy" and the imprecise use of words often fail to rise above journalese in Ted Hughes, and this is a characteristic problem of contemporary poetry— associated with its failure to find a truly creative theme.

Further philosophical problems—which are, I believe, at the centre of the issue of the survival of poetry—may be made clear by taking a recent poem by Hughes published in a book devoted to poems and passages about animals, *The Animal Anthology*, edited by Diana Spearman, ("royalties . . . devoted to the work of the Fauna Preservation Society"). It is called *The Last Migration*. On the face of it, the poem is a bitter warning to man, who takes on the role of God, and is devoted to unmake the world. He is the "God of the steady gaze", and he swallows up all life on the earth with his rifled bore, through the "vortex and rifling of the Word"—the explosion of his gun, and the "tiny hole of God's eye-pupil", his eye looking along a gun.

However, there is a curious contradiction in the poem: the Irish Elk, for instance, dies "back" into extinction through man's aiming eye, it seems, because its strange form was a "mistake". Here, it is not that man is damaging and destroying a nature whose complexities and mysteries he does not understand or respect. It is rather as if Ted Hughes supposes the world is to be unmade by man, because it is so full of the ugly, hideous and ponderous errors of God. The animals die because they were "unbelievables" —and the poem conveys the impression not that man should improve his creative perception, but that man's eye is to be totally equated with the "unmaking" gun, and that there is thus an inescapable inevitability about the destruction of the world by this

107

new god. It is as if the Un-Creator is the final outcome of "evolution":

> So God died. And a new god
> With narrowed eyes,
> Carrying the Word reversed,
> Gazed across the earth.

When Nietzsche said "God is dead" he meant the religious concepts and modes by which God could be found: he wanted a new source of moral values. In Hughes's universe God *is* dead: and man, having taken his place carries the "Word reversed": inevitably man is the Unmaker, the Unword. The earth "is cluttered with unbelievables".

> There stood the Irish Elk,
> A ponderous machinery of pain,
> A purposeless castle of gristle . . .
> How had the sea, that throws crabs up, thrown this up?
> Had those antlers fallen from a star?
> Had those eyes come from the moon?

This animal had

> clattered to some other draughty standing place
> With its absurd furniture and snow-proof eyelids,
> Staring around without comprehension,
> Like an error from timelessness . . .

It is often suggested, in popular pseudo-biology, that the dinosaurs were "mistakes", and so perished. Those who take this view seem to have forgotten that these strange prehistoric creatures successfully survived 190,000,000 years, while man seems unlikely to survive his first million. Ted Hughes's attitude to the strange animal the Irish Elk seems to be as patronizing; it is "ponderous", a "machinery of pain", "a purposeless castle of gristle", "thrown-up" with "absurd" furniture. It "stares around without comprehension"—and in this is an implicit denial of those strange but marvellous capacities for "positionality" displayed by the most humble animal.

Is the sportsman who has taken over God's role, then, simply removing God's errors from the world?

The narrowed eye, the God, spoke
Calling the Elk back.
And the scene was amended
As the furniture collapsed, and those eyes accepted the verdict
Like a hero's, without change of expression,
As the Elk's blood smoked, pulled back through the tiny hole
Of God's eye-pupil.
It lasted a few minutes and the Elk was unravelled.

But Hughes seems unable to find any satisfactory relationship between God, man, and the natural world. Is man now God?

God turned his gaze slowly,
And the Aurochs dropped to its knees, astounded,
Meeting His eye
And He called back the Aurochs,
It struggled to rise, it wanted to charge,
It thought He was only a man,
But it had already begun to leave the earth . . .

Then the Passenger Pigeons, and then the buffaloes

began to converge
Toward the sudden hole in the centre
Drawing, with a tumbling final thunder,
Through the rifled bore . . .

Hughes certainly conveys by his strongly active language
(struggled, converge, sudden hole, tumbling final thunder) the
power of the gun, the ruthlessness of the man-hunter, and even
generates a certain pity for the animals which cannot understand
what is happening. But there is also a strange false strength,
yielding a satisfaction in the caricature, which omits, in its black
purity, any recognition of creative potentialities in man, by which
he might be persuaded to live in harmony with the animals. Life
in Hughes's world is not evolving creatively, and his creatures are
not enjoying or using the world, towards boundless multiplicity
of forms and vitality, higher being, and richness. The animals, in
his world, are strange, stupid and alien: man is total uncreating
hate, as if this were the inevitable and final manifestation of
Evolution, gone wrong, too: [2]

And God saw everything He had unmade and Behold
It was what He wanted.

And then God spoke to the whole world,
And right around the world, the waters trembled
And began to move . . .

If confidence in perception fails, then the world can become a terrible place, which must always then be greeted by a defensive aggressiveness, unless one is to be overwhelmed by it. In a short story by Sylvia Plath, *The Wishing Box*, the protagonist commits suicide because, she feels, she cannot throw her imagination over the world:

> The utterly self-sufficient, unchanging reality of the *things* surrounding her began to depress Agnes . . . she felt choked, smothered by these objects whose bulky pragmatic existence somehow threatens the deepest, most secret roots of her own ephemeral being . . .

Ted Hughes's *Gog* in *Wodwo* is an extension of this feeling to the "whole universe" (*Wodwo*, 1967, p. 150). The first part is a sardonic rejection of the claims of religion. The title of the poem is not *God* but *Gog*—incidentally implying that the poet is concerned with primitive gods, and that the idea of god is a primitive one: Gog is the kind of primitive non-existent entity to whom Wandlebury Hill was devoted—so is God. There is also an invocation of Mr Eliot's "Keep the dog far hence . . ." and the cliché that dog is but god backwards:

> The dog's god is a scrap dropped from the table.
> The mouse's saviour is a ripe wheat grain.

In *Thrushes*, Ted Hughes's "vitalism" involved the use of animals to depreciate human qualities. The human being's grasping after meaning is ridiculed here by implying that it is a simple self-deception for man to hear the voice of god in his world. He hungers for meaning: but only as a dog worships his piece of fat cut from our steak. We worship our delusions.

> I woke to a shout: "I am Alpha and Omega".
> Rocks and a few trees trembled
> Deep in their own country.
> I ran and an absence bounded beside me.

In *The Waste Land*, there is a third figure walking beside the two characters in the fifth section: "Who is the third who walks always beside you?" This is an echo of the figure of Christ at Emmaeus. But in *Gog* it is an *absence* that bounds beside the protagonist, who seems himself to be a dog-like animal.

Who then shouted? It was an error, apparently, to hear it:

> Hearing the Messiah cry
> My mouth widens in adoration

—but only like the dog's or the mouse's, adoring their scrap of food. The trees and rocks only seem to tremble. They are "deep in their own country" and this country is that of "matter in motion".

> How fat are the lichens!
> They cushion themselves on the silence.
> The air wants for nothing.
> The dust, too, is replete.

> What was my error?

The material world, the air, the world of plants—these have no yearnings for meaning or God. The dust, having satisfied itself on death, as it were, is replete: it asks for no meaning to transcend death. What is the "error" of that kind of animal that goes on asking for meaning?

> ... My skull has sealed it out.
> My great bones are massed in me.
> They pound on the earth, my song excites them.
> I do not look at the rocks and stones, I am frightened of what
>   they see.

> I listen to the song jarring my mouth
> Where the skull-rooted teeth are in possession.

The Caliban-like animal self of the poem is totally absorbed in his bodily existence, and this "seals out" even his spiritual aspirations which (in "error") made him think that the voice of God spoke from Creation. His reality is teeth and skull, predatoriness and bones, death. Even his song seems alien, it merely jars his mouth. He is merely physically excited by this song, dissociated from all meaning. He does not look at the rocks and stones, because what they see can only be as dead as themselves: what

111

frightens him is that he would only see himself as they see him—petrified.

The only consolation for the absence of a God or a sense of meaning, for this Gog-Wodwo creature, is that he is massive: "I am massive on earth." We have the same feeling in *Wodwo* (the poem) itself: "What am I doing here in mid-air?"

How am I known in a world over which I can throw no meaning: how can it know me?

> Do these weeds
> know me and name me to each other have they
> seen me before, do I fit in their world?
> ... I've no threads
> fastening me to anything ...
> ... if I sit still how everything
> stops to watch me I suppose I am the exact centre ...
> (*Wodwo*, p. 183)

The world simply "*is*", is matter in motion, and the human consciousness thus has no continuity in it, does not belong in it, has no threads fastening "me" to anything. Experience here is experience fragmented as Hume fragmented it with no experiencing "I". This is biologically untrue: from the point of view of the life-sciences man must be seen as the most remarkable and mysterious *product* of the natural world, and his links with all things are being continually illuminated. His experience of the world is united by the "I": this is not to endorse anthropocentricity, about which Hughes is ironic. But his poetry denies, in its insistence on dissociation, the imaginative links between man and his world. If, as Coleridge declares in his *Biographia Literaria*,

> The primary IMAGINATION I hold
> to be the living power and prime
> Agent of all human Perception ...

then the world in *Gog* is one in which imagination has failed. In this poem the protagonist has suffered that fate which Sylvia Plath dreaded: the triumph of the thinginess of things over our power to invest them with significance. Why does the mother appear lamenting in *Gog*?

> My feet bones beat on the earth
> Over the sounds of motherly weeping ...

112

Both Sylvia Plath and Ted Hughes seem to assume that we will understand when they refer to the mother. Yet in truth their invocation of the mother is only explicable in the light of the "schizoid diagnosis": she is the mother for whom the unborn self or regressed libidinal ego yearns. Here the mother is lamenting the failure of the protagonist to find meaning, which is also a failure of his need for "creative reflection": it is these needs which are denied by the Caliban-ban-ban stamping of the feet-bones.

The protagonist in *Gog* sinks into indifference and oblivion:

> Afterwards I drink at a pool quietly.
> The horizon bears the rocks and trees away into twilight.
> I lie down. I become darkness.
>
> Darkness that all night sings and circles stamping.
>
> (p. 150)

In the darkness only a restless aggressiveness is left. The protagonist takes on darkness to himself and becomes it, singing and circling with a nihilistic impulse, to deny the mother's weeping, the need for meaning and the horror of the universe reduced to an unrelievedly materialistic one.

In Section II this universe becomes malignant. Ted Hughes will not allow us to redeem the dead Cartesian-Newtonian cosmos:

> The sun erupts. The moon is deader than a skull.
> The grass-head waves day and night and will never know it exists.
> The stones are as they were. And the creatures of earth
> Are mere rainfall rivulets, in floods or empty paths.

All life is but chance fluxes, in rivulets falling like rain, or caused by flood, or following empty paths in evolution. This is a complete denial of all the complex and creative processes of life: such a view would have horrified the Darwin of *Zoology of The Voyage of the "Beagle"*. (1840). But this is the inevitable consequence of the impact upon the poet of those philosophical attitudes which regard poetry as "misrepresentation". "All poetry is misrepresentation", said Bentham. But as poetry has been rejected since Galileo, along with all our inward life, while, increasingly, ideas from science have daunted us, stripping the world of meaning, the emergence of human creative consciousness as a primary force in the world must be denied, too.

113

Today, we are in the midst of a revolution, as Marjorie Grene insists: a revolution of life against dead nature—"a revolution founded squarely on the disciplines concerned with life: on biology, psychology, sociology, history, even theology and art criticism". Seventeenth-century thinkers had to free themselves from bonds of scholasticism: we have to free ourselves from the "bonds of Newtonian abstraction"—to dare not only to manipulate abstractions but to *understand*.

This is Blake's cause: but Ted Hughes is on the other side! Not for him the new revolution of understanding and imagination outlined by Marjorie Grene:

> The conceptual reform in which we are now engaged must restore our speech about the world to intelligible discourse and the world it aims at describing to significant and coherent form.

In Ted Hughes's *Gog* even the most intense visions of meaning are nothing: "The atoms of saints' brains are swollen with the vast bubble of nothing." Human spiritual yearnings are mere swellings of nothing-bubbles in the brain. Yet, of course, human meanings and yearnings exist:

> Then whose
> Are these
> Eyes,
>   eyes and
> Dance of wants,
> Of offering?

The eyes are the yearnings for "creative reflection", for the search for meaning in the eyes of the mother, as yearned for by Sylvia Plath—yet met by a moon that is "deader than a skull", as here. Human beings are all "wants" and seek continually the possibility of "offering", of "love and reparation". But just as Sylvia Plath, yearning for the mother's eyes as in mirrors, could only find the face in them to be a kind of death, so all these yearnings are death:

> Sun and moon, death and death,
> Grass and stones, their quick peoples, and the bright particles
> Death and death and death—
> Her mirrors.[3]

114

Hughes's is indeed the universe of modern science, of the Newtonian ideal, which has turned scientific procedure into "a mystic chant over an unintelligible universe". But Hughes makes poetry this kind of futile chant, too: dissociated from the real world as a kind of encapsulated mental rage.

So, in Section III we give way to the joys of this kind of hating. This is a characteristic *false solution* in our time, to the loss of meaning: the dynamics of hate that go with a schizoid response to a schizoid world. The danger is that what Jungians call the "alien psychic factor" may take over, and plunge the individual into destructiveness, as it did Sylvia Plath.

Before we analyze the Section III of this poem we must explain to the reader what is meant by the "schizoid diagnosis", since, I believe, many works by Ted Hughes, like those of Sylvia Plath, cannot be understood and placed, unless we make use of the new insights from psychoanalysis. This is so because writers like Ted Hughes have been encouraged by fashion, and by the advocacy of critics like Alvarez, to employ schizoid modes, and to give themselves over to forms of expression and moral inversion which have an effect on themselves and their art which cuts them off from regeneration. This seems true from the work of those who have examined this kind of problem (Guntrip, Winnicott, Fairbairn, Laing, and Marion Milner). I have dealt with the schizoid problem in art in my book on Mahler and in *Sylvia Plath: Poetry and Existence* (1976). It should be clear that in making a schizoid diagnosis I am not saying an artist is sick or mad: I am saying that he is expressing a characteristically modern problem of self and meaning, to do with weakness of identity, and sometimes taking false (hate) solutions based on an inversion of morality arising from the schizoid problem.

The "schizoid problem" is not, as many people think, following popular ideas, a question of "split personality", but of *weakness of identity*, of emptiness and meaninglessness. According to Guntrip, an individual who has not adequately experienced love from his mother in his own right, feels a vacancy or emptiness of identity. He can also feel himself to be a "mechanism". In terms developed by Winnicott, we can say that in the absence of adequate "creative reflection", the individual has not been able to see himself developing into a human being, "becoming", through responsiveness in the mother's face (an image clearly running throughout Sylvia Plath's work). The infant's need is for the mother to "be for" him, for the kind of responsiveness he needs is one which belongs to "female element being". It is not a mere question of breast-feeding, or bodily contact, or demonstrative love, but a response to the infant which conveys to him his own substantiality of existence, his own quality of emerging *being*, in terms of "having a presence in the being of the other" (Buber): by *liebende Wirheit*. This meaningful interaction generates a creative responsiveness to the whole world.

An individual who has not experienced this confirmation in "encounter" feels empty at the heart, however successfully he manages to deal with everyday life. Guntrip quoted an efficient and successful university lecturer, who came to him and said, "I am nobody"—and this dreadful sense of being nobody, of not being, may be found in a great deal of modern art: in the paintings of Francis Bacon; in Mahler's music; in Kafka and Beckett. But the problem is not merely to be dismissed as neurotic or "ill": it is a characteristic problem of man in the modern world, and is part of the whole failure of creative being in our era which these artists express, and are able to do so because they experience intense schizoid states themselves.

At the heart of this emptiness of identity, there often lurks the image of an unsatisfied, unreflected, hungry baby—waiting for the time when it can be brought to birth. Guntrip writes of how schizoid patients dream of a little baby, or a puppy, perhaps locked in a steel drawer or in some place hidden tightly away, which they care for, deep in themselves, which will someday be born. In Sylvia Plath's *Poem for a Birthday*, this is "Fido Littlesoul": in Ted Hughes it is "Littleblood", (in the last poem in *Crow*) that pulse of life which tells one that one is alive, even when one feels "nobody". This is what Fairbairn called the "Regressed Libidinal Ego", an unborn dynamic in the Self, seeking to *begin*.

"Littleblood" is the pulse which the protagonist of Sylvia Plath's novel *The Bell Jar* feels, as she stands by a grave, or comes round from a suicide attempt, "the old brag of my heart: I AM I AM I AM". Littleblood in Hughes's poem is regressed, "Hiding from the mountains in the mountains. . . ." In *Littleblood* this hidden little creature is "wounded by stars", and is menaced by the "leaking shadow / Eating the medical earth". This brings us to the outward projection of the inner vacancy, the relationship between inner emptiness and the (Newtonian) dead universe. When man feels a "nobody", he also feels that the universe is nothing: and by comparing Fairbairn's account of schizoid conditions with Michael Polanyi's essay *Beyond Nihilism* in *Knowing and Being* (1969) one may obtain a historical perspective, whereby the two feelings are connected: the feeling of inner worthlessness and meaninglessness on the one hand, and the feeling that the universe is nothing and that all is meaningless on the other. There is thus a continual historical connection between nihilism, and the utterance of nihilistic or morally inverted attitudes to human existence, emerging from schizoid individuals and from sceptical views of the world such as those implicit in strict scientific positivism. This can be called a "pathological" view itself because it embodies an essentially schizoid view of existence, emanating from over-intellectualized structures. As Fairbairn says, a great many intellectuals are schizoid people. Such people escape into intellectual systems, because they cannot "be" in their own whole bodies-and-beings. But the intellectual systems they devise (those of Sartre and Bertrand Russell are representative examples) are imbued with schizoid attitudes—and this means they are full of emptiness and hate, moral inversion, and a sense of futility and worthlessness.[4]

But as compensation for these dreadful feelings, an inverted morality develops. As Fairbairn points out, because the schizoid individual has had such a dreadful and empty experience of love, he has come to the conclusion as an infant that *love is harmful*. Within himself he feels there to be a monstrous hungry mouth—with all the power of the "mouth-ego" of the child—which threatens to eat up everyone and everything, out of sheer urge to survive. Because of this voracious mouth of the "Regressed Libidinal Ego", the schizoid individual comes to the conclusion that it is *wrong to love*, because it is so dangerous, and so it is *better* to live *by hate*. Here there are two motives: one is *moral*: because it is so dangerous to love, it is better and more moral to live by hate. The other is the *immoral* motive, which declares that because love is forever debarred from him, the schizoid will live by hate, and "get what pleasure he can out of that". The symbolism of this predicament is sometimes evident in terrorist acts or cultural atrocities. A combination of such motives explains many terrible tragedies, arising from the predicament of the schizoid individual who must live by hate.

This hate is the link between the schizoid problem and philosophies of life based on natural scientism, which I am examining behind the failure of confidence in poetry today. Where individuals cannot feel a sense of strength of identity based on love and reciprocity, they feel that their own human sensitivity, even their creativity, is dangerously vulnerable. These aspects of their make-up are generated by identification with the mother, and by enjoying her "creative reflection" of their emerging selves. So, their emotional and creative potentialities belong to woman, to the feminine, and to the female elements in everyone's identity, in both men and women. Woman and "female element being" thus become targets of hate in a schizoid culture (as is clear all around us today), because they symbolize the dangerous vulnerability of love.

In self-defence against vulnerability, the schizoid individual tends to "armour" himself, as Reich called it. He surrounds himself with a defensive wall of hostility, and black toughness—often clearly symbolized by the uniforms aggressive groups wear, from the Nazis to today's *"blousons noirs"*. In philosophies of life today this defensive manifestation is rationalized in various ways, but fundamentally it is supported by the fashionable view that man's primary reality is his instinctual life of sex and aggression, and belief in his basic "animal" nature. As Guntrip points out, this "model" of human make-up is used by us to conceal the more frightening problem, of our inner vacancy and lack of meaning. He believes that the Freudian "instinct" model is essentially yet another version of the Pauline—of an "unruly" aspect of the self, identified with the "body", which needs to be controlled and ruled by the "mind". In the schizoid diagnosis, Guntrip believes, we discover that this model hides the truth: the very idea of a "struggle" helps us to conceal from ourselves the fact that what we most fear is our weakness, our emptiness, our lack of a sense of meaningful existence a view endorsed in *Dasein*-analysis, and by existentialist thinking as in Rollo May's *Power and Innocence*.

In a sense, of course, to feel strong in such ways is also an

118

avoidance of responsibility. We excuse ourselves by saying we are "victims" of the impersonal forces which "drive" us. The universe itself is seen as a vast process of chance, in which matter in motion simply explodes and collides: life itself simply "happened" by the sun's rays accidentally affecting a passive mud. But here there are complex doubts. E. W. F. Tomlin argues that consciousness could not be a product of mere chance (*Living and Knowing*). In *Darwin Retried* Norman Macbeth points out that evolutionary theory cannot explain how the eye developed: it is far too complex an organ, and needs to be wholly developed to "work", so that it could not function (certainly not to ensure "survival of the fittest") in intermediate stages of evolution, or by degrees. Despite huge unsolved evolutionary questions of this kind, our "art" culture at all levels simply accepts theories of chance and necessity and "blind" evolution, and bases its general philosophy on them. The pessimistic implications are swallowed, because the implicit model seems to offer a brutal strength to the identity, to enable us to avoid contemplating our inner emptiness. And today many in the Arts and Humanities evidently feel, as Ted Hughes seems to, that they must serve the schizoid moral inversions of hate, as "truth".

I have tried to show, in previous works, how the "false solutions" of hate, based on pseudo-male aggressive "strengths", can distort culture. In commercial culture, hate-solutions can be quarried for profit (cf. *The Masks of Hate*). But, as Guntrip says, "it is the weak who hate: only the strong can love". Moral inversion and fanatical immoralism can thus encourage those with weak identities and insecure feelings about existence to adopt the postures of hate—and this can lead to "collective infections", of which one is the "black" tendency of today's fashionable culture. In *Sylvia Plath: Poetry and Existence* I have shown how delicate is the balance between true and false solutions to the problem of existence, and how persuasions to cultivate one's psychosis can contribute to self-destructive dynamics in an artist. It is possible for the false self, or malignant animus, to overwhelm even the individual's quest for authenticity and the true self.

Sylvia Plath's sometime husband, Ted Hughes, stands on a similar knife-edge, not least because he has adopted a view of the

119

universe which is nihilistic and from which it seems impossible to escape. Attention to philosophical biology makes it clear that this view is inadequate and false. Yet it makes Ted Hughes feel that his "Regressed Libidinal Ego" has a hopeless task, seeking for meaning, in a universe which consists of nothing but blind chance interactions of "matter in motion". "Littleblood" in the last poem in *Crow*, is the life that goes on, unremittingly, in this desert, the life-force-infant in oneself that continues to live despite the frailty it shares with all living forms:

> little boneless, little skinless
> Ploughing with a linnet's carcase
> Reaping the wind and threshing the stones . . .

All human effort is futile, bringing no harvest, because of death, and the ultimate running down of the world by universal entropy. All forms of life are mere chance experiments, and we share the terrible experiences embodied in these endless experiments:

> . . . drumming in a cow's skull,
> Dancing with a gnat's feet
> With an elephant's nose with a crocodile's tail . . .

God, who set all these chance mutations off, is (in *Crow*) a "cruel bastard", indifferent to the huge aeons of suffering he has caused —while Crow is the malignant joker who arranges the ghastly experiments, as God sleeps.

All this seems, by Hughes's language, his references to science, and his "vitalism", to be based on "biology". But his biology has not even advanced to the neo-Darwinian stage, and certainly not to that of Portmann and Plessner, biologists who see man as belonging to a higher dimension, inherent in his actual anatomy, of walking upright and being "open to his world".[5] His biology is certainly not that of Teilhard de Chardin who talks of "levels of being", and something like the emergence of consciousness as a manifestation of a dynamic complexity which seems to be seeking to realize itself. Ted Hughes's biology knows nothing of that universal life-process that Leavis calls the "nisus" of which one important element is the natural kind of conscience or "responsibility to life" he calls the *"ahnung"*. Indeed, that special level of being which, as men, we know, is absent from Ted Hughes's universe. His "philosophical anthropology" cannot "find" man, with his vision and creativity of "becoming". So, in his view of the universe he has adopted the most pathological view of science, what we may even call the most *schizoid* scientific view, which has as it were, substituted almost pure "male element doing" for being. He cannot "be-in-the-world", but exists only in an intellectual mind-system from which all creative elements have been eliminated as dangerous. Consciousness itself is a burden: resignation the only posture:

> Grown so wise grown so terrible
> Sucking death's mouldy tits . . .

There is no benignity of being, in a universe to which one belongs, and in which one meaningfully exists. The only milk in the universe is death. Man can only be a contender, cultivating the hate in himself, and having his horse's feet shod with "vaginas of iron". That is, all the weak, female, elements in himself are to be beaten into pseudo-male, aggressive, strong defences, and vulnerable creativity trampled under foot.

The syndrome is well-known to the psychotherapist. Guntrip reports a patient from a case-history:

> I feel now that my physique is weak and girlish, but I felt I was becoming masculine when I got a motor bike. Now I have a car but I still phantasy myself as a ton-up youth taking a shadowy girl on the pillion. . . . When I feel anxious I still put on my leather jacket and tight belt round my waist and look at myself in the glass and feel tough and masculine. . . .
>
> (*Schizoid Phenomena*, p. 256)

Such an individual compensates with his pseudo-male toughness for an ego-weakness left by inadequate creative reflection by the mother: so what he fears most is femininity in himself and others. Yet because of the regressed libidinal ego within himself he wants to be reborn, and will continuously yearn for the womb. But because he is "too big to go backwards" (as Sylvia Plath says of herself in *Poem for a Birthday*) this impulse to regression feels threatening: thus, the vagina, the wound in woman's body, will seem the most terrible threat of all.

Many of these images are found in Ted Hughes. In *Crow* (in *A Childish Prank, the Crow's First Lesson*) the vagina threatens to strangle man, and to lure him to death. (Interestingly enough, this symbolic image appears currently on a French film poster, and on a programme for a play at a fringe theatre, March 1976). Now, let us turn to Part III of *Gog*. Here the horseman gallops

> Out of the wound-gash in the earth . . .
>   shaking his plumes clear of dark soil.
> Out of the blood-dark womb, gallops bowed the horseman of
>   iron . . .

He is the "blood-crossed" knight, the Holy Warrior, hooded with iron, the seraph of the "black edge". The images are characteristically fascistic—for the horseman chooses to base his defiant posture on hate and a denial of all human qualities (as Rauschning said, "We will have no weakness or tenderness in our youth!"). He turns his enmity against all weaknesses, of sensitivity, female element vulnerability and the snares of relationship:

> Through slits of iron his eyes search for the softness of the
>   throat, the navel,
>   the armpit, the groin.
> Bring him clear of the flung web and the coil that vaults from
>   the dust.

From the dust we came, and unto dust we shall all go. It is this life-coil, which is us in our mortality, that the horseman seek to escape. He does not want to be human, and shuns the "flung web" of the claims of love, as a gladiator avoids the net.

In this poem, the poet is turning by identifying with his horseman-hero and his ruthlessness against the human need for dependence and love. But in the light of *Dasein*-analysis he is also turning against human *meaning*. The quest for ultimate *meaning*—the grail—is here being assaulted by a poet because the quest for meaning is a manifestation of the existential anguish he associates with the unborn infant within us:

> Through slits of iron, his eyes have found the helm of the
>   enemy, the grail,
> The womb-wall of the dream that crouches there, greedier
>   than a foetus.
> Suckling at the root-blood of the origins, the salt-milk drug of
>   the mothers.

The horseman seeks to destroy the dream, which is the Grail, which is within a womb-wall: human creativity. Our mouth-hunger is drawing greedily at the question of the origins of life, of the ultimate problems of existence. Yet this is rejected as "the salt-milk drug of the mothers". To someone to whom primary maternal preoccupation seemed a terrible experience, the normal human need to be satisfied by meaning, through love, seems terrible, an ever-unquenched thirst, that must be destroyed. So the horseman becomes a kind of armoured Ned Kelly hero in this poetry.

In these images we have a characteristic archetypal image of our culture. Humanness itself, sensitive, feminine, vulnerable self is identified with the hungry regressed libidinal ego, the unseen weakness that threatens one's existence by its love-hunger, its existence-hunger. The hunger to exist, with all its oral power to suck the inside out of the mother and others (the "object") is confused with the hunger to find the meaning of existence. The Grail, and ultimate love, are the Enemy: the greatest human capacity, to seek transcendence, is contemptuously rejected as a drug or feared as "this dark thing that sleeps in me/looking out with its hooks for something to love" (Sylvia Plath, *Elm*).

Love is the chief enemy, to the "horseman", sealed in his neo-fascist hate. Under the surface of the verse is the *vagina dentata*, the *fanged* grail. All the signs of love—the dipped glance, the kiss —are menaces:

> Shield him from the dipped glance, flying in half light, that
>   tangles the heels,
> The grooved kiss that swamps the eyes with darkness.

Dipped glances fly like bats at twilight and tie up one's ankles: the kiss is grooved like a weapon, and threatens to overwhelm with blindness. Love is the most dangerous force in the world: against it the hero must set intellectual constructions—thought— constructions of hate.

> Bring him to the ruled slab, the octaves of order,
> The law and mercy of number.

Birth is a menace, too:

> **Lift him**
> Out of the octopus maw and the eight lunatic limbs
> Of the rocking, sinking cradle.

123

Man and woman between them have eight limbs (two arms, two legs each). This octopus, of their sexual conjunction in procreation, creates a foetus, and this process is like an octopus that sucks the protagonist's blood, which is what the grooved kisses also threaten:

> The unborn child beats on the womb-wall.
> He will need to be strong
> To follow his weapons towards the light.
> Unlike Coriolanus, follow the blades right through Rome

Coriolanus is a characteristic figure, who toughens himself, even by processes developed from his infant proclivities: so, here, the regressed libidinal ego, that is, the infant self in the ego that has retreated as if in the womb (confused with the infant in the Grail womb), is advised to *armour* himself, like Coriolanus, if he is to survive.

Armouring means developing a total distrust of all normal values: he must cut through these by cynicism:

> And right through the smile
> That is the judge's fury . . .

The seeming benignity of justice is really a mask for hate. The smile may be merely the demands of dependence: "That is the wailing child . . .", or love that is disguised by pretty fairings. But this smile is really demanding conformity: and is hungry hate under the disguise, a hungry snake.

> That is the ribboned gift . . .
> That is the starved adder

Even the intentionality of dreams is to be distrusted:

> That is the kiss in the dream
> That is the nightmare pillow . . .

Creativity is to be distrusted above all: the "seal of resemblances" being *metaphor* itself:

> That is the seal of resemblances
> That is illusion
> That is illusion . . .

Here we have a poet virtually declaring that the most deceitful, menacing, damaging and unreal force in the world is *poetry itself*!

124

So the armoured horseman triumphantly tramples over femininity, petrifying it, destroying its claims:

> The rider of iron, on the horse shod with vaginas of iron,
> Gallops over the womb that makes no claim, that is of stone.

The most creative and delicate forms of love and creativity in woman's body—are despised, wrought into iron, to shoe his horse. This trampling on the despised woman's creativity echoes the symbolism of *Playboy*, and the toughness of the "horseman" is that kind of toughness. By all the weapons at his disposal he attacks the toothed grail, the hungry mouth, the foetus in the womb—all symbols of dangerous love.

> He follows his compass, the lance-blade, the gunsight, out
> Against the fanged grail and tireless mouth
> Whose cry breaks his sleep
> Whose coil is under his ribs
> Whose smile is in the belly of woman
> Whose satiation is the grave.

These lines depict the grail of the horseman's quest as a man-trap *vagina dentata* or toothed vagina that is also the endlessly-demanding maw of the regressed libidinal ego or unborn baby, in the Self. In Sylvia Plath's *Elm* she fears its "malignancy". In Ted Hughes's *Crow* the woman's body threatens to eat or strangle one: in *Orghast* it is the focus of hate. The cry of a baby, out in the world, "whose cry breaks his sleep" evokes the mouth-hunger within: the coil of this baby in "under his ribs"—it is his own guts, his own mortality. It is this new being, seeking to be reborn, who seems to smile in the woman's belly. Its life hunger is dangerous, the goal of the regressed libidinal ego is so powerfully sought, that it seems like a death-wish, and, in hungering to be reborn, actually comes to be *acted out* as a death wish. Moreover, the horseman wishes the created child dead, and the womb-woman dead.

There could be no more powerful expression of an excited desire that woman, the child in her womb, her creativity, femininity in general, and all creative attributes associated with woman,

125

including *poetry*, should be put to the sword, or petrified, in the ruthless career of the hero:

> Out under the blood-dark archway, gallops bowed the horse-
> man of iron.

Gog is certainly a strange poem for a poet to write. Its very energy expresses the schizoid maxim which W. R. D. Fairbairn expresses: "since the joy of love is barred to him, he will give himself over to the joys of hating and get what pleasure he can out of that"—the "immoral motive" in the inverted schizoid logic that has caused so many tragedies. But this is also a consequence of the blankness of our predominent philosophy of existence and its implicit nihilism, in its effect on the poet, as he cultivates the "violence" within him, as a source of "strength".

In *Gog* (and *Crow*) we have expressed the deliberate choice of a meaningless world, a deliberate rejection of a spiritual dimension, a deliberate choice of male "hardness", a deliberate rejection of the feminine of the child and new life "whose cry breaks his sleep". And, in the end, a deliberate rejection of poetry and the imagination virtually as "misrepresentation".

This is the price to pay for accepting the "scientific" universe. The penalty is the loss of the power of symbolizing itself. The capacity to symbolize is an achievement, and it goes with the accomplishment, in the normal child, of processes belonging to the normal stages of development of discovering the world and oneself, and the capacity to use culture in the benign processes of inter-relation. To revert to "acting out", and to the modes of hate, is to revert to delinquent behaviour that can achieve nothing—just as in a classroom a disturbed child will stop painting, and upset his water, tear the paper, or throw his brush at the teacher. Abandon-ment to schizoid modes thus leads to a loss of the essential fastidi-ousness of the artist—his concern for *meaning*—now a general feature of our culture.

Fastidiousness was the mark of some of Ted Hughes's early work. In *Wodwo*, for instance he ends still searching for the human-ness he cannot find in himself, and he is comically modest about the hope of ever finding it:

> What am I? Nosing here, turning leaves over . . .
> . . . again very queer but I'll go on looking.

But he is still content to be modest in a delicate quest for answers to the question, "what is it to be human?" In *Full Moon and Little Frieda* our attention is rivetted by the exactness of the words to small, delicate moments in experience:

> A cool small evening shrunk to a dog bark and the clank of a
>   bucket—
> And you listening.
> A spider's web, tense for the dew's touch.
> A pail lifted, still and brimming—mirror
> To tempt a first star to a tremor.

Here the mirror of the bucket's surface is a common-place object which is yet full of meaning. A version of the reflecting mother in domesticity, it is a symbol of female element capacities *to be*—still and brimming—and *seductive*. The seductiveness has the gentle quality of tenderness that can "tempt a first star to a tremor". In the farmyard, near the river of blood of the cows (which are "balancing unspilled milk")—the girl child is reflected upon as a female creature. She has within her the capacities to reflect, and so, like the surface of shivering water in the bucket, as it is lifted, she can call out a "first star" by "tempting". She creates a new moment. The first star is the first star to appear in the evening, and it is a symbol of the first lover to be called shyly out by the little girl's capacities for "encounter". (Sylvia Plath's comets, symbols of infant gestures crossing great gulfs of nothingness, seem to be in the background).[6] To call out stars by the power of "encounter" is also to call out meaning—and here, in this delicate poem of understatement, the universe has meaning because a child is looking at it. There in the heavens is the moon-mother, which the universe has created: " 'Moon!' you cry suddenly, 'Moon! Moon!' "

The "word" here is not malevolent, but creative: it *intends* the perceived moon, and creates it: placing it in the heavens:

> The moon has stepped back like an artist gazing amazed at
>   a work
> That points at him amazed . . .

In such a poem we have great strength—the strength of true creativity. The creativity is rooted in love, and the recognition of

127

the creative power encounter has, to give meaning to the universe for us.

Full Moon and Little Frieda is a poem of great strength and beauty: yet it belongs to the evanescent moments of everyday, loving, experience. And the strength of this art can be underlined by placing alongside it Lewis Mumford's emphasis on the way in which consciousness can give the world meaning. Indeed, the universe is only of concern because man perceives it, and seeks to give it meaning. Without that light, it is nothing:

> For man to feel belittled, as so many do now, by the vastness of the universe or the interminable corridors of time is precisely like his being frightened by his own shadow. It is only through the light of consciousness that the universe becomes visible, and should that light disappear, only nothingness would remain. Except on the lighted stage of human consciousness the mighty cosmos is but a mindless nonentity. Only through human words and symbols registering human thought, can the universe disclosed by astronomy be rescued from its everlasting vacuity. Without that lighted stage, without the human drama played upon it, the whole theatre of the heavens, which so deeply moves the human soul, exalting and dismaying it, would dissolve again into its own existential nothingness, like Prospero's dreamworld.
>
> (*The Myth of the Machine*, Lewis Mumford, p. 33)

Such fastidious attention to the true nature of human existence as we find in *Full Moon and Little Frieda* would, however, seem "pallid and artificial"[7] beside the schizoid exaggeration of *Crow*. The negative dynamic is there in *Wodwo* already, for the horseman in *Gog* whose mount is shod with "vaginas of iron" gallops on towards the harsh treatment of the "rows of vaginas" in *The Battle of Osfrontalis*. This black figure is galloping away in terror from the "female element" so creatively perceived in *Full Moon and Little Frieda*. So from one book to the other we cross a gulf, from a delicate perception of the creativity of a child's human vision, to a coarse hysteria, which denigrates human encounter in the language of the gutter press: "Horrors—hairy and slobbery, glossy and raw" (p. 86).

Crow belongs, like Ken Russell's buboes and manhandled actresses in his films, to the "acting out", the forfeiture of symbolism, and the literalism that menace the future of the Arts

128

today. The harm done to poetry is profound. The collapse of poetic language is at one with the damage done to the delicate web of "encounter" between human beings especially in the sphere of those female elements of being which establish *liebende Wirheit*, loving intersubjectivity, as a source of human potentiality and freedom.

In *Crow*, for instance, sexual relationships are reduced to grotesque acts of meaningless violence, in which every word is exploited for the juice of repulsiveness, or hate, which it can yield ("sniff . . . fasten . . ."). Primitive schizoid fears of mutual incorporation are evoked, so that (as often) under the "excuse" of a reference to the nuclear bomb, there can be an "acting out" indulgence in a primitive vision of the Primal Scene (i.e. sadistic parental intercourse)[8]

> They sniff towards each other in the emptiness.
> They fasten together. They seem to be eating each other.
> But they are not eating each other.

This is a regression to the infant's primitive fears of a schizoid kind, to a primitive belief that sex is a mutual eating which brings threats of annihilation. It makes no reference at all to the humanization which ameliorates such fears in us: "They have begun to dance a strange dance . . ." This meaningless act, taking place between two ghastly creatures, done "without guest or God" is Hughes's only gesture in *Crow* towards survival. If man survives, it will only be as a monstrous mutation who has no consciousness of his own sexuality, no capacity for choice, but is simply at the mercy of hideous instinctual drives. This survival is one which is only to be seen, cynically, as the futile but determined proliferation of monstrosities. Hughes is bitterly ironic:

> And this is the marriage of these simple creatures—
> Celebrated here, in the darkness of the sun . . .

The "human form divine" in *Crow* is utterly without redeeming features. In *Full Moon and Little Frieda* we have intentionality and love making the universe—and making it love her in return. In *Fragment of an Ancient Tablet* the emphasis is on the animal below-waist reality that undercuts human meaning in the face. The Human form is (*"above"*) "Well-known lips", "her brow, the notable casket of gems", a "word and a sigh"—but ("*below*") "The belly with its blood-knot" . . . "gouts of blood and babies". Conscious human woman is reduced to disfigured or bloody genitals.

> Above—the face, shaped like a perfect heart.
> Below—the heart's torn face . . .
> (*Fragment of an Ancient Tablet, Crow*, p. 85)

The "ticking bomb of the future" is her womb with its creative urge that can only lead to the "population explosion" and the ecocatastrophe, by determinist drives. The woman's vagina looks like a brutal wound. In many such works today—and not least in poetry—men seem to be obsessed with disgust at female sexuality. Moreover, combined with masculine protest is the impulse to put this femaleness in human nature to death and the sword. So

> Burning
> burning
> burning

(in *Crow's Last Stand*) becomes not a compassionate incantation over the sterility of a civilization (as in *The Fire Sermon*), but a statement that *all creation* is *doomed by entropy* (and the sooner the better). All that is left is a passive eye recording—and unwillingly staring at the meaninglessness of nothingness:

> there was finally something
> The sun could not burn . . .—a final obstacle . . .
> Crow's eye-pupil, in the tower of its scorched fort.
> (p. 81)

The seeing eye in *Crow* does not give meaning to the universe: the eye of the creature who has "given himself up to the joys of hating" can only doggedly view the malignancy of everything. One of the most malignant things about Hughes's blank universe is its refusal to allow the seeing eye to lose its terrible capacity to see.[9] In such attitudes there is a "longing for non-being", but one which sees, as does de Sade, with loathing, that love—and the universe—will, alas, persist, even despite the most intense dynamics of hate, in the attempt to destroy it.

In this brutal universe (which is the world of Edmund in *King*

Lear) Crow is that-in-the-self-which-endures: a knot in the dynamics of the self by which it is hoped to survive. Crow is a split-off knot of "masculine protest": a dissociated, black, hate-based, pseudo-male form of doing—paranoid—schizoid, ruthless, incapable both of suffering and of being violated. This split-off indestructible self is the schizoid split-off self we invent when, say, under shellfire, it seems to hover above us, out of our bodies —and will, by magic, survive even if the body and self are annihilated, a form of magic. It was no doubt spun out of personal suffering. That this Crow-self is one aspect of Ted Hughes himself becomes clear with some of the poems added to the latest edition of *Crow*: for instance on p. 79 the poem is called *Crow Paints Himself*—but the "I" has the voice of Hughes himself: "My thin shoesoles tremble. . . ."

The magic Crow becomes a creature in the Cosmos, who is even outside God and God's power: outside natural law. Ted Hughes, talking to George Macbeth on the radio about Crow called him "a childish hanger-on to the events of Creation". We could interpret this to mean that he is the kind of nightmare creature a child might imagine, who plays tricks of a malicious kind and is not always under control.[10] He was "created by God's nightmare" —so, he is not the product of dream and vision, but like a nightmare that comes unbidden. He "tries to become a man" and is "ready to turn into I don't know what". In the inner world of Hughes's fantasy he is the embodiment of the "alien psychic factor". He resembles Sylvia Plath's detached animus-Daddy, in some respects, as a black, male, phallic force of hate ("I fly about like clubs!"). It is thus significant that Crow bears human male genitals on the cover of Ted Hughes's book.

He is "indestructible" says Hughes, in his radio talk, "like Horatio". In this we may glimpse the self-curative element in *Crow*. But surely nothing in fact could be further from Shakespeare's Horatio's balanced and sane embodiment of values than Crow? The comparison shows that the cynical nihilism embodied in Crow seems to Hughes an embodiment of the truth. Crow is the "rubbish of the earth"—he is subjected to the worst humiliations, to see if he can endure: he is "outside God"—and so, outside the flux of created life in time, in which alone we can find our freedom and responsibility. He "tries to become a man". But it would

131

be terrible if this split-off Bad Male Imago did so, for then it might become total destructiveness (or hate)—which is perhaps what Ted Hughes fears, and defends himself from by his ambiguous view, as by talking as if Crow weren't "him", or "his". But, he admits, "once he's exposed he's finished". So long as the identity sustains the sense of being a horseman, "shod with vaginas of iron", it can fend off the paranoid dangers of cosmic malignancy. But, as with the patient in the black jacket, the purpose is to hide emptiness. Crow, thus, is a false-self defence against "unthinkable" fears. But if he were to be seen as a mere empty skin hiding an inner emptiness, everything would collapse into nothingness—or so it feels to Hughes. So, he must cling to Crow and identify with him, as he does with great success and popularity.

Despite his capacities for survival, however, Crow is no more than a passive "contender", without *potentia*, without the power of finding meaning in his world, or finding authenticity. He is merely put to the test of all manner of hostilities—like woman in pornography, representing the weak and despicable humanness which is feared, as likely to betray us, and so is subjected to hostility and assault again and again, triumphed over, in the hope of gaining control. Crow is thus continually subjected to experiments and yet (like Lady Lazarus) cannot really ever be destroyed, even when he becomes nothing:

> It was a naked powerline, 2000 volts—
> He stood aside, watching his body go blue
> As he held it and held it . . .
>
> The earth, shrunk to the size of a hand grenade
>
> And he held it and held it and held it
>
> BANG!
> He was blasted to nothing.

This is from *Truth Kills Everybody*: the truth is Proteus ("steaming . . . stinking"). The truth *is* "bulging Achilles", the oesophagus of a shark, a "wreath of lashing mambas, a screeching woman, Christ's hot pounding heart". It is, we might say, an infinite variety of forms of hate, structures identified with the "animal organism"—existence reduced to nothing but the matter and functions of which it is composed, without consciousness. Even

Christ's divinity is reduced to the final moment of entropy. Whatever the truth of Crow or the truth of that which Crow confronts,
he never becomes the kind of truth in the world recognized (over
the subject of bird migration) by the philosophical biologist:

> . . . if we consider all the aspects of these migratory phenomena
> in their immense variety, it becomes increasingly plain that they
> surpass elementary practical needs, such as the preservation of the
> species. All necessity is transcended in these great formative pro-
> cesses, into which tellurian events are integrated as wonderful
> alarm signals for the awakening and enrichment of organic life in
> time. The passage of clock time, meaningless in itself, is employed
> for the enrichment of life. It need hardly be added that human life
> is a magnificent configuration of time in the same sense, offering
> in its successive ages ever new possibilities of development in time
> and hence of living riches.

(*Time in the Life of the Organism, Man and Time,* by Adolf Port-
    mann, Princeton University Press, 1957, quoted by Grene,
    p. 42).

From here we begin to gather clues, as to how we might overcome the nihilism that *Crow* urges upon us. In the light of the new
biology and the new philosophical biology we can see that what
Hughes takes for "brutal truth" is out of date, and in fact arises from
the belated effects in the Humanities of out-of-date nineteenth-
century natural science. So, if we do some work on philosophical
problems, we can expose both Crow and his creator, and "finish"
them, in their attempts to lock us in an inescapable idolized despair. As Bernard Towers points out, one major problem is the
impingement on cultural thinking of two scientific concepts: the
theory of Evolution and the second Law of Thermodynamics. As
this scientist says, while many "literary" people could not be expected to quote the Second Law with accuracy, or to give an
account of evolutionary theory,

> the literary culture has understood more clearly, and grasped more
> honestly, the real implications of (the) scientific world picture
> (derived from these two concepts).

(*Concerning Teilhard,* p. 94)

This world picture, Towers says, is outlined by Sherrington:

> The living energy-system, in commerce with its surround, tends
> to increase itself. If we think of it as an eddy in the stream of

energy it is an eddy which tends to grow; as part of this growth we have to reckon with its starting other eddies from its own resembling its own. This propensity it is which furnishes opportunity under the factors of evolution for a continual production of modified patterns of eddy. It is as though they progressed toward something. But philosophy reflects that the motion for the eddy is in all cases drawn from the stream and the stream is destined, so the second laws of thermodynamics says, irrevocably to cease. The head driving it will, in accordance with an ascertained law of dynamics, run down. A state of static equilibrium will then replace the stream. The eddies in it which we call living must then cease. And yet they will have been evolved. Their purpose then was temporary? It would seem so.

(Man on His Nature)

So, we have a paradox, of proliferating manifestations of life, and of the increasing "complexity of consciousness"—but aimless and doomed. As Towers says:

The idea that because of the very nature of things the only possible ultimate future for man is annihilation, has crept like a paralysis through our culture. . . . Important writers in modern literary and philosophical movements have accepted this profoundly pessimistic vision as the true one. Mankind as a whole is a dead duck. Significance must be sought, if at all, in analysis of the isolated individual—and this at a time when the individual, once he has arrived at his own most certain death, is looked upon as no more than a bag of bones undergoing the much more probable process of thermodynamic decay.

(Concerning Teilhard, p. 95)

Yet, as Towers says, in taking such views from science "we have been led astray by the inadequate scientific understandings of the past". What we have to examine here are the literary person's highly subjective seizure on scientific theories which have their own inadequacies—and the literary person's extrapolation of these to forms of general philosophy in which sphere they have none of the validity or authenticity which science (justifiably) claims as the "one uncontestable intellectual authority in our time", in its own sphere.

Moreover, while science (as Towers says) goes on—despite its laws which clutch at the heart with their cold fingers—cheerfully believing in progress, the effect of its false extrapolations is to make *cultural* men, and even poets, feel hopeless, as scientists never do. Moreover, as science develops new and more adequate theories, these do not affect the "cultural" person, who is now locked, in any case, in a nihilistic world-view that feels "strong", and which he finds it hard to relinquish.

Today, there is no authentic reason in science or philosophy, to see the world as an unintelligible and alien cosmos, in which man is not at home, and which seems "designed" to torment him with his nothingness (although that there could be anything like "design" is exactly what is denied). Whether or not there is a God there is no cause to call Him a "cruel bastard". Indeed, it is absurd—and some would say a paradox of impertinence—for the most conscious and complex creature in creation, Man, who in a sense makes the cosmos intelligible and meaningful by being conscious of it, to see that universe and himself as pointless. He is the one product of that universe able to perceive its nature, to look backwards and forwards, and to create a future. Yet his reward for this mysterious gift is to declare that everything simply *is*, and is simply nothingness, himself included! Such a denial of the wonder and miracle of being in existence, inheriting the "mansions of consciousness", and given *potentia*, is surely the most blameworthy of all acts?

Moreover, if we fall victims to unconsidered and questionable philosophical assumptions based on these half-understood scientific theories, we also surrender our freedom. If we accept the determinism implicit in mechanism and the nihilism implicit in positivism, and feel unable to escape from nullity, then we become victims of circumstance, and, in consequence may suffer from what E. K. Ledermann calls existential neurosis.[11] We may feel we cannot exercise our creative will and so become prevented from exercising our freedom in existence, because we lose our sense of authenticity. This is the deeper objection to the nihilistic postures of contemporary art: they imprison us, and deprive us even of finding our potentialities through the arts themselves. It is clear that Hughes has been overcome by this paralysis. His characteristic protagonist undergoes only futile suffering:

> Grinning into the black
> Into the ringing nothing
> Through the bones of his teeth

135

> Sometimes with eyes closed
> In his senseless trial of strength . . .

Ted Hughes's man is a "bag of bones", a skull, whose endurance of cosmic infringement is absurd. Man is a "useless passion" and the poetry is poetry written to this thesis. His "contender" man, hanging on in this pointless existence, is evidently unable to exert his freedom or authenticity: sometimes he simply hangs on with closed eyes.

Again we may compare the view of the philosophical biologist:

> The whole biological development of a typical mammal has been re-written in our case in a new key: the whole structure of the embryo, the whole rhythm of growth, is directed, from first to last, to the emergence of a culture-dwelling animal—an animal not bound within a pre-determined ecological niche like the tern or the stag or the dragonfly or even the chimpanzee, but, in its very tissues and organs and aptitudes, born to be *open to its world*, to be able to accept responsibility, to make its own the traditions of a historical past and to remake them into a foreseeable future.
>
> (Marjorie Grene, *Approaches to a Philosophical Biology*, p. 48)

This is the creature seen and cherished by existentialism, who defines himself by his choices, and whose primary impulse is to fulfil his *potentia*.

By contrast, in our fashionable literary culture, man is everywhere a passive victim—as he is in *Crow*. Man is the victim of a God, whose most fundamental acts of creation are either cruel jokes, or accidents to which he is indifferent. God sleeps on his problems while human bodies lie around without souls"

> Dully gaping, foolishly staring, inert
> On the flowers of Eden.

Crow bites a worm in half: "God's only son." The worm is God's only son, because the only thing God begat with full deliberate awareness in Creation was death. So, it is Death that is bitten "Into two writhing halves. . . ." Here we have the Death Instinct with a vengeance lying behind the id-instinctual drives of sex, in Hughes's "philosophy".

> He stuffed into man the tail half
> With the wounded end hanging out.

136

He stuffed the head half headfirst into woman
And it crept in deeper and up
To peer out through her eyes
Calling its tail-half to join up quickly, quickly
Because O it was painful . . .
                    (*A Childish Prank, Crow*, p. 19)

Here the face of woman in love is the face of death which has eaten its way up from her genitals, after being bitten in half by Crow, so that what looks out of her eyes is the face of hungry death! The man in desire is possessed by penis-death, seeking to join with the death-worm in the woman.[12] Their coupling is a brutality, half-awake, half-asleep, the involuntary act of a fragmented worm, outside themselves and their volition:

Man awoke being dragged across the grass.
Woman awoke to see him coming
Neither knew what had happened.

God went on sleeping

Crow went on laughing.

                    (p. 15)

God is indifferent to the creation of our most creative act: that in which we find our deepest love and meaning. Sex was a practical joke thrust on us by God's nightmare, as a prank of his deathly voraciousness. So, in Ted Hughes's world, love is no source of meaning: it is just another cruel, absurd, futile joke at our expense.

Once we unravel the trick of inverting every value and every positive, from a philosophical formula based on an absurd mis-use of science and nihilistic ("old") existentialism, *Crow* appears rather as a foolish paranoid *blague*, than a genuine poetic exploration of experience. (This explains why students discussing the poems begin by being appalled—but end by giggling). Moreover, it is a *blague-à-thèse*. The *blague* is simply to invert every value, on the basis of reductionism. For instance, the poet simply turns birth on its head and calls it *A Kill*. So perverse, so exaggerated in a Grand Guignol way, is this negativism that, despite its logical appeal (belonging to what Polanyi calls "the logically stabler state of complete moral inversion"), it becomes increasingly unconvinc-

ing as one becomes familiar with it. Instead of being "equipped
with nimble limbs", Crow is "Flogged lame with legs". He is not
born into consciousness but "Shot through the head with balled
brains". That is, his brains are in his head like a lump of lead
or "balled" in the sense that they simply follow his testicles, or are
"ballsed up".

> Shot blind with eyes
> Nailed down by his own ribs . . .
> Clubbed unconscious by his own heart.

The body is not only a burden, as it is to Hamlet: it has been
thrust on one by violence: life itself is a malicious stab, only seen
in a flash as one drowns in one's own blood.

> Seeing his life stab through him, a dream flash
> As he drowned in his own blood . . .

To be born is to be split open and crashed on to the earth, as if
jettisoned by an air disaster:

> . . . letting the cry rip through him as at a distance
> And smashed into the rubble of the ground . . .

But at the moment of birth, it is not that the neonate comes
into the light, but ". . . everything went black". Everything is
given up to blackness:

> Black was the without eye . . . a black rainbow
> Bent in emptiness—over emptiness . . .

And agony—"In the beginning was Scream . . ."
It is true that fleetingly Crow is begotten, born and flies—but
as a mere survivor or victim:

> But flying . . .
> Trembling featherless elbows in the nest's filth . . .

The message of the poems is that "one is" merely, and that the
world "is"—there are no levels of being; there is no transcendence
of the weight of one's guts: there is no meaning and no values.
The message of Samuel Beckett's cult of inanition has sunk dis-
mally home—so that Ted Hughes himself is "seen" by "God's
nightmare", Crow—in *Crow Alights*, as a nothing.
The universe is nothing but a herding of meaningless nothings:

138

Crow saw the herded mountains, steaming in the morning.
And he saw the sea,
Dark-spined, with the whole earth in its coils . . .

The stars are "mushrooms of the nothing forest"—little pulses that spring up in a vast emptiness, "the virus of God". And he shivered with the horror of Creation. . . ." This "horror of creation" is a phrase which coarsely prejudges the particular posture Ted Hughes adopts.[13]

Fortunately, we are on the threshold[14] of a new scientific and philosophical view which both finds the complexity and mystery —but also finds man at home in the universe. The creative writer needs urgently to find such new views of man and of mind. This is not to demand a new anthropocentricity—but to demand a greater awe, which is capable of tasting the immense responsibilities loaded upon man by his role as the seer of what otherwise would be unseen, and his capacity, through consciousness, to search for some understanding of the potentiality in matter that he represents. This, again, raises immense problems of the nature of knowledge itself.

As Leavis says:

> The creative nisus is essentially heuristic: the *ahnung* that informs it is not to be identified with the apprehension of a telos or ultimate goal. The new knowledge and the new sense of the real to which it leads involve a new apprehension of possibility, creative impulsion and goal. Blake's reaction against Newton and Locke represents the really momentous new development associated with the complex spiritual and cultural eruption that we call the Romantic Revolution—eruption of ideas, impulsions and intransigently conscious human needs. His compellingly presented conception of an ultimate human responsibility . . . recommends itself peculiarly to our needs at this crisis of human history. . . .
>
> (*The Human World*, No. 7, p. 6)

Unless we are able to revise our concepts of knowledge, and rediscover our new stance towards the universe, we may perish; any corruption of our attitudes here jeopardizes survival. As Leavis continues:

> Essential or Blakean responsibility manifests itself in the full acceptation recognition that the directing *ahnung* implicit in life and the

nisus that has led to the achieving of mind and anticipatory apprehension and initiative are to be thought of as . . . pre-eminently represented by humanity and continually recreated in response to change, in the human world, and it entails of its very nature the recognition that (in Collingwood's words) it "must ultimately depend for its existence on something other than itself" (*ibid.*, p. 6).

In *Crow* Ted Hughes renounces this creativity, and this responsibility: his mood of "giving himself up to the joys of hating" is arrogant and self-indulgent. Not only is Creation a reality to be regarded with horror, it is a hallucination.

In the hallucination of the horror
He saw this shoe, with no sole, rain-sodden,
Lying on a moor.
And there was this garbage can, bottom rusted away,
A playing place for the wind, in a waste of puddles.
There was this coat, in the dark cupboard, in the silent room,
    in the silent house,
There was this face, sucking its cigarette between the dusk
    window and the fire's embers
Near the face, this hand, motionless
Near the hand, this cup.

Ted Hughes himself is "man" here, as seen by Crow. *But what Crow sees is all there is:* there is no denying it,

Crow blinked.   He blinked,   Nothing faded.
He stared at the evidence.
Nothing escaped him. (Nothing could escape.)

While posturing as "the contender", Hughes also tries to lock us in the reductionist vision of man, as seen in the perspective of the ironical (and "realistic") Crow. No-one can escape from their state in existence: nothing must escape our "objective" view of this. Crow lets none of this reality escape his ironical penetration. Blink as he will, the truth will not be dispersed. Nothing can escape the prison of the "objective" view—or must be allowed to.

It is time for us to reject this new imprisonment, and to expose its sentimentality and cowardice. By now, after *Endgame* and the opening scene of *Oh! Calcutta!* (by the same author) with the human bodies lying among garbage, naked, hasn't it all become as cliché, as boringly empty, as the language of Crow? Don't we too obviously expect to find that abandoned "garbage can"? (Why the Americanism? Why not "dustbin"?). The other properties in the scene are very old ones, "playing place for the wind" from earlier poems like *Nocturnes* by T. S. Eliot, expressing the schizoid dehumanization of the contemporary urban environment ("dry and curled and ready to snap", "vacant shuttles weave the wind"), though here they are used not to prompt our attention to spiritual emptiness: rather to prevent us from escaping from a sense of being imprisoned inescapably in our own paralysis.

Any attempt to recover from paralysis is caricatured by Ted Hughes.

> When God, disgusted with man
> Turned towards heaven.
> And man, disgusted with God,
> Turned towards Eve,
> Things looked like falling apart.
> But Crow   Crow
> Crow nailed them together . . .
> . . . heaven and earth creaked at the joint
> Which became gangrenous and stank . . .
> Crow
> Grinned
> Crying: "This is my Creation",
> Flying the black flag of himself.

When the crucifixion occurs, a great moment of meaning in our civilization, Crow reduces it to a stinking corpse: the only alternative to belief is a cynicism rooted in scientific realism. Crow "starts in on the two thieves". When there is a battle, Crow "has to start looking for something to eat". He may weep, but in spite of himself he must stab at living substance and eat it: cut off this ingestion

> Came the eye's
> roundness
> the ear's
> deafness.

Here we may examine the guilt expressed, at living, and especially over *eating*. Not only, as in *Littleblood*, is Ted Hughes living and

141

breathing in spite of himself: he must, in order to live, eat. So he must endure the anguish of being aware of the way in which living things must consume others—while at the same time being aware of his own consuming need for others (his dependence) and his need for meaning. Yet to him, as to Sylvia Plath (cf. *Tulips*) there is from time to time a dreadful apprehension of the eye that must and does see—and yet sees no meaning: the ear that hears, and yet is deaf. There are images of "life without feeling alive"—of life as it feels to the schizoid individual. So, we may trace Ted Hughes's sense of passive victimization to schizoid fashions, while the cynicism merely gives a ticket to egoistical nihilism (appalled by nothingness, one simply "starts in" on anything going).

The poem *Lovesong* gives a clue to the obsession in *Crow* with eating, and the guilt and anguish bound up with it. *Lovesong* is a statement of the primitive fear bound up in the schizoid individual, of the harmful consequences of love. It is a poem that does not really belong in *Crow*, because it has to do with human experience not in *Crow*'s cynical dimension. But it provides a useful clue. The fears expressed are those of "implosion"—of the schizoid fear that the hunger in love will prove so demanding that it destroys the identity and even the existence of the other. It is also, of course, an expression of the sucking, biting and incorporative-sadistic impulses lurking beneath any sexual relationship, not least in phantasy. But because these are associated with the Regressed Libidinal Ego, they express the fear that love is so dangerous as to threaten annihilization:

> He loved her and she loved him
> His kisses sucked out her whole past and future or tried to
> He had no other appetite
> She bit him she gnawed him she sucked
> She wanted him complete inside her
> Safe and sure forever and ever
> Their little cries fluttered into the curtains. . . .

The last line makes the sucking a sexual act. In the end, after this mutual eating (such as the child imagines the parents' sexual act to be), "In the morning they were each other's face. . . ." I have discussed the mutual intensity of such identification, in discussing Sylvia Plath. Ted Hughes says of himself and his wife that they

142

felt they wrote poetry "out of the same brain". Such close identification is also very frightening and often brought intense problems of envy, as are expressed in *The Wishing Box*, a short story
by Sylvia Plath: and her poem *The Shrike* in *Two Lovers and a
Beachcomber*, where one may glimpse the ferocity of the envy of
a partner's creativity. In many places, she deals with fears of
the intense consuming hunger of the Regressed Libidinal Ego, "All
Mouth".[15] The guilt and fear about eating may be seen in relation
to this fear of close identification.

Hughes sees the world as being full of incorporation which
makes the world seem too terrible: this arises from his own fear
and guilt, combined with a reductionist philosophy:

> The swift's body flew past
> Pulsating
> With insects
> And their anguish, all it had eaten.
>
> The cat's body writhed
> Gagging
> A tunnel
> Of incoming death-struggles, sorrow on sorrow.
>
> And the dog was a bulging filterbag
> Of all the deaths it had gulped for the flesh and the bones.
> It could not digest their screeching finales
> Its shapeless cry was a blort of all those voices
>
> Even man he was a walking
> Abbattoir
> Of innocents—

This is both an expression of a truth of animal existence: that
everything, to live, must prey. But at the same time it is reductionist, in that it makes the cat *nothing more* than a tunnel of guts.
The dog's cry here is only "shapeless"—yet this is not so, for a
dog has many voices, in its capacity to give tongue, its signal
gestures, its encounter rituals, its enjoyment of its world, its
selbstdarstellung.

Crow knows of moralistic injunctions against living at the expense of others. Ought he to aspire to the light?

> Crow thought "Alas
> Alas ought I
> To stop eating
> And try to become the light?"
>
> But his eye saw a grub ...

But, despite his idealism he becomes a victim of his drives, of his savage nature. He weeps, but he cannot escape—so, "came the eye's roundness", of voracious predatory vision, and the ear's deafness to screams of the dying: everything begins with "Scream". There is no escape from animality, and moral aspiration is inevitably defeated by biological "impulses".

The origin and continuance of life in *Crow* is in hate—and yet one cannot die, but can only live through the anguish, despising oneself for eating, while being driven in other ways by one's "natural" instincts. Whatever choice one makes, one is guilty. With this view of man's "reality", Hughes must inevitably continually make an attack on the possibility of love. It is inverted, simply, to become hate.

So, when God tries to teach Crow to say "love", the result is a leaping forth from the world around the most energetic manifestations of hate:

> God tried to teach Crow how to talk
> "Love," said God. "Say, love"
> Crow gaped, and the white shark crashed into the sea
> And went rolling downwards, discovering its own depth ...

This means that "If I open my mouth to speak of love I am afraid that hate will leap out at me in the world". It also means "A split-off embodiment of hate like Crow could never learn love"—but it is also by implication cynical about the idea of a God who can prate about Love, having made a world that is so full of incorporative viciousness.

Yet the biology, as so often in Hughes, is faulty. Alvarez says Ted Hughes writes "like a nature poet gone blind": we might rather say that he writes like a nature poet who throws his own anthropormorphic cynicism over the world he sees, and takes from biology *only* what justifies hate. Biologically, most creatures are sparing in their predatoriness, and this is perhaps more remarkable than hate: it ensures survival, and is only one aspect of a vast symbiotic complex.

> "No, no," said God. "Say Love. Now try it. LOVE".
> Crow gaped, and bluefly, a tsetse, a mosquito
> Zoomed out and down
> To their sundry fleshpots . . .
>
> > (*Crow's First Lesson, Crow,* p. 20)

But the "moral" here is crude—for why should the less attractive aspects of Creation, less attractive that is to *man*, be seen as symbols of that which makes "Love" a reality, to be denied in favour of hate?[16]

From this inept philosophical-poetic biology Hughes slips into making human love, procreation, and encounter disgusting forms of impulse, unwillingly experienced, and mutually destructive:

> "A final try", said God. "Now, LOVE."
> Crow convulsed, gaped, retched and
> Man's bodiless prodigious head
> Bulbed out onto the earth, with swivelling eyes
> Jabbing protest—
>
> And Crow retched again, before God could stop him.
> And woman's vulva dropped over man's neck and tightened,
> The two struggled together on the grass.
> God struggled to part them, cursed, wept—
>
> Crow flew guiltily off.

Human birth and human love are the creation of a mistake of "God's nightmare"—which God would have prevented if he could—and which are the product of a retching attempt to pronounce an unspeakable concept! Yet inter-relationship is the basis of autonomy in the higher animals, while love is the basis of all man's freedom and creative power.

In *Crow* it is as if Ted Hughes is saying, "This—Crow's—is a view of existence from which I cannot dissociate myself and which menaces me". ("Nothing escapes: nothing can escape"). Since universal entropy swallows all, all one can do is to hang on, like the Contender, in a dumb and futile doggedness—until one becomes that grinning skull which concludes a pointless life.

A poem like *Examination at the Womb Door* rests on the view that death an entropy swallow everything and make it a nullity. Yet it could be rewritten entirely from another point of view:

> What created these complex, well-adapted
>   feet, with their capacity to grasp,
>   feel, touch?
>   —Life.
> What developed this pattern of
>   muscular positionality, that
>   keeps upright and flies?
>   —Life.
> What gave this creature a trial in
>   the evolutionary process?
>   —Life.
> What has emerged from this planet as
>   on no other yet discovered?
>   —Life.
> What is the most significant outcome
>   of the cosmic flux?
>   —Life.
> —and the consciousness that serves it!
> In what can we find a sense of
>   meaning that makes death
>   and entropy irrelevant, in
>   terms of the need to exert
>   a quest for authenticity in
>   the face of temporality?
>   —Love.
> What is it that is of interest and
>   concern to us in the way
>   non-being is not?
>   —Life.
> What is it that gives Life meaning?
>   —Death.
> It is no wonder, then, that any creature
>   just born is of greater significance
>   than death?
> Pass, Crow.

I do not claim that that is a poem. But it does, I believe, indicate that to make a successful poem in the positive quest for meaning in such a vein, would require something more serious

146

than *Crow*, more complex than its crude, simplistic jokes, and its reckless nihilism.

For *Crow* is a serious attack on our existential seriousness. It offers to warn us of the destructive potentialities in experience— and yet it is only a black joke. At times it reads like a *Private Eye* parody of poetry, rather than like poetry itself.

In *Conjuring in Heaven*:

> So finally there was nothing.
> It was put inside nothing . . .
> Chopped up with a nothing . . .
>   nothing more could be done with it
>
> And so it was dropped. Prolonged applause in Heaven.
>
> It hit the ground and broke open—
>
> There lay Crow, cataleptic

However, it is only fair to say that in places one becomes aware that there *is* a serious psychological problem behind *Crow*—which is that of the female element itself. The protagonist is recognizably the creature of Gog and Wodwo, and behind all the braggadoccio there is an admission, here and there, of the underlying weakness. As in *Littleblood*, among all the Grand Guignol props (which belong to the posture of pseudo-male "bad thinking") there is a recognition of the needs of the unborn creature, the Regressed Ego, Littlesoul, who needs to be reflected. This is a problem of finding the "significant other" in woman, while eliminating the burden of "mother":

> There was a person
> Could not get rid of his mother . . .
>   (p. 70)

In the welter of bloodthirstiness and hate, one may detect even in *Crow* the record of a desperate struggle to relate, and to "find the woman". Since love is so dangerous, the pursuit of love gets out of hand, and becomes an outrage. But woman, all the same, despite the substitution of hate for love, is found to be at the heart of the failure of meaning in the universe—though any quest for love and meaning must inevitably turn out to be a bloody catastrophe. Two poems which engage with these problems are

Crow's Account of St. George (pp. 31–2) and *Criminal Ballad* (pp. 38–9) whose subjects are similar: and in the end both falsify the problem and its solutions.

The first poem links the desperate quest for meaning in relationship to the feeling (taken in from science) that the universe is meaningless.

> He sees everything in the Universe
> Is a track of numbers racing towards an answer . . .
> He refrigerates an emptiness,
> Decreates all to outer space
> Then unpicks numbers.

The science of this scientist-protagonist is "a mystic chant over an unintelligible universe". Although the scientist delights in his quest for truth, by rational processes, he is haunted by the spectre of a demon

> with tweezers of number
> He picks the gluey heart out of an inaudibly squeaking cell—
> He hears something. He turns—
> A demon, dripping ordure, is grinning in the doorway . . .

(p. 31)

The scientist tries to exorcise the demons by concentration on his manipulations of the organic stuff of life, genetic engineering. But, we may say (whether Hughes was aware of it or not) the scientist could very well be haunted by a number of demons. First, his "numbers", despite his passion, "answer no serious questions at all" (Husserl). Secondly "cutting the heart in two" with a "knife-edge of numbers" is a schizoid activity that separates "objectivity" in an unreal way from the realities of the subjective: it is an offence against the whole mystery of existence. Moreover, the apparent rationality of his science thus denies the irrational questions—or, we could say, the questions of telos, nisus, *ahnung*, origin, and unquantifiable aspects of being-in-the-universe which (as Roger Poole argues) science since Galileo has merely thrust aside and denied.[17]

I believe Ted Hughes does not grasp this, and has for his own reasons clung to objectivity and reductionism—and so to determinism, while at the same time simply falling into the irrational. His scientist's Devil is a paranoid split-off, representing Hate, and

148

the *malignancy* of the universe: he *is* Crow, in one sense. But in another, it is a malignancy which Hughes himself projects over all life, because however he positions himself towards it, it fills him with guilt (as it does in the philosophy of Heidegger and Sartre.) This devil is one which Hughes uses, indeed, to denounce, in his Grand Guignol way, all the positive dynamics of the universe:

> A bird-head
> Bald, lizard-eyed, the size of a football, on two staggering
>   bird-legs
> Gapes at him ...

The scientist smashes it, and it displays the shark-face of the demons of Hieronymous Bosch and Breughel

> The shark-face is screaming in the doorway
> Opening its fangs ...

The Scientist can be as tempted, just like a St Anthony, because his own incantations are really a form of mysticism. But the awfulness of the Devil here is a psychotic vision:

> A belly-ball of hair, with crab-legs, eyeless
> Jabs its pincers into his face. ...

—and when he destroys it, it turns out to have been "his wife and children". The image is like that in a horror film, and the trick at the end traps the reader in a paranoid-schizoid fantasy. As in some of the more psychotic poems of Sylvia Plath, the dynamic entities, instead of being seen as aspects of inner experience, leap out and inhabit the world, menacing us. So, the aggressive counter-action seems justified, but then turns, as in a nightmare, to have an appalling consequence. There is no escape.

The scientist would seem to be haunted by his own incapacity, and the incapacity of rational science, to embrace the irrational, and all those areas of darkness which we should call ours, like Prospero, but often fail to accept. So far so good. But then, as in films which exploit the irrational and horrendous, the entities of evil, like monsters or demons, seem to get out of hand. The scientist cannot cry, "Thou thing of darkness I acknowledge mine!" He attacks and murders the demon—and the thing that lies in its blood is his wife and child, his own creative life. So, there seems

149

no path of "embracement", to use Buber's word, but only confrontation with the darker side of existence which culminates inevitably in the destruction of love-objects. There is a parallel to be
drawn with Sylvia Plath's conflict with her animus: instead of
embracing "Daddy", she castrates and destroys him, and so leads
the way to the destruction of herself.

In Hughes's poem he challenges our view of moral struggle,
by calling this Crow's account of St George, and implies that it is
hopeless to try to resist the powers of darkness by being "good".
He seems to be saying something like this: "However much the
scientist concentrates on his rational interpretation of the truth
of the world, another truth will confront him—the truth of that
hate which is embodied in the shark, and in the malignancy of
universal entropy. If he tries to exorcise this threat to his sanity, he
may well find himself attacking and destroying the objects of relationship in his life which are significant to him, and in them
creativity and the future. If he turns against hate, he may find he
has killed love."

But, again, the polarity between the universe of numbers, and the
intractable evil of the demonic as if these were exclusive alternatives, depends upon the essentially naturalistic philosophy behind
the poem. There is another reality, which is that of the manifestations of creativity and consciousness in the universe which the
wife and child represent, and which are not to be confused with
the menacing spectres of darkness and evil. Their vulnerability,
and his dependence on them, are not to be confused with the
malignancy which seems to emerge from within ("looking out with
its hooks for something to love"). A great deal of harm is being
done in today's culture, by the exploitation of irrational fears of
the "demonic", which is presented not as a perverse projection
of those fears into split-off hallucinations (arising from the "alien
psychic factor"), but as evil realities in the world, coming from
some alien force.

What we need to arouse is not the capacity of the witch-doctor
to evoke spectres, or the hysterical projections of the occultist,
but the genuine capacity for creative vision of a William Blake.
One might expect a poet like Ted Hughes to champion Blake
against Newton. But what he does is to use his capacities to evoke
irrationality and chaos, leaving us no excuse except "racking

moments of smashing" in terms of a mental rage which can find no solutions to the problems of love and hate, meaning and non-meaning.

In *Criminal Ballad* the "mother", as in so many of Sylvia Plath's poems, has not given suck to the psyche: she becomes a mere mask, like Sylvia Plath's moon-mother. The result is a state of not-knowing-with-any-confidence-what-kind-of-creature-one-is, a schizoid state:

> the husband stared
> Through an anaesthetised mask
> And felt the cardboard of his body . . .[18]

The woman who should reflect is merely an object to be exploited and tortured: she merely calls to him (as so often in Hughes) from an appalling distance, "From the empty goldfish pond. . . ."

Again, the protagonist attacks blindly, in a desperate delinquent attempt to get through to reality: "His hands covered with blood suddenly . . ." he weeps: but only "Till he began to laugh . . ." (p. 39). The laughter here is a hebephrenic giggle, and the theme the futility of trying to relate and to find meaning. Love is fatal.

Some poems in *Crow* read like records of psychotic episodes, in which we may see the desperation, and the quest for meaning, survival, purity—such as the water makes in the Eskimo song, by desperate attrition:

> It came weeping back it wanted to die . . .
> Till it had no weeping left . . .
> Utterly worn out   utterly clear . . .

Hughes identifies with this water. But to this desperate quest woman must be sacrificed:

> Then, lying among the bones on the cemetery earth,
> He saw a woman singing out of her belly.

> He gave her eyes and a mouth, in exchange for the song.
> She wept blood, she cried pain.

> The pain and the blood were life. But the man laughed—

> The song was worth it.

> The woman felt cheated.

(pp. 92–3)

Winnicott speaks of how the fear of phantom woman in our unconscious life, the castrating mother, (who is also the mother in
ourself, and our female element, the anima) has caused infinite
suffering throughout history and the world. Hatred of woman is
today a predominant theme of our culture.

In this mood, to Hughes, sex is a cruel joke:

> Words came in the likeness of vaginas in a row—
> He called in his friends.
>
> (p. 34)

The coarseness of the rugby-pack's hostility to woman is now a
central feature of the sadistic debasement of woman in our
fashionable culture. Voyeurism is an O.K. indulgence:

> the faces
> Of two lovers in the seconds
> They got so far into each other they forgot
> Each other completely that was O.K.
> But none of it lasted . . .

Here the self-communing quiet voice of *Wodwo* has become a
dissociated obsessional mutter. What feels more secure than these
picked up and discarded moments is violence:

> The racking moments
> Of the man smashing everything
> He could reach

—that is, strength and reliability lie in giving oneself up to the
joys of hating—and to death, to a longing for non-being:

> The grin
> Sank back, temporarily nonplussed
> Into the skull . . .
>
> (p. 29)

In *Crow's Theology* these philosophies which declare that one
exists because God loved one are cynically denied

> he realised that God spoke Crow—
> Just existing was His revelation.

But in truth the existence of an indifferent universe of matter
suggest a "nature's roulette" that moves towards universal entropy
and death:

What spoke the silence of lead?

Crow realised there were two Gods—

One of them much bigger than the other
Loving his enemies
And having all the weapons.

Why, then, write poetry? To care so much, even to be cynical, even to try so desperately to shock us, to deny meaning and love as passionately as he does—all this denies implicitly Hughes's nihilism: as Camus pointed out, the advocacy of nihilism in any form gives the lie to nihilism. But it is a serious matter for poetry that at the hard core of *Crow* is a longing for non-being—for that death which alone (like the lead and the rocks and the silence) seems real. As Robert Daly says of the schizoid in the end it comes to seem to him that the only reality is death.[19]

The "striking" language of *Crow* disguises its falsity of theme. The "other God", of death, and entropy, does not really "have all the weapons". Indeed, if there is such a drift of mere matter, it is a nothing, compared with us who are aware of it: and in any case, what are we but matter become conscious of itself? We are not nothing, despite the death that overwhelms us personally, or when the Earth dies. None of our ultimate nothingness expunges such marvellous moments as when, like Little Frieda looking at the moon, we are conscious of the universe, of our own creation—and thus "make it" by our intentionality, by our creative perception. Our ultimate nothingness merely imposes on us an urgency of being responsible, aware, and fastidious—in our search for authentic choice and action. This is a responsibility, too, to the future, and to the survival of what can endure and survive.

If these things are so, then Hughes's wilful addiction to his false solutions shows him guilty of trying to undermine our sense of responsibility, and thus to harm us by damaging our freedom.

Ted Hughes's first sentence in his poem *The Last Migration* is "So God died. . . ." Man takes over, and unmakes creation, with a gun. With the collapse of faith since the middle of the nineteenth century a great deal of torment has centred round this question— of finding a focus for ethical values, if there is no God, no transcendental realm to vindicate absolute values.

153

But by saying "God is dead" Nietzsche did not mean to promote amorality or nihilism. On the contrary, he was, as Rollo May says, radically devoted, like Kierkegaard, to rejecting sick and dying deteriorated forms of theism and emotionally dishonest religious practices. Nietzsche sought to promote the self-realization of the individual in the fullest sense—and it was this that he meant by the "will to power". "It requires", as Rollo May says, "the courageous living out of the individual's potentialities in his own particular existence": "will to power is an ontological category, that is, an inseparable aspect of being." It is the courage to be as an individual (in Tillich's sense).

Rollo May quotes Kaufmann on Nietzsche at this point:

> Man's task is simple: he should cease letting his "existence" be "a thoughtless accident". Not only the use of the word *Existenz*, but the thought which is at stake, suggests that this essay is particularly close to what is today called *Existenz-philosophie*. Man's fundamental problem is to achieve true "existence" instead of letting his life be no more than just another accident. In *The Gay Science* Nietzsche hits on a formulation which brings out the essential paradox of any distinction between self and true self: "what does your conscience say? *Ecco Home, Wie man wird, was man wird, was man ist*—how one becomes what one is."
>
> (Kaufmann in Nietzsche, 1956, p. 133 ff., quoted by Rollo May in *Existence—a New Dimension in Psychiatry*, p. 31)

The central dynamic and need of life is this expansion, growing, bringing one's inner potentialities into birth in action:

> "*Not* for pleasure does man strive", holds Nietzsche, "but for power" . . . Joy is a *plus-feeling* of power.

This "power" is the power of authentic existence: the values of human life, as May insists, never come about automatically.

> "Individuality, worth and dignity are not *gegeben* . . . given us as data by nature, but *aufgegeben*—i.e. given or assigned to us as a task which we ourselves must solve. . . ."

May links this with Tillich's view—and that of Sartre, who insists that "you *are* your choices".

Kierkegaard, Nietzsche and Freud each deal, as May emphasizes, with problems of anxiety, despair, fragmentalized personality. What they sought was integration. We are today seeking for such wholeness. Much of what I have said could be related to Roger Poole's concern to indicate the inadequacies of "objectivity"—and to seek "the totality of problems, objective and subjective, by the *whole* thinker, taking into account all the evidence, both quantifiable and unquantifiable" (*Towards Deep Subjectivity*, p. 108). Only thus can "we attain that point of vantage by which we can give meaning to the world", rather than "let the world shove its meaning down on us". This requires an immense numinous effort on our part—not a lapse into paralysis.

Ledermann quotes Buber, in urging us to accept "the realm of the irrational", as a means towards finding an adequate position to realize our potentialities: "all comprehensibility of the world is only a footstool of its own incomprehensibility." This incomprehensibility, however, is not just negative.

> On the contrary, the person who knows the world outside or within himself without the use of his *ratio* gathers far richer knowledge than he can obtain with the aid of the rational principle: "What the most learned and ingenious combination of concepts denies, the humble and faithful beholding, grasping, knowing of any situation bestows. The world is not comprehensible, but it is embraceable: through the embracing of one of its beings" (Buber).
>
> (Ledermann, 1972, p. 72)

In *Crow*, Ted Hughes rejects the "embracing of the world and its mysteries" (though *Little Frieda* in the earlier volume is essentially about these). And indeed in it he turns bitterly against "embracing", and coarsely offends love. What is the effect of the lewdest and most banal poem in *Crow—Song for a Phallus*?

Sylvia Plath's *Daddy*, as I have tried to suggest in my book, is an act of giving herself up to the joys of hating, turning against the pseudo-male construct which alone holds her identity together by hate and aggressiveness. *Song for a Phallus* seems to belong to such a moment of Hughes *giving himself up to ultimate nullity*, a turning against life, in an orgy of nihilistic destructiveness. Ted Hughes evidently knows this kind of moment of smashing everything to pieces: the danger is becoming identified with it in his art, in *Orghast* and *Crow*. It is not that it expresses a loss of confidence in being, but that the indulgence marks a failure of confidence in all forms of normal being. Saul Bellow sees this, as an aspect of our culture, when he makes Mr Sammler say:

155

As long as there is no ethical life and everything is poured so bar-
barously and recklessly into personal gesture this must be endured
. . . there is a peculiar longing for non-being . . . why should they
be human? . . . The individual . . . seems to want a divorce from
all the states he knows. . . .

(*Mr. Sammler's Planet*, Penguin edition, p. 164)

The capacity to symbolize is given up, in a regression to schizoid
modes and acting out, "equation" modes—in which the audience
is assaulted as if it *were* the hated parent, rather than a collabor-
ative group of human beings, sharing a cultural exploration of
meaning through symbolism. Satisfaction is to be found in the
"impact" of the equation on the hated audience. In modern "art"
audiences are made to vomit, are assaulted, stunned or are sexually insulted or compromised, driven mad, rather than brought to
participate in a shared symbolic exploration of experience. As
James Baldwin says, "Contempt for the audience is the death of
art"—and it is this contempt that such attacks on today's
audiences display. In such a poem as *Song for a Phallus* Ted
Hughes both expresses a "longing for non-being", and gives way
to "acting out".

It would be interesting to have a comment from Faber and
Faber on this lapse. The English student, much influenced and
educated by the "Faber revolution", is confronted with verse that
would be poor as graffiti:

> You stay in there his Daddy cried
> Because a Dickybird
> Has told the world when you get born
> You'll treat me like a turd . . .

For what reason, we must ask, is the Oedipus myth expressed
in the language of the lavatory wall ballad or fourth form dirty
song? *Song for a Phallus*, indeed, might go down very well itself
in an obscene stage show (and has, in fact, been quoted to me in
defence of one):

> O do not chop his winkle off
> His Mummy cried with horror
> Think of the joy will come of it
> Tomorrer and tomorrer . . .

156

Indeed, this is close to the song in *Oh! Calcutta!*

> ... treat me rough, stuff me, Clarence
> Give me thrills, fill me, Clarence.

as are these stanzas:

> The Dickybird came to Oedipus
> You murderous little sod—
> The Sphinx will bite your bollocks off
> This order comes from God ...

> The Sphinx she waved her legs at him
> And opened wide her maw
> Oedipus stood stiff and wept
> At the dreadful thing he saw ...

Surely something strange has happened to English literary taste, for T. S. Eliot's (and Herbert Read's) distinguished publishers to bind up a ballad at such a level. Here we have a coarse (and coy) fantasy of the *Vagina dentata* offered not for some overall deep artistic purpose, but to make a lewd Rugby-song nonsense of one of the great myths of the world. There is here neither the invocation of past glories by contrast "Weia lala leia. . . ." nor recognition of the coarseness that has overtaken all England, and, indeed, western civilization:

> I can connect
> Nothing with nothing.
> The broken fingernails of dirty hands.
> My people humble people who expect
> Nothing ...

The dirty fingernails are themselves acclaimed as a "breakthrough". We could perhaps imagine *Song for a Phallus* scrawled by the carbuncular clerk himself, in a raucous moment in the pub, where he was consoling himself for the dinginess of his brutal encounter up the unlit stairs.

He, too, might have had an inclination for lewdnesses which depend upon being shockable:

> Then out his Mammy came herself
> The blood poured from her bucket
> What you can't understand, she cried
> You sleep on it or sing to it ...

—indeed the joke might have been taken from one of his office versions of *Mary Had a Little Lamb* ("and kept it in a bucket"). In publishing such unjustifiable obscenities Faber and Faber have done much to destroy the fabric of our response to several hundred years of English verse, to the delicacy and subtlety to which Eliot commended our attention. Such lapses of taste at a high level leave us unable to defend ourselves or "the people" at any level against debasement.

The language of the ballad is unbelievably banal ("All in their rotten bodies", "shrieked about the place"), and its debasement of the ballad currency destroys (say) *The Ancient Mariner* or *The Unquiet Grave* as much as stage obscenity destroys responsiveness to Shakespeare.

And, finally, Ted Hughes reveals that coarse view of the universe which really underlies his "vitalism" and his moralizing about Man's acts, the animals and love:

> And out there came ten thousand ghosts
> All in their rotten bodies
> Crying, You will never know
> What a cruel bastard God is . . .

The blindness of man in his driven pursuit of existential meaning in the face of his nothingness is reduced to ham rhymes which would hardly grace a pantomime at the Round House:

> Oedipus raised his axe again
> The World is dark, he cried
> The World is dark one inch ahead:
> What's on the other side?

The deep inner problems of the "regressed libidinal ego" and our hatred of woman's creativity are guffawed over, in the language of *She was Poor But She was Honest*:

> He split his Mammy like a melon
> He was drenched with gore
> He found himself curled up inside
> As if he had never been bore . . .

—but to what purpose?

The careful fastidiousness of genuine creativity is abandoned for a desperate and zany, but mental, sensuality—desperate because it can never supply the meanings which are sought in such (pseudo-male) ways. In such literature, language plunges into a coarseness which is an inevitable concomitant of desperation, while tendencies in the other arts, especially cinema and the "fringe" theatre, are indescribable. The danger is that sensibility may not be able to recover from such lapses. How would it be possible, for instance, to deal with a genuine problem of "true self being" in an atmosphere in which it is so acceptable to devote oneself to egoistical nihilism? It was Max Stirner who declared that he did not want to hear about people and their values: "the other—my food!" The phrase is from *The Unique One and His Property* which was published in 1845. But this is the motto of much contemporary art. If audiences are brought to feel that they have a "right" to indulge in any antic, whatever the cost to others, to taste, or to self-respect, then how can they possibly feel concern for the inner life of human beings, such as a genuine work of art inevitably requires? Again, Saul Bellow characterizes the kind of egoism I am referring to, in *Mr. Sammler's Planet*:

> the right to be uninhibited, spontaneous, urinating, defaecating, belching, coupling in all positions, tripling, quadrupling, polymorphous, noble in being natural, primitive, combine the leisure and luxurious inventiveness of Versailles with the hibiscus-covered erotic ease of Samoa. . . .

—and in his mocking tone, we find the recognition that it all leads towards meaninglessness, and the question which arises with Mr Sammler: "Who had made shit a sacrament?"

As yet, those who go overboard for debasement need feel no shame. The new fanatical immoralism has created an atmosphere in which sexual perversions, cruelties, and debasements of Humanitas and creative symbolism are acceptable, not least for polite dinner-party conversation. Behind this, there is the prevailing influence in the last decade of the mysterious power of the sexual deviant, to create an atmosphere in which people forfeit their individuality and self-respect, so that they may be seduced. Needless to say, such people have made good use of new and powerful media. This is not the place to discuss the problem, but there are clues in two important papers by Masud R. Khan whose implications are profound.[20] A great deal in our culture which has made

Crow possible has to do with sexual deviance, and the steady inversion of moral values (as by Genet, Burroughs, Tynan etc.)
Sexual deviance Khan sees as a form of play resulting from the
failure of developmental processes in the infant, with his mother.
"Winnicott especially stresses the necessity of a mother's capacity
to meet imaginatively, as well as affectively, the first creative
gestures of the infant-child and this forms the basis of the child's
true confidence in his evolving and crystallizing sense of self"
(Khan, 1968, p. 93). When these processes fail, sexual perversions
(including pornography) are one way in which the consequent
failure of a sense of self may be worked upon. But there are benign and malignant perversions. The "other" person in some perverted activity can never in fact cure a man "of his developmental
deviations in ego-integration resulting from the failures of maternal
care and provision" (Khan, 1964, 406). But "through the technique
of intimacy the pervert tries to compel and induce a regression to
dependence and instinctual surrender in his accomplice. . . ." In
our culture audiences at large have been made capable of accepting the grossest lapses, by the inculcation of this state of
"emotional surrender": they cannot summon any resources to
protest. And although it is a long way from the worst of today's
novel, stage and cinema, *Crow* was made possible by this strange
phenomenon of inculcated surrender—and so many respectable
teachers teach it in Humanities courses instituted to enrich sensibility and awaken the moral sense.

In the same paper, Masud Khan says that perversions are a way
of trying to avoid psychotic regression, so we may see the dynamics
of much contemporary culture as expressing an impulse not to
go mad. Those who do not accept it must face the fear of madness.
But in the meantime, many become enlisted in what Khan calls the
concoction of a "pleasurable negative identity". That is, they become seduced into pseudo-male false-self structures, based on hate
and nihilism. Again, *Crow* belongs to these, and inculcates a
longing for non-being. As Saul Bellow indicates, quoting Max
Weber,

> Specialists without Spirit; sensualists without heart; this nullity
> imagines that it has attained a level of civilisation never before
> achieved.

Yet this new barbarism is the consequence of the philosophical failure I am trying to trace in this book. As Polanyi indicates in *Beyond Nihilism* it leads to a scepticism which turns into nihilism and madness.

By his abandonment, in *Crow*, to the language and fantasies of the new barbarism, Ted Hughes attempts to frighten and dismay us; by his self-dramatising postures of pseudo-male strength; by giving himself up to the indulgence of hate (combined with the humiliation of woman) and by his assault on creativity. By this he has plunged minority taste in poetry—once a source of hope and regeneration—into the lurid darkness of Grand Guignol and gross sensationalism.[21] He has thus undercut the value of poetry in the present crisis, by serious devaluation. To devalue poetry so efficiently at this moment of wider barbarism is to devalue man. Poetry belongs itself to "female element being" as a source of creative potentiality and it is against this that Ted Hughes has turned, in a strange and anguished—but also irresponsible—longing not to be. This so-called "vitalist" has turned against human evolution, for the only hope for man is in his evolution as the *animal symbolicum*. We can only survive if we are able to exert our imagination on the world and give it meaning, largely through the Word. Hughes has coarsened the Word, and used it as a blunt instrument to imprison us in a sterile paralysis, in a dark universe, in which there is no hope for poetry.

NOTES

1. Some of this chapter appeared in the symposium *The Black Rainbow*, ed. Peter Abbs, 1974. There, however, it was seriously mutilated at the insistence of Olwyn Hughes, Ted Hughes's sister and literary agent.
2. In his poetry Ted Hughes seems to accept evolution and its philosophical implications as conclusive truth. In *Darwin Retired*, Norman Macbeth (1975) demonstrates that evolutionary theory is full of serious logical flaws.
3. These are met not by the gleams of loving eyes, but the *glitter* of weapons. "Her Mirrors" (i.e. Sylvia Plath's) are the mirrors of non-reflecting death.
4. The current mythology about menacing "black holes" in the universe shows scientific fact coloured by schizoid fantasy.

5. See also, John Vyvyan, *Sketch for an Evolutionary World-picture.*

6. See *The Night Dances,* in *Ariel.*

7. In *The Ways of the Will,* 1966, discussing the effects of schizophrenics on the psychiatrist, Leslie Farber says they make normal existence seem "pallid and artificial" because of the desperate drama of their attitudes to encounter.

8. In the sketch *Jack and Jill* in the American *Oh! Calcutta!* a man and woman measure one another's genitals (sadistically) and then he kills her by intercourse, walking off indifferent. See my essay "Who Dare Speak of Love?" in *The Use of English,* Winter 1973, Vol. 24, No. 2. It was interesting to note, after a *Times* Editorial attacking the development of hate in pornography, and linking it with a decline in Kenneth Tynan, that several people came forward to defend Tynan, against any suggestion that has well demonstrated an impulse to be cruel to women, though in this sketch it is actually acted out. In this we find evidence of the mysterious hold over people's minds the perverted elements in our culture are gaining and paralysing normal powers of perception and discrimination. Samuel Beckett, Edna O'Brien, Ionesco and Joe Orton all compromised serious stage art by contributing to Tynan's "despicable debasement of the language of sex" (Ian Robinson).

9. See in *Sylvia Plath: Poetry and Existence* (1975) discussion of her dread of the eye that "has to take everything in", as in *Tulips* and *The Wishing Box.*

10. See D. W. Winnicott's discussion of a child who had within him a split-off "wizard" who ordered him about, and to do wicked things (*Collected Papers,* p. 101 ff.).

11. F. K. Ledermann, *Existential Neurosis,* 1972.

12. See my comments in *Human Hope and the Death Instinct* on the feeling that the sexual act is a kind of death, found even in Freud.

13. For a related diagnosis see "Suicide: the Condition of Consciousness" by Masud R. Khan in *The Black Rainbow,* ed. P. Abbs, 1975, on Camus. The sickness of European culture Khan sees as "an egotistical alienation that is lethal in the end to the future of the individual as it is nihilistic of the traditions of the cultures he is reared in" (p. 90).

14. The movement has, however, been going on for a hundred years—some threshold! Brentano was born in 1838, Hussrl in 1859.

15. See *Sylvia Plath: Poetry and Existence,* 1976 p. 12 ff. and passim.

16. The symbolism (which is parallel) in such a film as *Jaws* is obviously not that of the pursuit of biological truth, but of inner voraciousness.

17. p. 107 ff., *op. cit.* See also E. K. Ledermann in *Existential Neurosis* on Buber's emphasis on the need to recognize and accept the irrational. Also E. W. F. Tomlin *Living and Knowing,* and, of course, the work of Michael Polanyi, and Marjorie Grene.

18. Sylvia Plath tells us in *Poem for a Birthday* she lives in a "dark house" made as a wasp makes its nest, by chewing paper. Elsewhere she says she is made of two grey papery bags.

19. See Daly, R., various papers on schizoid problems, quoted in *Sylvia Plath: Poetry and Existence*.

20. "The Function of Intimacy and Acting Out in Perversions", *Sexual Behaviour and the Law*, ed. Ralph Slovenko, Chas. C. Thomas, Illinois, U.S.A., 1964; "Reparation to the Self as an Idolized Internal Object" (a contribution to *The Theory of Perversion Formation, Dynamic Psychiatry*, 1968); Robert Stoller, *Perversion: the Erotic form of Hatred*, Harvester Press, 1975.

21. I refrain from giving an account here of spectacles in the present revival of Grand Guignol in Paris, involving guillotining and nuns caressing themselves sexually. As Phillip Rieff has said, one fears the implications of intellectuals claiming they must have the right to indulge in such sights.

6

Modern Poetry and the Death of Sympathy

> Where has the tree gone, that locked
> Earth to the sky? What is under my hands,
> That I cannot feel?
> What loads my hands down?
> (Going, Philip Larkin)

The sterility of Ted Hughes's development, in *Crow* and *Gog*, is but one feature of the widespread death of poetry in our time. Another significant figure is Philip Larkin. His *Whitsun Weddings* is perhaps his best known poem. It is the last of the six poems of his own which he included in his *Oxford Book of Twentieth Century Verse*, and is, in a way, his touchstone for the other poems he includes in it. The poem is of interest in the present context, because it is obvious at the end that Larkin feels he should be expressing a creative moment, in creative terms:

> And as we raced across
> Bright knots of rail
> Past standing Pullmans, walls of blackened moss
> Came close, and it was nearly done, this frail
> Travelling coincidence; and what it held
> Stood ready to be loosed with all the power
> That being changed can give. We slowed again,
> And as the tightened brakes took hold, there swelled
> A sense of falling, like an arrow-shower
> Sent out of sight, somewhere becoming rain.

In discussing this poem, I find students want to find something seminal, something transcendent, in those closing lines. But what defeats them is the language. It is not good enough: it cannot take

164

on the burden of the meaning that the poet wants to give the moment, before the train stops. The phrase "and it was nearly done . . ." might stand as a motto, or an epitaph, to the poem itself. It has a stillborn quality, such as Sylvia Plath attributes to her own lifeless poems.

> These poems do not live: it's a sad diagnosis.
> . . . They sit so nicely in the pickling fluid!
> (*Crossing the Water*, p. 35)

The train in which Larkin is travelling is full of married couples. For the train-ride they are all united, and will soon be unloaded or unleashed on London: what will happen?

> There swelled
> A sense of falling, like an arrow-shower
> Sent out of sight, somewhere becoming rain.

The vagueness is like that of Housman:

> Nor ask amid the dews of morning
> If they are mine or no . . .

> The happy highways where I went
> And cannot come again . . .

A generalized sentimental "poetic" emotion is expressed, which stands in the place of exactness, or of any focus on defined feeling. It is a groping after some appropriate feeling, rather than a poem which "had to be written" because the feeling *demands* organization and expression.

Of course, as a train slows down to enter a metropolitan terminus, one feels a kind of emotion *swelling*, and this may be called a *sense of falling*, since the human burden that has been carried along at sixty miles an hour will now be turned out on its legs. But how is this like an "arrow shower . . . sent out of sight"? The phrases simply recall

> I shot an arrow in the air
> It fell to earth I know not where . . .

But this, and Larkin's phrases which evoke it, are ridiculous. Of course, the newly-weds will all shoot off into odd corners of London, or to air-ports, and thence to foreign places. But what symbolic or metaphorical act, as if from classical myth, is indicated? People send single arrows into the air, as a kind of act of chance, like flinging a dice, to find treasure or some indication of the direction they should take. But who sends a whole shower of arrows? And what might they hope to gain from it?

And why do they become *rain*? London's "postal districts" in the previous stanza, are "packed like squares of wheat"—but this suggests wheat ready for harvest, and this doesn't benefit from rain. The rain is, of course, in the phenomenology of *The Golden Bough*, a symbol of fertility, and so the image may be of newly-betrothed couples being shot off into the unknown, the men to unloose their seed which will fall somewhere on fertile ground, yielding offspring. But, neither an *arrow-shower* nor *rain* are fertile in themselves. A shower of arrows, as at Crecy, can be hostile. It is all left very vague.

And what about that "somewhere"? Somewhere, somehow, the poet feels, there ought to be something here about fertility, promise, dignity, transcendence. It is, after all, a kind of epithalamion:

> At length they all to mery London came
> To mery London, my most kyndly nurse,
> That to me gave this life most natiue sourse . . .
> Against the bridale daye, which is not long:
>> Sweete *Themmes* runne softly till I end my song.

Since Spenser's *Prothalamion* begins

> Calme was the day, and through the trembling ayre,
> Sweete breathing *Zephyrus* did softly play . . .

The image of the arrow-shower and rain has obviously something to do with good wishes for the espoused:

> . . . they stood amazed still,
> Their wondring eyes to fill,
> They seem'd they never saw a sight so fayre . . .
> For sure they did not seeme
> To be begot of any earthly Seeds,
> But rather Angels or of Angels breede . . .

To quote Spenser—whether Mr Larkin meant his poem to be evoked or not—reveals the difficulties of a poet of the "New lines" movement, and a sometime colleague of Kingsley Amis (of whose work Mr Larkin includes four poems in his Oxford Book):

> The fathers with broad belts under their suits
> And seamy foreheads; mothers loud and fat;
> And uncles shouting smut; and then the perms,
> The nylon gloves and jewellery-substitutes,
> The lemons, mauves and olive-ochres that
>
> Marked off the girls unreally from the rest . . .

I am reminded of a sentence in one of Mr Amis's novels; of a schoolteacher looking at mothers; "she could not imagine any of them in the act which had produced these children." Why try to imagine, then, only to be cruel? The language has a certain coldness of detachment, in which there is an appeal to the reader to become enlisted in a particular denigratory attitude of the writer to his subject. In Larkin's poem, if we join him in this, it is not *our* mothers who are "loud and fat", nor do *our* uncles shout smut. Other people's, the "people's", mothers and uncles do. But there is more to it than class distance—for not only would *we* not wear nylon gloves, jewellery-substitutes or "lemons, mauves and olive-ochres". It is that we *know* that these are not the "right" things. There is a kind of vulgarity, bad taste, flamboyance, and attitude to sex from which we have escaped—and to which we can feel sneeringly superior.

The sneer is not so apparent in Mr Larkin's poem as it is, continually and arrogantly, throughout Mr Amis's work: it needs to be said firmly that anyone who indulges so persistently in sneering as Mr Amis does has no claim to be considered as a creative writer in any sense whatever, because the sneer is destructive of that sympathy without which there can be no living art. But there is a parallel cruelty in Larkin, a hostility under the surface:

> grinning and pomaded, girls
> In parodies of fashion . . .
> girls, gripping their handbags tighter, stared
> At a religious wounding . . .
> Just long enough to settle hats and say
> *I nearly died* . . .

The colours and fabrics worn by working class, or "ordinary" people are grotesque; they are actually awe-inspired by the idea of a wedding service, and are so foolish as to have awesome feelings about the significance of defloration; their language is full of commonplace clichés like "I nearly died" and this is very funny because it isn't a funeral, it's a wedding—but all the strange paraphenalia of working-class pseudo-ritual is here, weddings or funerals, it's all one, "they" are so comic with it. The girls especially are grotesque (do working class girls, or did they in the '50s, wear "pomade"?)—and everyone is seen as in a caricature, loud, fat, broad-belted, crease-faced and coarse: *grinning in parodies*.

The language of the poet himself is calculated at the same time to mark him apart, from the "bunting-dressed coach-party annexes". He belongs to the managerial class:

> That Whitsun, I was late getting away:
> Not till about
> One-twenty . . .

He takes the noise to be "porters larking with the mails" and "went on reading"; he is aware, with affinity, of someone running up to bowl. He is aware, on their behalf, of the sensitivities: but they, poor things, are oblivious in their lot:

> Thought of the others they would never meet
> Or how their lives would all contain this hour.

He alone is able to connect them in this way.

This detachment, with its air of superiority, is difficult to convey to students, I find—because of its appeal to them. It is an appeal from the half-educated to the half-educated—and this could be made even more clear in Amis, who has no feeling whatever for civilized values or for culture, except insofar as they enable him to feel superior to those at whom he sneers ("some rubbish by Brahms"—one must know Brahms to be able to say this, just as one must *know* Mahler to enjoy Mr Ken Russell's obscene and insulting film about him). This use of art to climb to a position from which one may give free rein to one's hatred of human beings is, of course, the death of creativity—and is the death of humanness too, since in such an atmosphere good feelings cannot survive. It is a manifestation of a radical *insecurity* that has turned spiteful and exerts a certain destructiveness against

168

the people—ordinary people—it fears. Reviewing Larkin's anthology I found myself beginning to compose a lampoon

> Amis, Larkin, Burgess and Co—
> England is paying for them now:
> The death of a thousand comic kicks,
> The death of creativity, the death of sex . . .

To drive the point home, about what is wrong with Larkin's tone, we may go back to Chapter XIX of *Martin Chuzzlewit* where Dickens introduces us to Sarah Gamp. Larkin's last stanza is, I believe, an attempt to open his heart to others, or about others, in a "Dickensian" way. But it comes out as dead generalities, as in Housman, because the heart is dead. Dickens is able to elevate his unattractive, working class, commonplace creatures to the level of tragi-comedy: like us, they choose, act, live and die—they "choose man" in Sartre's sense, and we are involved in their choice. Dickens does not merely caricature their grotesquenesses— he enjoys them, because he enjoys finding the gestures of joy and tragedy even in a "low-life" character. He sees them capable of "peak moments"—perhaps even more capable than us, as the stoker in *Dombey and Son* is more capable of grief than Dombey himself: or, like Jo in *Bleak House*, tragic figures even though they "don't know nothink".

> Mrs. Gamp had a large bundle with her, a pair of pattens, and a species of gig umbrella; the latter article in colour like a faded leaf, except where a circular patch of a lively blue had been dexterously let in at the top.

We may compare the "broad belts" and "lemons, mauves" of Larkin's working-class wedding guests. The reference to a "faded leaf" goes with Mrs Gamp's occupation—she too is mortal, as she goes about bringing children into the world, and laying out corpses.

> "And so the gentleman's dead, Sir!
> Ah! The more's the pity."

The patch let into her umbrella is of a "lively blue": she is not condemned for her silly olive-ochres, but seen as someone with a manic flair—using the same *dexterous* hands to mend her umbrella, as were used for birth and the final rites for a corpse. Dickens does not sentimentalize her:

169

She was a fat old woman, this Mrs. Gamp, with a husky voice and a moist eye, which she had a remarkable power of turning up, and only showing the white of. Having very little neck, it cost her some trouble to look over herself, if one may say so, at those to whom she talked. She wore a very rusty black gown, rather the worse for snuff, and a shawl and bonnet to correspond. . . .

And there follow the marvellous phrases about how, because she pawns her "weeds", "the very fetch and ghost of Mrs Gamp, bonnet and all, might be seen hanging up, any hour in the day, in at least a dozen of the second-hand clothes shops about Holborn". The comic effect of this is redoubled by the undercurrent of recognition—that the gin obtained by selling the clothes has been drunk in the service of sitting by actual dying men, whose ghosts they might be, hanging there.

Dickens writes about his characters with *affection*: even when he says, "The face of Mrs. Gamp—the nose in particular—was somewhat red and swollen and it was difficult to enjoy her society without becoming conscious of a smell of spirits." Both this, and the way he employs the phrase "a fat old woman" is a great distance from Larkin's "mothers loud and fat". Dickens' euphemisms ("difficult to enjoy her society") do not enlist one into separating oneself from Mrs Gamp in any defensive way, of patronizing or hating her: she goes "to a lying-in or a laying out with equal zest and relish": and there is a sense in which Dickens admires her for doing what we would flinch from—with or without "the nerve a little sip of liquor gives. . . ."

Looking back at Dickens, what strikes me is not only the greater concentration, the immediacy and directness—but the gravity he is able to command, even when being funny: "Mr. Mould the undertaker . . . a face in which a queer attempt at melancholy was at odds with a smirk of satisfaction; so that he looked as a man might who, in the very act of smacking his lips over choice old wine, tried to make believe it was physic."

To use such language, to effect such a response, obviously requires a set of values shared with the reader: it is funny, but also involves us in moral judgement, to encounter an undertaker who is satisfied with the money he makes from death, or even from the morbid occupation of his craft, while trying to look appropriately sad. There is nothing in Larkin's caricature of this subtlety—and

170

there cannot be, because he does not know what values to share with his reader, and can find no flow of warmth between himself and us, or his subjects.

So, it is not only that he keeps himself at a puzzled distance from his wedding subjects (Larkin seems clearly to be in a first-class compartment looking at second-class travellers): he also keeps himself at a distance from his readers. And this leads to a certain kind of linguistic *genteel* quality:

> A hothouse flashed uniquely . . .
> The next town, new and nondescript . . .
> All posed irresolutely . . .

There is a self-preservatory, somewhat mincing, note about the use of these words, a claim to belong to a culture from which low life may be laughed at safely by the higher educated. Yet the words are loosely used: "uniquely" is a characteristic exaggeration, as is that "irresolutely"—it is the hyperbole of the undergraduate or the "quality" press (a glimpse at *Isis* shows you how one turns into the other). It is only a shade away from saying "terribly" or "devastating": and as we come to examine the language closely it is that of the *Guardian* feature-article, bright, empty, cliché-ridden, very much concerned with conveying a "knowing" intelligence that knows nothing—knows nothing in the sense that Dickens *does* know about the world and human nature:

> my three-quarters-empty train . . . all sense / Of being in a hurry gone . . . blinding windscreens . . . where sky and Lancashire and water meet . . . the tall heat . . . canals with floatings of industrial froth . . . sun destroys / The interest of what's happening in the shade . . . out on the end of an event / Waving goodbye / To something that survived it . . . The last confetti and advice were thrown. . . .

And that, I believe, places it: the language of the "New lines" movement belongs essentially to the higher journalism. Like that journalism, it claims the right to ridicule, criticize, condemn and guy, without responsibility to values. The "psychology" of it belongs not to Dickens' kind of penetration into the strange mixture of human make-up as into Sarah Gamp's mixture of the pitiful, the brave, the dexterous, the mean, the compassionate. It is a psychology that diagnoses the self-deception of others, but leaves us with no deeper understanding of what we see; only a stance of a clinical detachment ("sociological" in tone):

> And, as we moved, each face seemed to define
> Just what it saw departing: children frowned
> At something dull; fathers had never known
> Success so huge and wholly farcical;
> The women shared
> The secret like a happy funeral . . .
> Free at last
> And loaded with the sum of all they saw . . .

The last phrase is crucial. Their view is different from his. Does everyone in every Whitsun wedding party fit so nearly the categories of the comic postcard—for the image is, surely, a Bamforth comic postcard picture of W.C. life? Had one talked to each couple, each man and woman, wouldn't one have found something quite different from the stereotype? Larkin takes it that his train is "loaded only with the sum of what they saw"—while what he sees is people who say "I nearly died", just as charladies on the stage used to say "My pore feet!"

And then he yearns to bless them, to go out benignly into their future, in a creative way, at the end of his poem. But he cannot, of course. Neither his language, nor his concepts, nor his emotions, nor his perceptions are good enough, deep enough, real enough, *attentive* enough and certainly not *intentional* enough, to allow him to do so. He sees there ought to be a sense of the "power that being changed can give"; but *he* is not changed, since he holds the whole train load at such arm's length. They *none of them*, thought of the others: he had to do it—he had to unite them all in his thoughts. But this *is* a "frail travelling coincidence" because it doesn't mean anything to him. He tries frantically to find some thought or feeling about them before he leaves the train, but fails, despite his references to "Stood ready to be loosed with all the power. . . ."

And, in truth, as throughout the *New Lines* movement, what one is left with is a feeling of impotence. Things have neither been seen, nor expressed: even the spoiled countryside is seen with a flat, cool detachment, without passion

> —An Odeon went past, a cooling tower
> And someone running up a bowl . . .

172

For a moment, this is what they see: and it is given as if they did not see it, or saw it with indifference. Weren't some overawed by the springtime light in the sky? Weren't some afraid of the dehumanization of that landscape? Weren't some of the gleams, even on windscreens, sparks of a new world? Larkin is not going to allow them, or himself, to see the world like that, not to see man like that. Especially not to see *girls* like that: a clumsy lurch across the stanza division marks his heavy contempt for their way of expressing their identification with the bride

> The lemons, mauves and olive-ochres that

> Marked off the girls unreally from the rest.

The word "unreally" is significant: the whole *New Lines* movement was devoted to "realism"—and this kind of realism impels Larkin to exclude all the transcendence he can from *The Oxford Book of Twentieth Century Verse*—such as Isaac Rosenberg's *Break of Day In the Trenches*, David Jones, or Seamus Heaney (and only one poem by Bernard Spenser). The realism of this Movement represents an obliteration of peak-moments, of becoming, of idealism, of creativity. Man *is* nasty, and brutish—and human nature *must* be sold short. So, the girls in the wedding parties are to be despised for displaying themselves as foci of sexual creativity (however awful their colours)—because *we* know sexual creativity to be something we darkly know about (as hidden showers of rain, somehow, somewhere) but *they* don't—for them it is all wrapped in superstitions ("religious woundings") or else the subject of smut. (In the name of this misrepresentation, our fashionable intellectual world in our time has overwhelmed the ordinary with a combination of brutal realism and gross obscenity, a concomitant of the kind of half-educated knowingness for which the "movement" stood).

There is a straining attempt in Larkin, to understand other people:

> Struck, I leant
> More promptly out next time, more curiously,
> And saw it all again in different terms . . .

But the puzzlement is not solved: again, it is a question of the connection between creativity and values, existential values. We leave Sarah Gamp aware of her Falstaff-like villainies:

173

"Mr. Sweedlepipe, take as much care of your ladylodger as you can, and give her a word or two of good advice now and then. Such", said Old Martin, looking gravely at the astonished Mrs. Gamp, "as hinting at the expediency of a little less liquor. . . ."

But she remains a target for our affection

Mrs. Gamp clasped her hands, turned up her eyes until they were quite invisible, threw back her bonnet for the admission of fresh air to her heated brow; and in the act of saying faintly—"Less liquor! . . ."—fell into one of the walking swoons. . . .

What Dickens knows is how *hard* life is for others, and how ordinary people share our weaknesses in dealing with it: but display a courage and zest of their own kind, and he is warmly aroused by their solutions to life's problems. It is this empathy Larkin cannot achieve: to him the "people" are

> Small-statured cross-faced tribes
> And cobble-close families
> In mill towns on dark mornings . . .

For them, "Life is slow dying". But the death is rather on his side, for the *Whitsun Weddings* not only displays the educated writer cut off from the people, but a man whose perceptions, curiosities and versifications cannot be creative, cannot find and communicate "the power that being changed can give" even though he knows he should. The human being in Mr Larkin's poem is not "the upsurge of creative time", but, alas, nor is the poet in his anthology of our time.

Whitsun Weddings might have been a kind of touchstone for Philip Larkin's choice in *The Oxford Book of Twentieth Century Verse*. Supposing in that anthology we turn to the last few poems? These may be compared with those by Thomas Hardy in the first few pages. What is then revealed is a catastrophe of sensibility, which is also a failure of philosophical anthropology.

Brian Patten is, apparently, a popular poet among young people. His two poems at the end of the anthology are called *Portrait of a Young Girl Raped at a Suburban Party* and *Ode on Celestial Music* (OR: *It's The Girl in the Bathroom Singing*).

If we compare these poems with those of Thomas Hardy at the beginning of the Oxford anthology, we notice that something

significant has happened to the word "girl", or rather, since Hardy
uses somewhat different terms, to "she" and "her" and the concept
of woman. Hardy was not unaware of the difference between conventional sexual mores and realities, as he shows in the ironic
poem about a girl who becomes a rich man's mistress, *The Ruined
Maid*:

> —"I wish I had feathers, a fine sweeping gown,
> And a delicate face, and could strut about Town!"—
> "My dear—a raw country girl, such as you be,
> Cannot quite expect that. You ain't ruined", said she.

To be "Victorian" is not to be incapable of fun about sexual
codes. But to Patten a girl is an object of another kind: there is
a significant decline in reaching out towards the "significant
other". "Woman lifts us up" Goethe said: by our time she has
become simply an object to stimulate a physical excitement. As
a "girlie" in the Rape poem she is just "a" girl; in the *Bathroom*
poem she is "*the* girl in the bathroom". Although Patten strives
to "meet" these women, to feel tender about them, and to have
(in the second one) passionate feelings towards them, they remain depersonalized, without unique human qualities, and the
shaft of attention which yearn towards them is bereft of meaning
—*it does not expect meaning*. They are objects, never encountered
as beings, certainly never as "woman"; here is a radical failure of
the capacity to relate to the "significant other", and thus of
meaning and relationship with the world.

It should be clear from all that has gone before that we cannot
separate our feelings about the world from our feelings about
relationship, about love, and "the significant other". In these last
poems in the *Oxford Book*, the "other" has no significance at all.
The last poem of all is about the failure of meaning itself, insofar
as it is possible, with such poor language, to discuss it. "The girl"
is singing in the bathroom, and it is not "celestial music"; she
does not inspire, she is "only" a girl. "You can tell"—that phrase
belongs to the common phraseology of English verse since the
New Lines "movement". Of his infant son's death Jon Silkin
writes, "There was no nobility in it or anything like that"—the
throwaway manner is characteristic of our time. After Amis, one
might say, we can neither be grave nor heroic, and writing is in-

capable of either tragedy or joy. The poet knows that in fact there can be transcendence: but he must joke it, and never be serious.

> You can tell. Although it's winter
> the trees outside her window have grown leaves,
> all manner of flowers push up through the floorboards.
> I think—what a filthy trick that is to play on me,
> I snip them with my scissors shouting
> *"I want only bona fide celestial music!"*
> Hearing this she stops singing.

Everything drowns in irony. The gesture at recognizing how a girl's singing can wring flowers out of an unprepossessing situation can reach at no more than something like a scene in an "absurd" comedy; the language rises no higher than "what a filthy trick" —the language of Amis comedy.

So, "the girl" becomes the girl in the advertisement who looks out of the window in her bath-towel, while the young man voyeuristically gazes in. The person, the muse, is reduced to "parts".

> Out of her bath now the girl knocks on my door,
> "Is my singing disturbing you?" she smiles entering,
> "did you say it was licentious or sensual?
> And excuse me, my bath towel's slipping."
> A warm and blonde creature
> I slam the door on her breasts shouting
> *"I want only bona fide celestial music!"*

The "absurd" comedy moves into something like titillating farce. It could be acted out, this humiliation of woman, on the stage; it parallels the insulting voyeurism of *The Sun*, and the gloating references to it on the radio in "Our Look at Today's Papers": this debasement of body-meaning is the staple of English culture from top to toe. Of course, we know what Patten means—even when the girl offered to merge the libidinal with the ideal, we (or he) rejected it. But what is rejected here is no genuine, creative eroticism (as we can see if we compare Donne or Wyatt) but a masturbation fantasy—or the fantasy of the "girlie" magazine, of a woman suddenly coming to one in smiling seductiveness. The slamming of the door on her breasts is meant to be an indication of failure on the part of the protagonist; but in its "cool" brutal-

176

ity it reveals the splenetic hatred of women that lies behind the impotence, the failure to be able to relate in terms of inter-subjective meaning, which afflicts not only protagonist, but poet. The consequent hate is everywhere acted out, with intellectual vindications. So, we move on to an old age of failed opportunities, obsessed in bitterness with futility—echoing *Krapp's Last Tape*:

> Much later on in life I wear my hearing-aid.
> What have I done to my body, ignoring it,
> splitting things into so many pieces my hands
> cannot mend anything. The stars, the buggers, remained silent.

The last phrase seems to echo Beckett: the dead universe of the Newtonian system is coarsely blamed for not singing. The reason for the failure is one which might be given by Freudian psychology or perhaps Reich—a failure to satisfy the body, while being over-analytical. The ageing protagonist is again listening for celestial music from "the girl's" daughter:

> Down in the bathroom now her daughter is singing.
> Turning my hearing-aid full volume
> I bend close to the floorboards hoping
> for at least one flower to appear . . .

"I do not think that they will sing to me", as Prufrock observed. But nowhere in the poem does this young man find what the essential fault is, which has prevented his protagonist from hearing the meaningful music for which he yearns. Nor does he penetrate in any insightful way to the spiritual impotence which afflicts our sexuality or our capacity to "have a presence in the being of the other". The yearning, and its defeat, are simply guyed.

In the penultimate poem in *The Oxford Book of Twentieth Century Verse* Brian Patten offers compassion to a girl who has been raped at a suburban party.

In discussing such a poem I find myself in such difficulties, whether in a seminar or in a book like this, because I often wish as now that I had never embarked upon it. The language is not only poor; it insults its subject in presenting it. The concept of human nature has sunk so low that it is as much as one can do to redeem it, let alone point out the utter impossibility of achiev-ing anything creative in such an atmosphere—of developing any truly creative theme. Yet here it is, enshrined, even immortalized, in the familiar blue and gold binding.

The poem is heavily derivative—for one thing, from *Whitsun Weddings* itself: it belongs to that kind of "realistic" account of what today's England is like, and it ends with a similar kind of sentimental gesture:

> When planets rolled out of your eyes
> And splashed down in surburban grasses.

What does this mean?[1] On a dull Sunday evening in suburbia, all this young girl's romantic yearnings, which were fixed to the stars, fell to earth. But why invoke a space shot by that "splashed down"? Why planets rather than stars?

The gesture at the heavens is an attempt to lift the poem to some "poetic" height, parallel with "It is the stars, it is the stars . . ." or "Let me not name it to you, you chaste stars" or something like that. But the matter is already too much insulted by its presentation.

> And after this quick bash in the dark
> You will rise and go . . .

"I will arise and go now" is echoed from Yeats's most anthologized and most unfortunate poem. Or perhaps Eliot is echoed

> Women come and go
> Talking of Michelangelo . . .

She is

> Thinking of how empty you have grown
> And of whether all the evening's care in front of mirrors
> And the younger boys disowned
> Led simply to this . . .

The "compassion" reveals the emptiness of the poem: the impossibility, in this medium of language (barely above the level of that of *The Daily Mirror*) of placing an act of drunken cruel sexual rapacity by the phrase "quick bash". We are in the language mode of Amis in the *New Statesman*: "having it off for nothing". Anyone who can speak or write so has entered into the paralysis of perception and expression whereby nothing can be said, because the human image has been so insulted, in the adoption of a

178

certain cold-blooded "objectivity". No "compassion" can overcome this language, because to use such language is to cut oneself
off from the flow of sympathy, the identification, necessary for
pity:

> Now you have left your titterings about love
> And your childishness behind you
> Yet still far from being old
> You spew up among flowers
> And in the warm stale rooms
> The party continues . . .

There is a dead banality in the presentation (spew up) which communicates a feeling of not being able to escape a predicament—a
situation, in fact, imposed upon youth by their exploitation by
commerce, by their separation from their parents; and by the
coarse literalism of our culture in general. So, there seems no-
one to whom this girl could go, either to prevent her rape, nor
to find consolation, either. At least, the brutal simplicity of the
poem conveys this, for history to note: and to note that the poet,
despite his heavy moralizing, does not even notice the absence
of adults, or of concern among the other youth, or apparently
see the schizoid isolation of the girl. The poet does at least note
that she has been driven out of her individual freedom into a
youth-cult mould:

> Confined to what you are expected to be
> By what you are
> Out in this frozen garden
> You shiver and vomit—
> Frightened, drunk among trees,
> You wonder at how those acts that called for tenderness
> Were far from tender.

There is an air about the moralizing, of desperation: and it is
probably because of this that young people like the verse of Brian
Patten. He tries to speak wisely, in the absence of all touch with
the values of civilization, of the appalling predicament of a youth
brutalized by exploitation. But he does not give up the spurious
pretence that youth has a "culture" of its own, and so he cannot
penetrate the essentially pathological state of her alienation. All

the girl has is the capacity, after being raped, of detaching herself from the young brutes who did it:

> It seems you saw some use in moving away
> From that group of drunken lives
> Yet already ten minutes pregnant
> In twenty thousand you might remember
> This party
> This dull Saturday evening
> When planets rolled out of your eyes . . .

But there is nothing in the language that can invoke any human values by which the event may be placed, or felt about. It hardly begins to be poetry. But it may be examined phenomenologically in a useful way, because it reveals such paralysis in poetry. The paralysis is evident in the flatness of tone, by which such an atrocity is coolly presented.

"Yet already ten minutes pregnant . . ." is so dead as to be almost psychotic in its numbness of tone. If she is "empty", the poet is emptier, to talk so coldly.[2] There is no imaginative capacity to find and examine the implications of life created under such circumstances. There can be no insight into the traumatic effects on a girl's feelings—will it only be that in a year's time she "might" remember this party? When she was minimally disillusioned, as the "planets rolled out of her eyes" and splashed down on the grass? The collapse of language and attitudes belong to the death of personal relationships and relationship to the world, insofar as those are conditioned by our culture (which does contribute inevitably to how people see themselves and their acts).

This is revealed clearly enough, if, as, I have suggested, we compare these final poems with those by Hardy at the beginning of the anthology. I don't mean, of course, to compare the great poems of Hardy, which I discuss elsewhere in this book. If we take a slight poem, for instance, *On The Departure Platform*, we find an attentiveness to significant moments between "him" and "her", which belongs to a totally different dimension:

> We kissed at the barrier; and passing through
> She left me, and moment by moment got
> Smaller and smaller, until to my view
> She was but a spot;

> A wee white spot of muslin fluff
> That down the diminishing platform bore
> Through hustling crowds of gentle and rough
> To the carriage door.

Hardy conveys a tenderness towards which Brian Patten can only gesture. He gives a sense of care and concern for "her", which needs to be preserved, in its fragility, in a difficult world: a sense of what she means to him, and the anguish of recognizing that she who is all to him can be only a little spot of colour and shape in a crowd. Elsewhere, "At News of Her Death"

> Not a line of her writing have I,
> Not a thread of her hair . . .

—this conveys a gentle sense of meaning in intersubjectivity which can only brutally be excluded from the world of Brian Patten. His own language ("bash", "spew") deepens the taboo on tenderness: Hardy is strong enough to dare that "wee". Yet the triumphant creativity of *After a Journey* or *Beeny Cliffs* is only possible if we begin from such gentleness. In the reduction of "the girl" to the status of object, and part-object at that, we may find one of the elements of the contemporary sensibility which have caused poetry to lose its bearings, in our dark night, to dehumanized sex. The Victorian was, by contrast, capable of a respect for the person we cannot now hope to emulate: and so, of a sense of meaning in life, emerging from significant relationships, to relationship with the Earth.

The contemporary apologist for fashionable nihilism will declare these things may be held apart—language, capacity to love, respect for the person, and meaningful perception. But this is the point of invoking philosophical anthropology: *they cannot be.* They are integral: and to divide them is darkness. In this darkness, there can be no hope for poetry—no hope for meaning in life, such as Yeats and Hardy yearned for and asserted when they could. If poetry has any point, it is that it is concerned to create a sense of meaning: it cannot exist if it proclaims *itself* that the reality of "instinct", or "matter" is superior to the truth of imagination and being, or brutality is a reality that must triumph over love.

I open my *Oxford Book* at random and find Philip Hobsbaum proclaiming, quite flatly, that truth lies between a woman's legs.

Moreover, the brutal realism of his poem destroys all the realities of vision, imagination and meeting: what values shall stand in the way of his pleasures (and ours, in enjoying his rape)?

> None, none. The awkward pauses when we talk,
> The literary phrases, are a lie.
> It was for this your teacher ran amock:
> Truth lies between your legs, and so do I.
> (*A Lesson in Love, Coming out Fighting*)

The earlier stanzas employ the word "romance"—but the very concept of romance, as embodied, say, in the tenderness of Hardy's anxious eye, watching "her" down the platform, is denied bluntly:

> Now on the floor, legs thrashing your dress
> Over your stocking-tops, your tight blue pants
> Bursting to be off at my caress,
> This is the underside of our romance . . .

What price now the "wee white spot of muslin" or the "air-blue gown"? The particularizations are ugly, and are meant to be ugly—ugly with that unrelieved, never-to-be-transcended "realism" that today dogs English writing. First, one unmasks decency, chastity, reticence:

> Sitting straightbacked, a modest Irish miss,
> Knees clenched together—even then I knew
> Your full mouth would open under my kiss,
> The line under your eyes gave me my clue . . .

The rhythm has a saucy bounce—saucy with the confidence of one taking an "ego-trip" in fantasied domination over the feared woman: one can find plenty of this in Amis. The seduction comes over as an act of predatory hate:—a "lesson" in the sadistic sense. It is vindicated by the fact that she *wanted* to be seduced. The triumph is the triumph of pornography, over that sensitivity one fears—and the language sinks to that of *Penthouse* and *Forum*:

> Which is the truer? I, speaking of Donne,
> Calling the act a means and not an end,
> Or at your sweet pudenda, sleeking you down.

The "sweet" is sickly, and "pudenda" sicklier: "sleeking you down" is the triumphantly perverted voice of the script-writer for stage sex shows. And perhaps the worst aspect of all is that use of education, rather of half-education—"knowing" Donne, "knowing" about means and ends, "knowing" that behind the simpering faces they all go to it like the soiled horse or fitchew, between their forks. (The willingness of Cordelia and the fool to die for love, and the irrelevance of that because love has shown itself greater than death, could not be understood in the same ethos—which is, it needs to be said, the ethos of our "new universities").

What one must say is that anyone to whom Donne, or poetry, or discussions of means, ends and values, woman or humanness *meant anything*, would not write like that. Anyone who pursued meaning and creativity in any serious—nay, in any comic or joyful sense—*could* not write like that, so glibly crowing, over an act of hate, the taking of another person like a thing.

> Labour is blossoming or dancing where
> The body is not bruised to pleasure soul . . .

The "blossoming" or "dancing" of creativity make their gains in the area of the subjective life, where from the body-life, the shadow, the unconscious, the "formative principle", symbolism enables the human being, enables his consciousness, to pursue meaning. By this creative dynamic, he transcends himself—groping towards achieved significances which do not die with the body: these, a musical phrase, a line of poetry, a great dramatic or symphonic structure, a painting—assert the *Dasein*: the "being there". I *was there*: and nothing can eradicate this trumphant moment when I was my true self, and spoke of this meaning, this peak-moment, this enhancement of my experience: Bonnard's woman in the bath, Hardy's ghost among the caves, Lawrence's moment among the breakfast roses: "This I constructed, upon which to rejoice, before I was swept away into nothingness."

This is creativity. From it can flow meaningful lives—in the sense that, inspired by the *Dasein*-moment, by the knowledge that life can be transcended, that nothingness can be overcome—people enriched by the joy and tragedy of art, can go back to their choices and actions in life, more aware of "authenticity", of rightness and trueness. They know better what it is to be human, and they have found a point in existence.

Acquisitiveness cannot give this feeling, nor can competitiveness, nor material comfort, nor sensual indulgence. The film can never give it, because its essential idiom does not come from the creative inward dynamics of a human consciousness, as word, painting-image and musical phrase do. The photographic age is an age of literalism, and this is killing our creative dynamics— destroying man's moral being, as we can see clearly enough if we look around us. The film of sexual organs in action is the final banality—the ultimate insult to creativity, in which "body is bruised to pleasure soul": with no transcendence possible, only a brute stirring in the loins.

Philip Hobsbaum's poem belongs to this ultimate reduction, inspired by the filmic, and the whole collapse of English writing to the level of believing "the truth" is "between our legs".

I am aware that I am rejecting Philip Hobsbaum's poem on different grounds from those employed by F. R. Leavis in (say) rejecting Browning. Leavis begins from inadequacy of diction, texture, rhythm—and from there comes to attack the actual persona and being of the poet. He declares that

> All that we can fairly ask of the poet is that he shall show himself
> to have been fully alive in our own time. The evidence will be in the
> very texture of his poetry   (p. 24).

So, he starts from the texture, and from there deduces whether the poet is or is not "fully alive". Here it may be that "current conventions" will not serve even to provide a start for a poet, or "current poetical habits" may interfere.

But what we *can* try to judge here is the truth and quality of a writer's model of man, what he thinks and feels about humanness (which will be bound up with what he feels and thinks of himself). And when a poet tells us "The literary phrases . . . are a lie . . ." and "Truth lies between your legs, and so do I . . ."— we can say that he is wrong. Moreover, we can say that he is wrong because he uses poetry to justify the indulgence of egoistical nihilism, for his imagery vindicates a pornographic exploitation of the other ("Your stocking-tops, your tight blue pants . . . your sweet pudenda, sleeking you down. . . ."). The blunt aggressive sensuality of his language is offensive to privacy, and vindicates a kind of rape.

Egoistical nihilism has become the philosophy of our culture

184

at large today: it is a mark of lost bearings like mariners drifting in a rudderless boat, resorting to cannibalism. Max Stirner has become our philosopher (*Der Einzige und sein Eigenthum 1845*):

> Let us seek in others only means and organs. . . . For me no-one is a person to be respected . . . but solely an *object* . . . an interesting or uninteresting object, useful or useless. The "other" is but an object to be "consumed", whose only relation to me is that of useableness, utility, use.

This is what "she" becomes, towards the end of *The Oxford Book of Twentieth Century Verse*: and if we turn to the language itself, it is that of "consuming time" as Stirner did, by "creative Nothingness" and "criminal frivolity".

Finally, perhaps, we could here look, distasteful as it may be, at a poem by Amis. I am particularly struck by his influence—on Larkin, on Brian Patten, on Philip Hobsbaum. It goes with the whole influence of reductionism in our time—bringing human experience down to the bones, guts and skin—the concrete—in denial of the spirit that transcends: man is waste matter, as in Sartre, according to the strictures of Gabriel Marcel (see *The Philosophy of Existence*, pp. 65–66), and this has led to the present obsession with perversion, as if distorted and contorted body-acts were the only meanings left to us.

Concomitant with the reductionism is the denial of potentialities, of anything, joyful or tragic, that transcends; anything that intends or moves forward to new potentialities in the "upsurge of time". And, as I shall try to show by my comparison with Hardy and Yeats, it is a form of disinheritance, of loss of past and future. The especial aspect of the corruption of the creative gains of the past may be studied in Kingsley Amis's poem *St Asaphs* (*Oxford Book*, no. 492). Evans, shaving, watches the children coming to school. A chestnut tree stands in his line of sight, "between the GIRLS entrance and 'Braich-y-Pwll' ".

> Not that he really wants to get among
> Schoolchildren—see, some of the stuff by there,
> All bounce and flounce, rates keeping an eye on:
> Forthcoming models.

That is, we are to find amusing (and "realistic") the portrayal of a low-life grubby character, who watches and bides his lustful time with the schoolgirls. He waits for May-time when he will see, voyeuristically, "just the odd flash of well-filled gingham". We might be doubtful enough about the way in which we are invited to join in this febrile excitement, in such a gloatingly "ironic" poem. We might make a mental note that, like so many manifestations in the contemporary world, there are forms of "irony" that involve us in giving assent to an indulgence in a cruel and destructive assault on human values and tenderness. Naturally Amis's poem lacks all attention to what one thinks, ethically, of a man who gloats on adolescent girls' figures, and lusts in his heart to use them. It is simply unfair, that he can't indulge more "freely" in his hate (Amis doesn't see it as hate). And then comes the pay-off verse:

> You can't win, Dai. Nature's got all the cards.
> But bear up: you still know the bloody leaf
> From bole or blossom, dancer from the dance.
> Hope for you, then.

What is evoked by the phrase "among schoolchildren" thus becomes not a record of Yeats's *creative* agony of mind, about the relationship between art and life, perception and reality. It becomes a joke for the "educated" adult chatting up schoolgirls, and how, with any luck, "Evans", the common little man, typical of "us", can avoid getting in a mess with some kid, by strictly keeping his masturbation fantasies to himself—or only seducing those who become bloody-well mature enough to enjoy it. The struggle in Yeats's mind, language, poetry, attitudes, imagery—all are corrupted, together with concepts of "English", and the words themselves.

The effect on Yeats's great poem is devastating; the tenderness and complexity of his images blasted. And this is one characteristic item in Cohen's anthology—which contains more than its fair share of material from not-poets and anti-poets, the effect of whose works is to erode not only man's image, but creativity itself.

If poetry matters, it is surely because it can help offer us a sense of meaning, not least in the realm of relationship, as against the predominant emptiness of meaning in a schizoid world. What happens if poetry makes a deliberate assault on the meaning of intersubjectivity?

Often, today, what is accepted as poetry "includes" a kind of expression which I can only see as anti-poetic, and seriously damaging to poetry and the expectations of the audience, not least because it seriously damages the realm of "meeting" to which poetry belongs as "encounter" itself.

Here one can perhaps usefully refer to Coleridge's pronouncement on Sterne, which might equally apply to Amis and many prevalent figures in today's London literary scene:

> There is a sort of knowingness, the wit of which depends—first on the modesty it gives pain to; or, secondly, on the innocence and the innocent ignorance over which it triumphs; or, thirdly, on a certain oscillation in the individual's own mind between remaining good and encroaching evil of his nature—a sort of dallying with the devil—a fluxionary act of combining courage and cowardice, as when a man snuffs a candle with his fingers for the first time, or better still, perhaps like that trembling daring with which a child touches a hot tea urn, because it has been forbidden; so that the mind has in its own white and black angel the same or similar amusement, as may be supposed to take place between an old debauchée and a prude,—she feeling resentment, on the one hand from a prudential anxiety to preserve appearances and have a character, and, on the other, an inward sympathy with the enemy. We have only to suppose society innocent, and then nine tenths of this sort of wit would be like a stone that falls on snow, making no sound because exciting no resistance; the remainder rests on its being an offence against the good manners of human nature itself.
>
> (*Works of Samuel Taylor Coleridge*, Nonesuch edition, p. 420)

Amis is one who has eminently settled for "offence against the good manners of human nature itself": but the offence goes deeper —for it sells out the poetic to a world of acquisitiveness and empty materialism.

Or we may put alongside the quotation from Coleridge, this from Philip Pacey, a Librarian and Humanities lecturer in a College of Art:

> it does appear to be the case, that it is possible for us, as a society, to retreat from risk; to make a hero of our False Self and its art-against-art; and perhaps we are especially vulnerable at the present

time. For the materialism which Blake saw beginning is in full swing. The interests of those in power is to drive a wedge into the divided self of each one of us, to split-off our false self and exploit that as their puppet—in its anxiety to conform it is so easily manipulated. It is in their interest to make us dissatisfied with those small miracles which can show us more in a grain of sand than they can ever contrive to offer, and, through pornography's distorted image of woman, so evident in their advertising, to mock the feminine element of being . . . the feminine through which we would enter into a feeling of oneness with each other and all Nature. . . . The wonder is that human naturalness has not gone under altogether; that the "feminine" in us can still lead to the true doing of creativity. That this is so says much for the strength of human naturalness in its own direction. . . .

("Art as Risk", *Transcript*, November, 1974)

The kind of poetry I have discussed in this chapter denies both the truths recognized by philosophical anthropology, and also turns its hatred on imagination, values, and man's higher nature— on "female element being" as an aspect of our creativity. It mocks all transcendence of our supposed essential brutality, as functional man: and yet this is the staple of our cultural diet, even as it is taught in schools and colleges. When such destructiveness can be accepted as poetry, and is the touchstone of our cultural life, there seems little hope for poetry. And the only way to dispel such an entrenched enemy is through the power that subjective disciplines, in the investigation of man's nature, can give us.

As I have said above, there are new ethical principles emerging from "philosophical anthropology". If we accept these "ethical statements", we can see many poems and novels written today as expressing inversions of human truth, and deliberate falsifications of human reality. As Rollo May says, encounter is the basis of decision and will: if poetry is abused as a form of encounter, this ethical principle is denied:

Responsibility involves being responsive to, *responding*. Just as consciousness is the distinctively human form of awareness, so decision and responsibility are the distinctive forms of consciousness in the human being who is moving toward self-realization, integration, maturity . . . *Decision*, in our sense, creates . . . a pattern of acting and living which is empowered and enriched by wishes, asserted by will, and is responsive to and responsible for the significant

188

other-persons who are important to one's self in the realizing of the long-term goals. If the point were not self-evident, it could be demonstrated along the lines of Sullivan's interpersonal theory of psychiatry, Buber's philosophy, and other viewpoints. They all point out that wish, will, and decision occur within a nexus of relationships upon which the individual depends not only for his fulfilment but for his very existence. This sounds like an ethical statement and *is*.

(Love and Will, pp. 267–8)

If art denies the need for the significant other, and denies the link between this "nexus of relationships", between *responsiveness* and *responsibility*, then it forfeits its right to exist. Rollo May declares that our capacity to be free—in the sense of making true, responsive, and responsible choices—depends upon accepting this need for relationship, while an adequate awareness in our consciousness also depends upon it. If poetry denies these ethical statements, then it is denying the essential quality of consciousness, it denies freedom.

But not only do many poems written today deny these qualities in our life: poets even write poems abusing their own craft, rejecting (not least by the poor blunt language they use) any hope of transcendence. A characteristic poem here is Peter Porter's *What A Lying Lot the Writers Are* from *Once Bitten Twice Bitten* (1961):

> To put it all down now I take my pencil up
> And a bilge of hate can be sluiced up top.
> I have no time in a bored lifetime
> To love a body in its sour confines
> Because the love is a meeting place
> Of impossible pictures as a disputed face.

This kind of dull destructiveness requires an energetic rebuttal from philosophical anthropology in defence of poetry, because at every point the writer is wrong.

Peter Porter goes on, in his rejection of all that creativity stands for:

> But people make metaphysics out of this
> And play among bodies with such or thus . . .

The reality (as with Philip Hobsbaum) is the body—functional man. It is wrong (Porter asserts) to pay attention to man's

189

higher qualities or his moral being: the reality is his brutal need to be acquisitive, among the wolf-pack:

> To be above the tearing fingers of the ruck
> You need good teeth, a good income, good luck.

By contrast with this concrete reality, the imaginings of the writer are lies:

> This then is the lie: we write and perform
> Great solemnities in the mind's frame.

The lies are that

> The lovely are loved, the victims rail,
> Beds hold the sick and the hale free-wheel,
> Great events are remembered as history,
> Science understands us, we are free.

It will not do to believe these illusions: "Books tell us stories of friendship and love, / Animals and plants help us stay alive." But in fact

> Talking until the last minimum of death
> We praise God or opportunity or both
> But we die in the first room we see
> The bright locked world, the captivity.

The whole poem amounts to little more than a flat declaration that we are not free—and cannot be. We are captive in "the bright locked world", the "first room we see": that is, we live in the most immediate actuality, and there is no question of finding transcendence in the manifold mansions of consciousness. The "last minimum of death" is the measure of our mortal existence: as Marcel argues, when we can find nothing more than functional man, death represents only the scrapping of a machine that now becomes totally worthless: man throughout Porter's poem is but "waste matter". Science defines us, as "matter in motion". So literature is "lies", which disguise from us the way in which we are locked in the deterministic effects of "objective" forces.

But, as we have seen, the implication of philosophical anthropology, as expressed by Maslow, is that "man has a higher nature, and that this higher nature includes the need for meaningful work, for responsibility, for creativeness, for being fair and

190

just, for doing what is worthwhile and preferring to do it well"
(*Towards A Psychology of Being*, p. 222). Surely the poet should
be the custodian of this "higher nature", of responsibility and
creativeness—not submerge these in a "bilge of hate"?[3] Yet today
the poet destroys transcendence, and abandons hope, in the
general mess of forfeiture of the sense of anything to believe in,
and of hope.

For transcendence, by contrast, we may turn to someone for
whom there was no hope. The poet Isaac Rosenberg died in the
trenches, and must have known that he had little hope of survival:
so, the question of confidence in intentionality has no direct relationship with the actual circumstances of the writer. It is evidently
a question of his philosophy of life. In *Break of Day in the
Trenches*, the opening line conveys immediately the disintegration
in which the poet exists:

> The darkness crumbles away—
> It is the same old druid Time as ever . . .

Time goes on, bringing the dawn; and for a man who has been on
guard duty all night, the exhausted eyes can only register a
crumbled shadow. Time is an aged ritualist: the immediate moment
is full only of odd moments—incidents which are ironically manifest of life, or, rather, death in life, for against the progress of
slow druidic time, the soldier has nothing more than a continual
procession of last moments.

> Only a live thing leaps my hand—
> A queer sardonic rat—
> As I pull the parapet's poppy
> To stick behind my ear.

Why "only"? Because of the crumbling night, and the overweening
sense of Time's dragging length by contrast with the soldier's brief
moments: the threatening death implicit in these. "Only a live
thing . . ." (Perhaps we recall King Lear's "Why should a dog, a
rat have life . . ."?) The "live" and "leaps" with the slight labial
alliteration, express the vitality, and the shock of coincidence,
when, as the soldier makes his plucking gesture, a rat jumps over
his hand. He "pulls the parapet's poppy"—and here the alliteration emphasises the intentionality of the act. It is an assertion of

being alive, of plucking before he is plucked, of a manic flaunting in the face of death: to stick it behind his ear is a perky act of gaiety, a jauntiness, which declares, "I am still alive!" But the rat is "queer" and "sardonic" because it chooses that moment to make its comments: moving from corpse to corpse, it leaps over a hand that will soon be dead, just as this hand asserts it is not yet dead, by its symbolic gesture—which is also a little death, a plucking, of the live flower. (His death will be no more than that, a being-snatched-away.)

The rat, by its cosmopolitan indifference as to which kind of corpse it eats, exposes the difference between man and the neutral natural world.

> Droll rat, they would shoot you if they knew
> Your cosmopolitan sympathies

The rat also conveys a "sardonic" comment by its queer, droll, grinning indifference to the human conflict, whose point is brought into question.

> It seems you inwardly grin as you pass
> Strong eyes, fine limbs, haughty athletes
> Less chanced than you for life,
> Bonds to the whims of murder . . .

The handsome youths are not as free as the rat: they are chained to the random infliction of death, by an impersonal industrialized war. By contrast with the sardonic leap of the rat (which can go where it pleases), they are

> Sprawled in the bowels of the earth,
> The torn fields of France

Looking at the rat, the soldier sees a choric, ironic, grin. What does the rat see in their faces, as it moves about its cosmopolitan travels?

> What do you see in our eyes
> At the shrieking iron and flame
> Hurled through still heavens?

The heavy rhythm and aspirates of that last line and the next convey just enough gravity to convey the dread of death that underlies the poem's apparent easiness: "What quaver—what heart

192

aghast?" There is no doubt that the soldier is trembling and appalled.

But the gesture he makes is that of transcendence: a gesture towards *Dasein*:

> Poppies whose roots are in man's veins
> Drop, and are ever dropping;
> But mine in my ear is safe,
> Just a little white with the dust.

All the sardonic comment of the rat, and all the poet's dread, creates a powerful ambiguity around the word "safe". The last line, certainly, undermines it: the poppy is white with the dust of explosions. Its roots were in blood anyway. The plucking merely anticipates the dropping: emphasized by the line-break and the rhythm, we see a vision of a myriad of red flowers falling, like men falling and bleeding on a battlefield. In this, what can be "safe"? He has in fact accelerated the poppy's falling by plucking it: yet we know what he means. In a sense, the plucking and wearing of the flower says, "I am a man. I can find joy in a wild-flower, and I can make an assertion of being alive and free by wearing it in my ear. I have made this gesture in the depth of hell—and nothing can take the phenomenological meaning of this away, not even oblivion." The poem is, in a sense, the gesture and the plucked flower: and it is this courage, of wringing beauty and meaning out of hell, that poetry today has lost.

NOTES

1. The image is perhaps lifted from *Death of a Son* by Jon Silkin: "And out of his eyes two great tears rolled, like stones, and he died."
2. Compare Hardy's rich eroticism in the scenes of Tess's courtship by Angel; their kisses alter the polarity of their worlds.
3. This is not to give up scientific realism of the objective kind, but to find a better objectivity. As Rollo May says, "we must not give up the experience gathered on our journey through materialism which turned us almost to stone", "What is Existentialist Therapy?", *"Journal of Existential Psychology* (1967) p. 159, last vol.

7

What Can Creativity Do? W. B. Yeats's *Among School Children*

How do we begin to climb back painfully to a sense of the value of true creativity? By turning to the great achievements of the past in poetry. The problem I am examining in this book has been successfully grappled with by a few artists in the past—and only now, I believe, are we beginning to understand their success. I have tried to show how Mahler, menaced by the loss of faith, by a Godless universe, by nihilism, and by his own empty, or most cynical, dynamics of the self, struggled on to find a sense of meaning that could triumph over spiritual paralysis. The triumphs are only momentary: but they *are* triumphs which, transmuted into art, are permanent in the sense that they can be repeated—repeatedly enjoyed by us, as we re-create them in the hearing. The threat of chaotic non-meaning (often experienced in the first movement of Mahler's *Ninth Symphony*) is overcome and translated into joy on the one hand and tragedy on the other. Blankness is transmuted into creative meaning, and so into gratitude for having existed.

W. B. Yeats was experiencing much the same kind of problem in the twenties and the complex conflict in him is perhaps best examined in *Among School Children* (*Collected Poems*, p. 242), written in 1925 when he was sixty.

The poem follows the unfolding progress of a mood, underlying which is a powerful theme of continuity and creativity. He enters a schoolroom, and is faced by the wondering eyes of the children, and their creative exploration of their world. There is also the presence in the room of "creative reflection"—the care and concern of the nuns. Here Yeats is confronted by man's need to "have a presence in the being of the other"—and it raises a number of problems in his mind.

He is tormented by memories of his own need to find creative reflection in the eyes of Maud Gonne: his idealization of her, and the tragedy that overtook it, as she became a pseudo-male windbag, no longer beautiful, an empty scarecrow, such as he (he feels) now becomes himself.

This evokes deeper memories which underlie the poem, of that primary identification we experience in "primary maternal preoccupation". He remembers himself as a child, his feelings of togetherness with Maud Gonne, as they recall their childhood, and this brings him to the deepest and most buried theme of all: if primary maternal preoccupation fails, or is inadequate, does it not mean that all the quest for meaning which sets off from this area of "encounter" is pointless, too? Will not all such effort fail?

In Buber, Winnicott, and Guntrip, we find an emphasis which suggests that only through the primary relationship of infant to mother—being to being (the mother "being for")—can men find a sense of relating to a benign universe. But there is an additional problem. Since "God is dead", in a godless universe, the problem seems to become intolerable, not least because the language and forms of religion can no longer be the pathway to meaning, to feeling at home in the universe (which is what Nietzsche's phrase meant). So, for Yeats, it seems as if all human action and choice are meaningless, not least those self-mocking acts by which symbolism is exerted in the true philosophical quest: "old clothes upon old sticks to scare a bird."

This is a very revealing line, and we may link this poem to our general theme from that stanza. There, philosophy and poetry, in the quest for meaning and the truth of existence, are dismissed as futile. They are mere "old clothes upon old sticks to scare a bird": he identifies with this spectre himself, for he is a "comfortable kind of old scarecrow". His poetry, his attempts at meaning, like those of Plato, Aristotle and Pythagoras, are all futile attempts to scare off the real birds of prey—old age, time and death—who triumph. Death, and the nothingness it brings, not least to vision, is the most real thing in the world: poetry and philosophy can do no more than scare these away for a while. In

195

this attitude we see the triumph of nineteenth century natural scientism, of the Cartesian dismissal of poetry and man's creative powers (the "very roots of our being" as Marjorie Grene puts it), and of the laws of universal entropy. By implication, the poet is actually dismissing consciousness as an unreality—in the face of the primary realities of age, pain and mortality: of physical existence.

To dismiss the primacy of vision, consciousness and meaning is, of course, an agony for a poet. In the face of the enquiring eyes of children, and what they represent—human creativity—he can hardly bear the pain of feeling that his whole life has been devoted to a futile self-mockery. And so, by persisting in his effort to record and wrestle with the experience he actually transforms the anguish into a creative triumph which by its achievement in art, gives the lie to his own nihilistic tendencies.[1]

The symbolism of the poem is extremely deep, not least because it is coloured from the beginning by philosophical pondering. The nun's white hood, for example, is a symbol of the purity of the nun-teachers' care for the children, and the simplicity of their task, as they conceive it. The accusation of self-mockery later almost hurls itself against the white hood, which contrasts strikingly with the black rags of the scarecrows—of himself as an old man, and of the poems and philosophies he withers with contempt into *épouvantailles*.

Again, the word "cipher" is significant, since it implies gently that the achievements which the nuns care so much about are mere empty "O's." Yet the voice is as yet gently appreciative, and touched with wonder at the new developments in teaching "in the best modern way"

> I walk through the long schoolroom questioning;
> A kind old nun in a white hood replies;
> The children learn to cipher and to sing,
> To study reading-books and histories,
> To cut and sew, be neat in everything
> In the best modern way—the children's eyes
> In momentary wonder stare upon
> A sixty-year-old smiling public man.

The schoolroom itself is an image of intentionality, of preparation for the future: the "neatness" expresses a confidence (a

God-fearing Roman Catholic confidence) in the future of the children. The attention they give him is "momentary"—because they are not interested in old smiling public men, only in their own movement into the new, into the things they have created, into the future.

So, he begins to contemplate time, its promise, the failure to fulfil. But this arises out of recapturing the childlike empathy between himself and the woman he idealized. He looks round and wonders if Maud looked like this child or that child:

> I look upon one child or t'other there
> And wonder if she stood so at that age . . .

Why does he remember her at all in that setting? I believe there are a number of reasons, related to the themes I have examined above.

The nuns obviously idealize the children, as he idealized Maud. But there was a time when Maud was as beautiful as the children, as full of promise, as *idealizable*. Then, there is something like the idealization of a child in a man's idolization of his ideal object—she resembles the ideal child image into which men make their mother when they are small, and retain, as a kind of child image, in their mature life (see *Mary Rose* and my analysis in *Gustav Mahler and the Courage to Be*). The reference to Leda is here significant: she obviously belongs to the world of Gods and myth, in which a god could come disguised as a man, and so transcend the mundane into the ideal. It is, at any rate, this transcendent quality of which the children remind him, and remind him of how, once, with her, he had at times been able to enter into the particular kind of joy and tragedy of which childhood is capable, and which adults can recapture in remembrance—together with the memory of capacity for intense identification, primary at-oneness, which is possible in childhood, too:

> it seemed that our two natures blent
> Into a sphere from youthful sympathy,
> Or else, to alter Plato's parable,
> Into the yolk and white of the one shell.

This is a memory of recapturing in an adult relationship moments resembling the primary identification of which Buber writes:

The ante-natal life of the child is one of purely natural combination, bodily interaction and flowing from one to the other. Its life's
horizon, as it comes into being, seems in a unique way to be, and
yet again not to be, traced in that of the life that bears it. For it
does not rest only in the womb of the human mother. Yet this connection has such a cosmic quality that the mythical saying of the
Jews, "In the mother's body man knows the universe: in birth he
forgets it", reads like the imperfect decipherment of an inscription
from earliest times. And it remains, indeed, in man as a secret
image of desire. Not as though his yearning meant a longing to
return . . . but the yearning is for the cosmic connection, with its
true *"Thou"*, of this life that has burst forth into spirit.

(Martin Buber, *I and Thou*)

In the "cosmic connection" for which Yeats yearns is the secret
of the meaning of life, "the knowledge of the universe". He had
re-experienced this sense of meaning in talking with Maud about
childhood tragedy: and the moment is almost brought before him,
among the actual children there at that moment:

> And thinking of that fit of grief or rage
> I look upon one child or t'other there
> And wonder if she stood so at that age—
> For even daughters of the swan can share
> Something of every paddler's heritage—
> And had that colour upon cheek or hair,
> And thereupon my heart is driven wild:
> She stands before me as a living child.

His own vision actually materializes her, the swan-one, who is
superior, being god-touched, to ordinary beings. But there is a
strange touch here: "daughters of the swan"—so that Ledaean
means procreated by the swan. So, Leda now becomes Maud
Gonne's *mother*. Elsewhere he writes of Leda and the Swan

> A shudder in the loins engenders there
> The broken wall, the burning roof and tower
> And Agamemnon dead.
>   Being so caught up,
> So mastered by the brute blood of the air,
> Did she put on his knowledge with his power
> Before the indifferent beak could let her drop?

> (*Leda and the Swan, Collected Poems*, p. 241)

198

Maud Gonne is idealized as half-goddess: her body was Ledaean. But in this other poem there is a suggestion that in creating her, a male "brute blood" engendered hate and chaos—not least by the lust which turned to indifference as soon as it was satisfied. The passage from this other poem is relevant, because it shows Yeats had insight into the schizoid nature of Maud Gonne's political intellect—engendered in her by "false male doing".

We see this other side of the idealized object in Stanza IV of *Among School Children*:

> Her present image floats into the mind—
> Did Quattrocento finger fashion it
> Hollow of cheek as though it drank the wind
> And took a mess of shadows for its meat?

The fifteenth century as a period of art in Italian history was a period of the development of humanist realism. The Ledaean idealization of classical sculpture, presumably Yeats means, gave way to the Renaissance attention to the reality, the anatomy, the mutable mortality. The recognition of the temporal brings awareness of nothingness—the wind, the mess of shadows which the human being takes in, even as he eats and drinks and enjoys life.

This image of the time-worn real woman is evoked, also, by the beauty and youth of the children. The contrast threatens, too, to evoke his bitterness: but he turns self-pity aside with a wry irony:

> And I though never of Ledaean kind
> Had pretty plumage once—enough of that,
> Better to smile on all that smile, and show
> There is a comfortable kind of old scarecrow . . .

To the nuns and the children he is not going to show his anguish of mind: he is outwardly smiling. But the irony is directed at the smiling nun's false innocence, too.

And so he bursts out, declaring that a mother, having suffered her birth pangs, would not be able to bear her pains, if she knew how her child was never going to fulfil her hopes. But this is a strange and tormented stanza. For what Yeats has been yearning for is that original creative togetherness of primary identification: and yet here he reveals an extremely negative attitude, to psychic parturition and care. The image he presents is as far as one can get from "creative reflection", and must be seen as a schizoid picture of one's origins.

For one thing, "honey of generation"—the sweetness of desiring to procreate and the sweetness of sex—have *betrayed* the child into the world: it is a "shape", a lump of life-stuff,

> And that must sleep, shriek, struggle to escape
> As recollection or the drug decide ...

I find in poetry seminars that many students refuse to accept the painfulness of this and sentimentalize it. But the "that" refers to the "shape", and it is an almost hostile image of a baby which has been unwillingly and painfully thrust into this world, and which can only bear it (and often *cannot* bear it)—by sleeping, screaming with pain if it remembers the shock of being born, or having its misery stifled by drugs. This is a totally negative picture of infant existence and points to a deep disturbance in Yeats about birth and infancy.

If a mother who had coped with this infant anguish could see her son at sixty—would she think him a compensation for the pains of labour, or the uncertainty of his growing up? It is a very disturbing and bitter stanza, and reveals that the yearning for adequate reflection, for sympathy and togetherness (expressed in life in his idealizing fascination with Maud) is a yearning to complete the processes of psychic birth, and to experience the love he had insufficiently experienced in infancy—in the sense of the mother's capacity to "be for" her child.

Incidentally, the poem reveals that in Yeats's mind "creative reflection" (between nuns and children, himself and Maud, mother and child) runs parallel to artistic creativity—as is clear from the line

> Both nuns and mothers worship images ...

But if a mother's reveries are mocked by the old scarecrow a man becomes, when sixty winters have fallen on his head, so perhaps all attempts through symbolism to find meaning in life are "old clothes upon old sticks to scare a bird"? Yeats expresses a distrust of man's primary need for symbolism: a terrible predicament for a poet.

> Plato thought nature but a spume that plays
> Upon a ghostly paradigm of things;
> Solider Aristotle played the taws
> Upon the bottom of a king of kings;
> World-famous golden-thighed Pythagoras
> Fingered upon a fiddle-stick or strings . . .

There are totally different modes of interpreting our existence in the world. Plato's view is distrustful of the uncertainties of our existence: as Marjorie Grene says, he "had to turn his back on the changing world of sensible things and affirm a pre-natal confrontation with truth. His certainties lay in a vision beyond and opposed to the everyday, visible world."

However

> For Plato's greatest pupil, for Aristotle, the platonic starting point, the thesis that "sensible things are always in flux and there is no knowledge of them" was itself a mistake, and so the intellectual conversion away from the perceptible world to the really real of the Forms was illusory and unneeded. The source of certainty, Aristotle believed, is with us and around us in the nature of things, and in the natural concordance between our own intelligence and the world.
>
> (*The Knower and the Known*, p. 36)

In Yeats's poem Aristotle is dismissing Plato's paradigm-spume concept as Dr Johnson dismissed Bishop Berkeley's idealism, only by beating the material behind of youthful Alexander, instead of kicking a great stone.

Pythagoras believed in the transmigration of souls, "appears as the revealer of a mode of life calculated to raise his disciples above the level of mankind, and to recommend them to the favour of the gods" (*Everyman Classical Dictionary*). This attempt to transcend the human by claiming to be half a god is ridiculed by Yeats—together with artistic creativity, which is here but "fingering" on a "fiddlestick". The word "star" is important in "What a star sang"—for by this irony Yeats implies that a star is the mass of gas revealed by objective science. It is "fiddling" and make-believe ("What . . . careless Muses heard") to try to make reality anything else than what it is. Things only are, and pass. We may reject Plato's uncertainty, but Aristotle's certainty is essentially based on the mundanity of whacking knowledge into boys, while Pythagorean mathematics or songs are but invention.

201

All human intellectual endeavour is but a mockery, in the face of the mess of shadows and the wind of nothingness, that blows us all into oblivion.

The next stanza (VII) thus ends in a howl of despair:

> Both nuns and mothers worship images.
> But those the candles light are not as those
> That animate a mother's reveries,
> But keep a marble or a bronze repose.
> And yet they too break hearts—O Presences
> That passion, piety or affection knows,
> And that all heavenly glory symbolise—
> O self-born mockers of man's enterprise . . .

In the first four lines the poet almost seems to prefer (as in the Byzantium poems) the aesthetic achievement because of its deadness and "repose". (There is the assertion behind the reference to devotional imagery that there is no God or Christ behind the images.) But the reality of the symbols is admitted—because they too break hearts, as much as unfulfilled promise in a child breaks the mother's heart. And then he bursts out at them as "Presences", the objects of passion, piety and affection, which symbolize heavenly glory—burst out at them *because* they are real *in this*.

The poet is, as it were, overcome by the primary reality of meaning (despite its quality as being a self-born mocker of man's enterprise), and then admits that creativity *can* succeed, even if we cannot find where it is, or in what sense it succeeds:

> Labour is blossoming or dancing where
> The body is not bruised to pleasure soul,
> Nor beauty born out of its own despair,
> Nor blear-eyed wisdom out of midnight oil.
> O chestnut tree, great rooted blossomer
> Are you the leaf, the blossom or the bole?
> O body swayed to music, O brightening glance,
> How can we know the dancer from the dance?

The word "labour" inevitably picks up the reference to birth in Stanza V, and the theme of relating birth and child care to creative effort all through the poem. Creative effort *does* yield a blossom, does create a dance, when the body is not being punished or pained to yield pleasure, or where beauty does not have the blighting quality of desperation. Desperate sensualism, or beauty wrung from a desperate compensation for nihilism, are not the successful sources of creative meaning: nor is a painful scholarship, coughing in the ink.

But there *is* transcendent meaning. One cannot particularize or divide it into its parts. It does not lend itself to fragmentation, but is all of a piece in its wholeness, and belongs to a whole natural process, to "life". The chestnut tree is a "being-in-the-world" and it is impossible to say its beauty *is* "in" this feature or the other. The individual is a being-in-the-world like that and his sense of meaning is to be found in that continuous wholeness.

There is a meaning in the dance, but it transcends the facial expression, and the body of the person dancing: we cannot make a split between the dancing individual (who is mortal) and the dance he or she dances: somehow, meaning is wrung from these processes, and this meaning, this *wholeness in existence* cannot be destroyed by the objective or natural scientistic philosophies which lurk in the background of the poem. The wholeness Yeats expresses in the chestnut tree and the dancing dancer symbolize the wholeness of meaningful existence, such as is found by "creative reflection" and exists above the flux of time: in those last images he finds a benign sense of *Dasein*, which he seems earlier in the poem to believe impossible. Yet in the tree and the brightening glance these are found, in no sphere of idealization, or "god-whisper", but in the normal surroundings of the natural world and the natural creative activity of man. The effect of the last stanza is like that of the final bars of *Das Lied Von Der Erde*, and brings us, after all the torment and uncertainty of the poem, to acknowledge that there is meaning to be found, naturally, by the exercise of perception, consciousness and creativity, as natural functions of man, which can overcome his mortality and suffering.

NOTES

1. Something of the same happens in *Sailing to Byzantium* where the richness of teeming life in the texture of the poetry gives the lie to the arid groping to become transmuted into art "out of life" expressed there.

8

Thomas Hardy and the
Meaning of Existence:
After a Journey

In *New Bearings in English Poetry*, as we have seen, F. R. Leavis is strangely negative about Hardy. ". . . there was little in his technique that could be taken up by younger poets and developed in the solution of their own problems" . . . "his originality was not of the kind that goes with a high degree of critical awareness: it went, indeed, with a naïve conservatism." These strictures may be re-examined in the light of what has happened in the forty years since: what still stands out as strength, in the first half of the century? It is certainly not the "techniques" of Ronald Bottrall or his kind of "critical awareness"—indeed, the critical awareness of the *Scrutiny* movement produced hardly any creativity at all. And what has "naïve conservatism" to do with poetry in the modern world? Eliot was a conservative, and Pound was a reactionary: the former ended in a strange creative denial of creativity, the latter had no creative theme. The more naïve poets—Edward Thomas, Isaac Rosenberg, Robert Frost—have been among the best, and some of them have recorded the greatest catastrophes to consciousness more effectively than the most sophisticated (or whatever may be the opposite to naïve). Empson's poetry fades, despite its "critical awareness", as time goes by, because of its emotional emptiness hidden under the intelligence which *Scrutiny* acclaimed in him. Edward Thomas wears better.

Was Mahler "naïve"? I find myself a possible likeness between Mahler, the Hardy of *Vestigea Veteris Flammae*, and the stoical Chinese poetry translated by Pound and Arthur Waley (poetry which interested Mahler in German translation, and in which he found the clue to his escape from nihilism). And this comparison gives me a feeling that what Leavis calls naïvety is often an artist's greatest strength: the strength to recognize the essential inner weakness—"Littlesoul"—associated with the struggle for meaning.

Of course, Leavis pays Hardy some appropriate tributes: he is a "Victorian poet who wrote great poetry evincing an intense concern, not with a world of day-dreams, but with the human situation as it appeared in the light of modern thought. . . ." But he "did not impinge until it was too late"—too late for what? Mahler is only just coming into his own, and I believe this may be true of Hardy. But at the end of the century

> By then the stresses incident to the most sensitive and aware had shifted and altered. Hardy is now seen to be truly Victorian—a Victorian in his very pessimism, which implies positives and assurances that have vanished. He inhabits a solid world, with the earth under his feet. He knows what he wants, what he values and what he is (p. 57).

—and here Leavis quotes the concluding lines of *After a Journey*, declaring "I am just the same as when. . . ."

> Compare this poem, or any of Hardy's best, with, say, one of Edward Thomas's (a representative modern sensibility), and Hardy's solidity appears *archaic* (p. 57, my italics).

Hardy (Leavis goes on) is "a naïve poet of simple attitudes and outlook" and references to I. A. Richards on the neutralization of nature follow. His greatness lies in the "integrity with which he accepted the conclusion, *enforced, he believed, by science*, that nature is indifferent to human values . . ." (my italics). His greatness lies in the *character* with which he faced this, according to Leavis. As I try to suggest above, this is to underestimate the philosophical-poetic achievement.

As we now realize, from philosophical anthropology, it is not so much that nature is indifferent to human values, but that the predominant view of nature spreading from science had itself lost touch with human values, excluded the dimensions of man's spiritual and moral being, and denied meaning—yet without any qualification to do so, since science is not a general philosophy.

At the same time, however, the universe had become "godless", not only because it was no longer, after Huxley and Tyndall, for some, possible to believe in the old naïve way—but because (as Nietzsche was pointing out) the very texture and fabric of disciplines of belief and moral exploration had gone dead. The loss of a literal belief in an ("objective") after-life is a parallel process.

The most surprising element in Leavis's account of Hardy is the implication that (once more) he is to be valued for his *character* rather than anything that may be called *intelligence*. In this I believe we may note the over-exaggeration in Leavis of "mind" of the kind he can judge, or supposes he can. There is a kind of thinking—even a very simple, quite deeply felt and even naïve thinking—which is profoundly intelligent, not least in its deceptive simplicity. This kind of thinking is manifest in, say, the last song in *Das Lied Von Der Erde* or the *Kindertotenlieder*, in Edward Thomas's *The New House* or *Old Man* (which Leavis commends), and in the poems of Bernard Spencer. It is unassuming, but it has great strength, not least in that it often moves out of immediate time, and the immediate anxieties of the generation, into the timeless realms of man's tragic predicament: *"Was war wirklich im All?"*

In this area of thinking, Thomas Hardy loses nothing by comparison with Edward Thomas: there is no doubt Hardy is the greater man as Thomas would be the first to recognize. Moreover, the closing lines, with their "I am just the same as when" rest on no solid ground of Victorian security of values, but are won by an astonishing creative victory, over nihilism and despair. Pessimism is not the thing to commend Hardy for.

I have argued elsewhere that Leavis places too high a value on "character". Character is nothing: it is impossible to solve the *Dasein* problem by character.[1] What does triumph is the assertion of *having been*, in the here and now, in a meaningful way, and this requires not only aliveness and integrity but the kind of thinking I have spoken of, the achievement of a particular stance, a certain kind of structure that not only "accepts" and "confronts", but which moves forward, in "intention", to establish a sense of meaning which can never be swallowed up by the grave, or be overwhelmed by indifferent matter. It stamps, as it were, the ineradicable fact of one's creative existence on matter, and thereby humanizes it, gives *it* meaning:

> Primaeval rocks form the road's steep border,
>   And much have they faced there, first and last,
> Of the transitory in Earth's long order;
>   But what they record in colour and cast
>   Is—that we too passed.
>
> <div align="right">(<i>At Castle Boterel</i>)</div>

In *At Castle Boterel* the assertion seems merely asserted—confidently enough. But in *After a Journey* it is much more creatively enacted, and conveyed as an experience—by no means naïve or belonging to "simple attitudes".

From philosophical anthropology we learn that our perception of a benign and meaningful world is at one with our capacity for love, from the first encounter with the mother to adult sexual relationship. When the love object dies there is obviously bound to be a serious wounding of the capacity to believe in a benign world. It may be relevant here perhaps to note that Christians when dying, or widowed, often have the power to believe, often almost with rapture, that they will be reunited with their loved ones in a world the other side of death: to them, the most important thing in their whole existence, is to be back in encounter with the significant other, as a manifestation of togetherness with God (an aspect of love made clear in the Marriage Service). By contrast those who have no faith often find the world so empty and meaningless when the loved one dies that they simply die too. But to those who have no faith, and for whom there is no transcendent realm, no afterlife, and no God, the loss of the object by death may seem the ultimate blow to the one focus of meaning in existence, the meaning of love. Their sense of meaning attaches itself to the uniqueness of the other, whose irreplaceable quality yields a sense of the uniqueness of the Self, and thus a *Dasein* quality to one's life. Sweep the other into oblivion, and nothingness threatens to overwhelm the *being there* quality in the self:

> Till in darkening darkness
> The yawning blankness
> Of the perspective sickens me . . .
>
> <div align="right">(<i>The Going</i>)</div>

The unappeasable reality of things, of matter and the sun going on indifferently, threatens to overwhelm—and cannot be softened by benignity:

> while I
> Saw morning harden upon the wall . . .
> All's past amend,
> Unchangeable. It must go.
> I seem but a dead man held on end
> To sink down soon . . .

The comparison suggests itself with that plangent clarity of King Lear's final utterances, in a poetry Shakespeare developed—an immense achievement—to express the ultimate self-know-ledge, of oneself as tragically mortal, ephemeral—with only the fragilities of love and creative values within one's grasp, to transcend "the promis'd end". It would seem strange to speak of "technique" in Hardy's *Poems of 1912–13*: yet I believe that now is the time for us to study the artistic achievement that they represent. For one thing, I believe, that, unlike what we have in the evident employment of conscious technique in Pound, Eliot and Ronald Bottrall, Hardy's language takes its forms from the deepest inward voices, those of "being", like Mahler's themes in his last symphonies. The "voice" of the above stanzas quoted from *The Going*, for example, are like King Lear's "I pray you do not mock me. . . ." They could not have been achieved by conscious deliberation, but spring spontaneously from a deep inward engage-ment with the most profound agony of being.

Being able to use Hardy's "technique", or to benefit from his art, becoming able to use it towards one's own originality, as grist to one's mill, as it were, therefore depends not upon simply study-ing his idiom or verse-forms, but on understanding his art in the deepest sense. And this is a question of understanding his thought, which is profoundly existentialist: the *Dasein* problem is given in the first word of *After a Journey*:

> HERETO I come to view a voiceless ghost;
> Whither, O whither will its whim now draw me?
> Up the cliff, down, till I'm lonely, lost,
> And the unseen water's ejaculations awe me

The search is for *being there*: he and she were at this spot forty years ago, before the marriage and before the marriage became a mockery. He is seeking something out of time and out of space: but yet something to be found only in time and space (hence *After a Journey*)—by re-enacting the wanderings of the first courtship. He tries to pin his attention down to a particular configuration: "the spots we knew . . ." and this requires a creative manipulation with time.

Thus "hereto" as the opening word of the poem pins it to the going-to-that-spot, as an intentional act, devoted to convincing himself that once, there, then, was a meaningful encounter.[2]

But part of the intention is to view what cannot be seen, and to hear what cannot be spoken. He does not say he came to view a *faceless* ghost, but a *voiceless* one: yet there is enough of the sound of "face" in "voice" to suggest it, while *voiceless* just creates enough tension of expectancy, to convey to us the mood of groping for confirmation in which he goes to Pentargon Bay. "Whither" conveys the puzzlement of the quest—and, as with many words in the poem, makes us feel the absoluteness of his recognition that she is nowhere. Yet he stumbles about, and the verses enact it. "Up the cliff, down, till I'm lonely, lost . . ."— the absence of her, faceless, voiceless, is exacerbated by visiting the cliff paths where she is not. The only springing lively movement there is that of the waves, their sudden flowings, with their slapping sounds, into the empty caves, unseen, too.

The line "And the unseen water's ejaculations awe me . . ." resembles Wordsworth's line: the same kind of long, unexpected word speaks itself of the desperate urge to find meaning, almost as if by physical act, where none is: "That spot which no vicissitude can find. . . ." Up and down the cliffs he finds an emptiness where he had hoped to find her. Suddenly, from time to time, as he tries to call her image into being, and as he wishes she were there, alive, he hears a surge of water slap on to the wall of a hollow cave beneath his feet. The word "ejaculations" is here onomatapoeic. It also conveys, in an existentialist sense, "thrownness"— they met here in such a way by chance as to become able to assert a meaningful love against the state of being thrown—*abandonnés* —into the world. Like Wordsworth's "vicissitude", it conveys a feeling in the body, an experience of "felt thrownness". Now, in that state, she has been thrown suddenly into death. In the coarse ethos of our world the sexual meaning of "ejaculate" is a barrier here to a proper response: but the ambiguity of the word, its strangeness, includes the sexual sense—for we are, after all, concerned with a relationship in which for many years that love for the "significant other" was consummated by his ejaculations in her womb. The rock caverns are her womb, which is now dust in the tomb: and the wave's ejaculations are the only pulse of life in this hallowed place, where they once existed. And these pulses of the surging ocean cannot awaken life, any more than Wordsworth's "vicissitudes", happenstances in existence can ever stumble into the other world of the other side of the tomb, or on her, "deep buried in the silent tomb, that spot. . . ." The dead loved one is in another dimension that no physical search or leap of life can find; he is left alone: *abandonné* indeed.

No wonder the poet says the waters "awe" him, for at this moment he is tasting the full dreadfulness of not-being. Yet, he tries to believe that she is not unalterably fixed in nothingness, but, like the wave-movements, still flits, tempting him, here and here:

> Where you will next be there's no knowing,
> Facing round about me everywhere . . .

There is no doubt at all as to where she is: she is in one fixed immovable spot, and her face (and capacity to reflect him) are forever gone into nothingness. But against this the intentionality of creative love exerts that extraordinary future tense: "You will next be", and the possibilities are left amazingly open!—"there's no knowing". There can, in fact, as the earlier poems make clear, be no doubt, that she will be "Heard no more again, far or near. . . ." But here there are no known limits to her living presence

> Facing round about me everywhere,
> With your nut-coloured hair,
> And gray eyes, and rose-flush coming and going.

We may compare Yeats's moment in *Among School Children*: "she stands before me as a living child"—both record a peak moment of recapturing the immediacy of the significant object. Of course, she was not "there" at Pentargan Bay: but she was "there" in his vision—and is "there" in the poem. She has thus been won from oblivion, since there can now be no doubt of her

Dasein-existence, of her living presence in his being, which, since we re-experience her in her life and beauty every time we read it, is now outside time.

As Sylvia Plath conveys in her poem *The Night Dances*, in what else, other than in glances, signals, evanescent communications, looks and caresses (even in the exchange of flesh and ejaculations), does love exist, does creative reflection "exist"? We see ourselves "having a presence in the being of the other" in her "gray eyes, and rose-flush coming and going". And if the memory of those responsive echoes is as strong forty years after as a few hours after—Death, where is thy sting, or grave thy victory?

The effect of this courageous assertion of her living existence in his inward eye, is deeply moving—so deeply moving that this is perhaps one of the most difficult and taxing poems to read aloud. (Of what other poems of this century can one say that?) And the tension between the re-creation of her, and the indifferent awfulness of the slapping waters is a tension of existentialist thought about the nature of existence of a kind we are only beginning to become able to understand. If this is simple and naïve, then so are Marcel, Binswanger, Buber, Frankl and Maslow.

It is hardly surprising, after the triumphant achievement of the first stanza that the second should begin: "Yes": he has "found" her.

> Yes: I have re-entered your olden haunts at last;
>   Through the years, through the dead scenes I have tracked you;
> What have you now found to say of our past—
>   Scanned across the dark space wherein I have lacked you?

Here there is a clear admission that his creative effort in this art is to bring the relationship back to life and significance, through the "dead scenes". These are not only the scenes of her actually dead, but the scenes of their marital deadness. The vision at the end of the first stanza is a vision of love: but now there is a huge problem—which is that of many years of alienation in the years between. The ghost is voiceless, and she cannot find anything to say; but if he wrestles a little harder with time, perhaps he can find a point of vantage (perhaps by entering into her perspective as a young girl, his bride) from which he may be able to alter the awfulness of the dark spaces—the space after her death, the space after their love became blank.

> Summer gave us sweets, but autumn wrought division?
>> Things were not lastly as firstly well
>>> With us twain, you tell?
> But all's closed now, despite Time's derision.

Here he unflinchingly admits the failure of the relationship: is that how it looks to her (in *The Going* perhaps the deepest agony is in not having a chance to talk to her, to put this dead period in the relationship into place)? In Hardy's poems there is often a paranoid touch (*Honeymoon Time at an Inn*, *In a London Flat*) by which individuals seem to be tormented by malicious forces, and in *The Interloper* he expresses a tormented distress at the intrusion into his wife's life, and into his marriage, of mental illness. And it is this bitterness that makes him speak of "Time's derision". Time is also derisive in mocking him over his dedication to his love and the meaning of his marriage: if he tries to assert that the most meaningful thing in his life is this love, Time can mockingly say—"Well, you lived with her for forty years and for the latter part of that time you were estranged, and it was no marriage at all." But, whatever Time may say now, there is no more living relationship in time to be experienced. All one can do is to take it out of consecutive calendar time, and examine its meaning in the timeless dimension. Is there now anything of the *Dasein* to assert? The moment in the second stanza may be compared with the outbursts of irony directed against his own achievement of a sense of meaning in Mahler's Symphonies—as in the Third movement of the *Ninth*.

> I see what you are doing: you are leading me on
> To the spots we knew when we haunted here together . . .

How, in our age of coarse sensualism, can one convey how "leading me on" here has a sexual connotation, and represents an encounter with the spirit of a woman who entices libidinally, even after her death—in the pursuit of meaning?

But now she joins him in the quest for "being there", for "having been there": it is as necessary, to give meaning to her life as well as his. The word "haunts", however, gives the line an astonishing vibration: when they were actually hanging about those rocks, were they then less real, more ghostly, than they are now? Was their vagary then, mooning about in love, a rehearsal for the present haunting, when a frail old man ("faltering forward"—*The Voice*) follows a ghost he conjures up in his own mind, only to become lonely, lost?

But, again, so intense is his quest, that he actually recreates the "being there":

> The waterfall, above which the mist-bow shone
> At the then fair hour in the then fair weather . . .

How can one convey the impression of this line, with its intentional insistence on the word "then", and its strong rhythm, which actually draws that past, poignantly, into the immediate present, and asserts its definite quality of having-been-ness, and having-been-meaningfully, into the present? Yet the waterfall and the mist-bow shining are but images of moments that pass away, peak-moments of transcendence as they may be: water falls (slaps, is thrown), a mist bow is dispelled or vanishes as the sun goes behind a cloud: neither can be grasped. (Yet, of course, in *Under the Waterfall*, it is clear that Hardy has powerful associations with a waterfall into which, as lovers, they dropped a pic-nic glass from which they had taken wine, almost as a kind of sacred communion.)

Even then, when everything was so fair (and as firm as the line's rhythm emphasizes), they were mortal in the midst of transcendence: the joy itself was only a "spume that plays". Even then, just as there are awful caves under his feet, there were caves and hollow voices:

> And the cave just under, with a voice still so hollow
> That it seems to call out to me from forty years ago,
> When you were all aglow,
> And not the thin ghost that I now frailly follow!

Again, the complexity nearly overwhelms the reader with emotion, though it is perfectly kept within bounds by Hardy's simple language and quiet intimacy of voice. The cave continues to speak of death and nothingness—as it did then, and has ever since. It tells him now that his quest is hollow—the consonantal and other sounds that enact the meaning in "voice still so hollow" don't have to be stressed for their perfect qualities in the art. Their hollowness challenges the rose-flushing image: but he asserts it again by his "all aglow"—and this in turn is contrasted with himself in his elderly frailness, the frailness of his hopes, and the wraith that she is—conjured up only in his mind, and seen only in projection over the rocky shore.

The word "ignorant" may be associated with Leavis's word "indifferent": the seals and birds go on being creatures living in the skin of their immediate sensations and life-worlds. They don't have the agonies of consciousness, and don't see his ghost:

> Ignorant of what there is flitting here to see,
>   The waked birds preen and the seals flop lazily . . .

Ignorant means "not aware of", but also has that slight bitterness we attach to the word "indifferent"— they are brutish, and he can't throw over them any pathetic fallacy of their understanding of the human drama being played out on the shore all night. As dawn comes, they simply live as "beings-in-the-world": "preen" and "lazily" suggest a pace of existence quite different from the tense attempt of the man to wrestle with the actuality of time. Animal time is that of simply responding to the growing light, of enjoying bodily existence: *preen* and *flop* belong to the simple rhythms of natural existence, like *ejaculate*. This reality "lours": it stands in the way of his attempt to throw his own meanings over the world. The reality of the hazy whitening of the light makes it more difficult for him to sustain his projection of her ghost.

> Soon you will have, Dear, to vanish from me,
>   For the stars close their shutters and the dawn whitens hazily.
> Trust me, I mind not, though Life lours,
>   The bringing me here; nay, bring me here again!
>   I am just the same as when
> Our days were a joy, and our paths through flowers.

It seems to me extraordinary for Leavis to say "He inhabits a solid world, with the earth firm under his feet" and that it is "characteristic" that he should end his poem thus. As we have seen, at various moments throughout the poem, a hollow awfulness of nothingness and non-meaning menaces any security he can call up or create. But in these closing lines he admits that this existential anguish, generated in him by her "calling", is perhaps the best source of solutions to the *Dasein* problem. "I mind not / The bringing me here; nay, bring me here again!"—again, as in the word "hereto" we have the sense expressed that the solution to the haunting possibility of nothingness is to be found in attention to "the then fair hour" by walking over "the spots we knew when we haunted here together", contemplating "together", as the most fruitful source of meaning.

It is out of this suffering—the suffering of trying to exert intentionality against insecurity—the possible loss of all significance —that Hardy wins his sense of continuity. It is as an individual faced with utter dissolution that he says "I am just the same as when", not as a Victorian secure in his values, and secure on firm earth.

The declaration, "I am just the same as when . . .", has been won through an agony. He has won his way back to the time when their love was meaningful: and in the absence of any meaning in the world of water, rock and animals, he is brought to recognize that meaning is to be found only in himself, and in what he can throw over the world—as he throws her ghost out into it, to transform or endow it with significance. Having found this centre in himself, in his memory, of that strong time ("the *then* fair hour . . ."), he establishes a sense of continuity which is out of time, is not broken by Time's derision and the "dead scenes": he comes into touch with the joy that was, those peak-moments, that transcendence, that gave the world meaning

when
Our days were a joy and our paths through flowers

The strength of those closing lines is that of achieving *gratitude for having existed*: as I try to argue in *Gustav Mahler and the Courage to Be*, this is as much as may be achieved by the non-believer: by escaping from quotidien time, from the reality of the predominance of present "reality", he can achieve a sense that nothing can destroy the fact that one has existed and that, from time to time, there have been transcendent moments in which a sense of meaning has been grasped, evanescent as may be, that are indestructible.

As Viktor Frankl says, "The problem of meaning in its extreme form can literally overwhelm a person. . . . The candle's being (Heidegger would say: 'Vorhanden-Sein') may be interpreted as a process of combustion. But man possesses a totally different form of being."

> Human existence takes the form of historical existence. It is—in contrast to the existence of animals—always placed in a historical space (a "structured" space according to Ludwig Binswanger) and cannot be extracted from the system of co-ordinates governing that space. And this frame of reference is always governed by a meaning, although that meaning may be unspoken, and perhaps altogether inexpressible. . . .
>
> (*The Doctor and the Soul*, p. 27)

Hardy's greatness was in being able to express it, in direct and immediate language—albeit in a poem of immense complexity. And in doing so he wins a victory over both meaninglessness and death: over the dead world of our thinking. As Frankl says,

> temporality . . . is therefore not only an essential characteristic of human life, but also a real factor in its meaningfulness. The meaning of human life is based upon its irreversible quality. . .

Frankl speaks of the full gravity of responsibility that every man bears throughout every moment of his life—it is, finally, to that sense of grave responsibility to which Hardy's art contributes. At a time when egoistical nihilism has overtaken us, not least by a deliberate assault on such gravity, such linguistic care, such deep and courageous *thought*, and such responsibility—to *life*, to use Leavis's own word—Hardy seems, in these late poems, to represent in poetry, like Mahler's music, exactly what our art needs today, to help give it bearings, by the restoration of creative man.

NOTES

1. Leavis quotes Lawrence approvingly when he says of E. M. Forster, "All he is left with is people".
2. See the poignant insistent rhythm, discussed on p. 213, of "the *then* fair hour, in the *then* fair weather . . ."

216

9

Conclusions

We cannot solve the problems of the failure of confidence in creativity, in poetry and criticism, unless we diagnose the philosophical malady behind it. Since the Galilean-Newtonian-Cartesian Revolution, men in our civilization have had to live in a world in which recognition of the subjective and intentional elements has been suppressed in the predominant view of existence. The world was to be known only literally, and all that man might project over it in terms of meaning was to be rejected as false. So, we are left in the end with Yeats looking out at a landscape in which the only myths and meanings are those he has artificially projected there himself, by unconvinced invention, while the reality itself seems meaningless (see *The Tower*).

Marjorie Grene quotes Portmann on "the apparatus of gleaming glass" in the modern laboratory, "the bright research laboratories and men and women in white (who) have acquired an almost symbolic value" and his emphasis on how "we must look again and see how great is the darkness out of which the light that fills the bright spaces of intellect wells up".

> We must try, in other words, to achieve anew a whole vision of our nature—a revision which by its very character research alone is unable to provide.
>
> (Grene, *Approaches*, p. 51)

It is this search for a new "whole vision of our nature" that is needed, to provide new bearings for the arts of today. A whole false, unsatisfactory way of seeing the world and our own nature has been the stumbling block to creative existence—even though there have been individual artists, like Blake, the Impressionists, Tolstoy, Bonnard, Turner, Dickens, Lawrence and Mahler, who have overcome the paralysis, by knowing the world and themselves by

217

the "other" disciplines, creating a new "life-world" in the dimension of the "category of life".

For the reality of the world is not in its "mathematical bones". While science is a human spiritual accomplishment, as Husserl emphasizes, by limiting itself to what has "objective" validity it has ceased to be able to answer any of the serious questions (see Husserl's *Crisis*, pp. 121 ff.). No wonder the imaginative artist feels hopeless if the one authoritative discipline of his time tells him that only the mathematical bones are real—and that they can answer nothing at all. The bright light of the intellect, despite its prestige and claim to exclusiveness, becomes an incoherent nothing—while that vast darkness, the "very roots of our being", though it is quite evidently there, cannot be explored by any valid "research", while both his creativity and the subjective disciplines which are the only way to explore the life-world, are falsehood, fables, fictions and lies!

It is this problem that lies behind so much sterility in contemporary writing. Of course, in all this, "commercialism" can be blamed for something—as Donald Davie blames it at the end of his book on Pound. But commercialism is but one aspect of our whole civilization. It has substituted "the sale of half-hose" for the Pierean roses, because of a general belief that things, possessions, and sensations are the way to a secure sense of identity and meaning. Our age demands the "prose kinema" because it cannot have the patience to wait for the deeper achievement of the poet or sculptor. But this is because of the widespread triumph of literalism, at deeper levels. If man is an organism in a merely matter-in-motion universe, as Marjorie Grene says, there can be no response but despair—and this may prompt a desperate attempt to fill the moment with sensation: "deep, surge, thrust, plunge", as the advertisement has it. To seek a feeling that one is "real" because one feels something may impel a kind of egoistical nihilism, and in this we may find a link between "objectivity" and the philosophy of Max Stirner, whose book *The Unique One and His Property* (1845) so disturbed Marx.

If God is dead, and the universe is "nothing", so that we are nothing, in the end, and there is no-one to whom to give an account, by what values should we respect others? Why base our values on love? Stirner's conclusion was that "I am the Creative

218

Nothing, the Nothing out of which as Creator I myself create every-thing: there is no-one to whom I need render account." (see Paterson, 1971, p. 218.) Stirner's attitude might be that behind much contemporary culture, and is expressed even in some of the poems I have discussed. We hear today from Conservative poli-ticians, about our "values" but it was these same people who offered us the Stirnerean slogan, "Having it good" not long ago—and in this inculcation of a ruthless acquisitiveness they were encouraging a philosophy of life in which there was nothing left to believe in except self-indulgence. A slogan on a T-shirt in a Cambridge shop recently declared, "If it feels good—do it!" As a philosophy this easily moves towards a denial of that human meet-ing from which all meaning and creativity flow. This was Martin Buber's answer to Stirner: Stirner teaches us that "true is what is mine":

> Here already lies hidden the fundamental principle of our day. "What I take as true is defined by what I am." To this, two state-ments may be taken as alternatives or as a combination—to Stirner's horror, certainly, but in logical consistency as an inescap-able interpretation. There is first the statement, 'And what I am is conditioned by my complexes,' and second, the statement, 'And what I am is conditioned by the class I belong to,' with all their variants. Stirner is the involuntary father of modern psychological and sociological relativism . . .
>
> (*The Question to the Single One*, Martin Buber: Will Herberg's anthology, p. 69)

At the back of the failure of our confidence in creativity is this kind of nihilism, as it is manifest in contemporary "objectivity", and the psychology, sociology and philosophy that uphold it. It is not commercialism, decadence or triviality that destroys us, but what lies behind these: "attachment to the concrete is a loss of the future." Attachment to "psychological" or "social" reality in terms of objectivity is a kind of nihilism that destroys the capacity to transcend oneself as functional man, or what Lawrence called "social man". But in revolt against this nihilism, those who (like Pound) know the answer to be in imagination and creative dis-ciplines, may hurl themselves into aesthetic self-cultivation, or into pedagogy, or into ironic expressions of a (schizoid) sense of superiority, or into the expression of poignant sadness and loss—but never produce more than a "rushlight". Can we do more?

I believe we shall never escape into confident creativity—or discover essential creative themes—until we have invoked and applied the kind of philosophical anthropology with which philosophers like Marjorie Grene have provided us. She offers a triumph which is one both of intelligence and sensibility over the anti-poetic forces (from Galileo, Kepler, Bacon, and the Royal Society to Huxley, Tyndall and Skinner) who have denied wholeness to man and the world since the beginning of the Renaissance. Pound rejected the Impressionists as "muzzy", because he was preoccupied with "form". But his "form" becomes for him a quest for a kind of "certainty" that runs parallel to the need for intellectual security that dogs "objectivity". The greatness of the Impressionists was that they were able to hold together a scatter of light, a diffuse vision, in an overall intentional concept, in the celebration of *humanitas*. Like Mahler, they were able to sustain a persistent sense of human creativity, even when disintegration threatened. In them the technical accomplishments, or "form", were the product of an idea of man, and a determination to enlarge potentialities. There is nothing yet equivalent in writing.

What positive steps can we take, to find our way back to a confident belief in creativity?

The first problem is to recognize our problems: the next to see that many decades will be required to begin to understand them and solve them—a situation which, incidentally, reveals the difference between the influence of Sartre and Merleau-Ponty. Sartre has led virtually the whole of our culture into mental rage, "endless violence", and an essential inauthenticity: preoccupation with nihilism, perversion, and even (as with his support for the violence of the Maoist and the Baader-Meinhoff causes, while he did not even endorse Maoism or Baaderism) radical inauthenticity. Merleau-Ponty (as Poole shows) suffered appallingly from political disillusionment when he discovered the truth of the Stalinist concentration camps—as, indeed, all of us must suffer when we read *The Gulag Archipelago*. But Merleau-Ponty is the much more serious philosopher, and between him and Marcel, Husserl, Frankl, May, and Maslow we may see the gates opening, on a new rediscovery of man's potentialities, and a new politics. Man's need for meaning comes to the centre of the picture: meaning is bound up with *liebende Wirheit,* and with the capacity to exercise one's authenticity and freedom—all of which are *possible* as they are not in Sartre and the "old" existentialism.

One principle the poet might well adopt, from the new existentialism and phenomenology, is "back to the things themselves", that is, back to the study of whole experience, of the nature of consciousness. As I have shown, many poets are paralysed not by their own "conditions", but by taking on the "scientific world view" and by wearing the distorting spectacles of positivism. Like de la Mare, they have given up trying to believe in the mystery of their own existence, under the pressures of what they believe to be the destruction of "belief"—out there, as if "belief" itself were an objective entity, and as if the meaning of the universe had been destroyed by science as a manifestation of consciousness.

But to return to the phenomena of consciousness, as "I" experience them, restoring my confidence in the "I" that unites my experience by having *my* experience, requires a philosophical act. Today we can even be persuaded that our experience isn't really ours: sexologists, for example, even speak of providing a "primer", to help people see what kind of experience they are having. B. F. Skinner writes a book on *Behaviourism* passionately arguing (virtually) that there is no such thing as an "I" with consciousness that can have such passion. A neurologist is reported by Polanyi to have jumped up and down with rage at a conference to declare, "We know one thing—ideas don't move muscles!" The "brain" is anthropomorphized, and talked about as if it were an autonomous creature or person "receiving" and "sorting" impressions "for" us, and somehow looking at the pictures inside our eyes and interpreting those "for" us.

So, we need to begin the painful process of putting the ghost back into the machine, and asserting roundly, in everything we do, that we exist in our whole uniqueness in the here and now, and that what is real is what is authentic for us in this immediate being-in-the-world, as "I". By contrast with what this "I" authentically knows, the mathematical concepts of natural science are by contrast inauthentic, and any quantified version of man, whether Skinner's, Kinsey's, Eysenck's, or that of the Departments of Health, Education, and Science (they are all Hume's) is not valid.

In this, we need recourse to philosophy, and the problem, whatever Dr Leavis may say, is not solvable without philosophy. Indeed, we may even go as far as to say that Dr Leavis's own refusal to recognize, foster, or find possible new creative themes over the last thirty years is itself a mark of a failure to employ philosophy in his literary criticism, while becoming obsessed with "character" (leaving him only T. S. Eliot and D. H. Lawrence as two facets of a phantom composite, around whose "character" he endlessly tramps).

The Phenomenology of Perception, Merleau-Ponty's classic, will be a key work, because it is a phenomenological work on perception which pursues the injunction from Husserl to return to the phenomena, to seek a new psychology of perception and sensation.

To Merleau-Ponty, perception is an existential act by which we commit ourselves to a certain interpretation of the "sense" of experience as it presents itself to us.

Husserl appears in the second sentence of Merleau-Ponty's great work. All problems amount to finding definitions of essences: the essence of perception, or the essence of consciousness, for example. But phenomenology is also an existential philosophy, which puts essences back into existence, and it does not expect to arrive at any starting point other than "facticity", that is the factual being of *Dasein*, being there in actual existence (as opposed to *Sosein*, essence). For this philosophy the world is "already there" before reflection begins. All its efforts are directed at reachieving a direct and primitive contact with the world and endowing that contact with a philosophical status.

We may see a parallel role for poetry, which, too, must "return to the things themselves". Merleau-Ponty asserts that

> I am not the outcome or meeting point of numerous causal agencies which determine my bodily or psychological make-up. I cannot conceive of myself as nothing but a bit of the world, a mere object of biological, psychological or sociological investigation. All my knowledge of the world, even my scientific knowledge, is gained from my own particular point of view (p. viii).

Yet in some of the poems we have looked at, whether the brutal ones of contemporary "realism", or those of a Yeats daunted by a world stripped of meaning, the poet can only find himself (and "the woman", often) as but "bits of the world", mere objects of scientific investigation. Merleau-Ponty helps to break this spell, along with Michael Polanyi. Even those mathematical chimeras of "objectivity" themselves sprang like armed men out of dragon's teeth—sown in the ground of consciousness by *tacit* processes. That is, the ghosts which haunt poetry sprang out of the same knowledge of the world which can only be rooted in the personal knower. Having been born, the scientific ghosts deny their origins, as by denying the "absolute source", the "I" which generates knowledge.

> I am, not a "living creature", nor even a "man", nor again even "a consciousness" endowed with all the characteristics which zoology, social anatomy, or inductive psychology recognise in these various products of the natural or historical process—I am the absolute source, my existence does not stem from any antecedents, from my physical and social environment; instead it moves out towards them and sustains them, for I alone bring into being for myself (and therefore into being in the only sense that the word can have for me) the tradition which I elect to carry on, or the horizon whose distance from me would be abolished . . . if I were not there to scan it with my gaze (p. ix).

It is through consciousness from the outset that a world forms itself round me and begins to exist for me. It is this first principle of existence that the poet must uphold—against the naïve and dishonest scientific points of view, according to which my existence is "a moment of the world's".[1]

In Merleau-Ponty we find many such new explorations of the relationship between the self and the world (an introduction to which may be found in the present writer's forthcoming studies in hand). But perhaps the most important aspect of his emphasis, where poetry is concerned, is his attitude to time. As we have seen, the paralysis in modern poetry belongs to a paralysis of time: this is clear even in its tenses. And with the failure of creative time goes a loss of creative will.

In Merleau-Ponty, as in Polanyi, knowing is essentially a telic phenomenon, a reaching out towards the future. Time, thus, as *lived time*, is telic in structure. In Merleau-Ponty we are not, as in Sartre or Heidegger, reaching forward in being-unto-death. We are, with a glance back at Husserl and his feeling for Intentional-

223

ity, biting into the future with our "protensions". We escape from
the atemporal world of Descartes and Hume, in whom experience
is fragments of sensation in beads of time, with no central experiencing "I". We restore the *stretch* of time, and bring the time
of the past to bear on the time of the present

> It is here that we see a future sliding into the present and on into
> the past. Nor are these three dimensions given to us through dis-
> crete acts: I do not form a mental picture of my day, it weighs upon
> me with all its weight, it is still there, and though I may not recall
> any detail of it, I have the impending power to do so, I still "have
> it in hand". . . .

And while we have this capacity to "recollect in tranquillity", this
is bound up with our capacity to move, shapingly, into the
future:

> Ahead of what I can see and perceive, there is, it is true, nothing
> more actually visible, but my world is carried forward by lines of
> intentionality which trace out in advance at least the style of what
> is to come. . . .

"We are the upsurge of time": in such emphases we have the clue
to escape, at last, from the appalling paralysis into which poetry
has fallen since the seventeenth century. As Marjorie Grene puts
it, "Protensions are temporal arches, curved times reaching back
from their goals to the steps that lead on to them":

> Though we cannot make our time
> Stand still, yet we will make him run . . .

The reference to Marvell enables one to make another point about
Merleau-Ponty's relevance to poetry—his embodiment, already
mentioned. Roger Poole says that he speaks of how

> our own body . . . wrapped in its own cocoon of meanings, estab-
> lished our meanings in the world, meanings which are picked up in
> a kind of criss-cross dialect by other embodied counter-subjects in
> the world.
>
> (Poole, *Universities Quarterly*, Autumn, 1974)

And this emphasis on body-meanings in creative time has widespread political implications which may be pondered in relation
to poetry

It is I who give a meaning and a future to my life, but this does not mean that this meaning and that future are conceptual (conçus): they surge from my present and from my past, and in particular from my present and past coexistence.

(Phanomenologie, p. 510)

We are mingled with the world and with other people in an inextricable intermixture: we are in an ambiguity between the "engagement" of history and our condition among others, and the disengaging freedom of our acts. All these insights into the dynamic aspects of our existence from Merleau-Ponty may be applied to any of the poems discussed in this book: for me, if I do that, I have a feeling as if of a stopped film being re-started: or perhaps of a log-jam in a river being released. The flood can move forward: as in the lovely image in Theodore Roethke's *Meditation at Oyster River*, itself a poem about finding one's way back into the natural world:

In this hour,
In this first heaven of knowing,
The flesh takes on the pure poise of the spirit . . .
I shift on my rock, and I think;
Of the first trembling of a Michigan brook in April . . .
Or the Tittebawasee, in the time between winter and spring,
When the ice melts along the edges in early afternoon.
And the midchannel begins cracking and heaving from the pressure beneath,
The ice piling high against the iron-bound spiles
Gleaming, freezing hard again, creaking at midnight—
And I long for the blast of dynamite,
The sudden sucking roar as the culvert loosens its debris of branches and sticks,
Welter of tin cans, pails, old bird's nests, a child's shoe riding a log,
As the piled ice breaks away from the battered spiles,
And the whole river begins to move forward, its bridges shaking.

(The Far Field, p. 18)

If only this could happen to the stream of poetry! For Roethke, as to Eliot in *The Waste Land*,

> The self persists like a dying star,
> In sleep, afraid . . .

The "centricity" of living things suggests another mode:

> The humming-bird, whirring from quince-blossom to morning-
> glory—
> With these I would be.

We urgently want to find ourselves being-in-the-world, like "The tongues of water, creeping in, quietly . . ." in Roethke's poem "Water's my will, and my way. . . ." His suicide, however, suggests defeat, as for so many poets, the self dying like a star in the Newtonian cosmos.

But besides Merleau-Ponty, there are many others who can now help us out of the impasse: Erwin Straus, for instance, with his phenomenological analyses of the mysteries of existence: Helmuth Plessner with his, of the signs and meanings of body-life in animals and men.

Yet in the early stages in this new development of the philo-sophical rediscovery we may come to feel overwhelmed with hope-lessness, not least, because the Arts in general have become so corrupt that they have largely moved beyond access of any re-humanization or even recovery of creativity. I quote from a letter from a university English professor and poet who prefers to remain anonymous:

> It may seem hopeless . . . my own shred of conviction that good drives out bad may seem to be overborne by the sheer monstrous mountain of nonsense and evil that piles itself up before our eyes . . . I had better say nothing of the more intimate trials of hoping and trying to write poetry, and at the same time finding that taste and opinion have turned violently and rudely against me and my kind. . . .

We are faced with a mentalized sensuality whose violence seriously inhibits our capacities to recover our bearings. Another professor poet writes to me of "the vulgarity, the insulting *obviousness*, of all this sexual innuendo". This new barbarism must first be dis-pelled, and there are signs that it is retreating (except on the BBC).

Strangely, if we turn to scientific writing we often find an attitude to existence which, by contrast, is a relief. Man there is more often than not still seen as creature of dignity and creative power. We may find celebrated in much scientific writing truths of human nature which emphasize man's unique situation and his unique responsibilities in the world, as in (say) the work of W. H. Thorpe, Dobzhansky, Bernard Towers, and Polanyi himself. Science has not lost its passion, but seems rather to uphold vision and faith.

Man's reaching out to the moon belongs to the same glad acceptance of these unfolding capacities—by which imagination can take us into an unforeseen future, which is yet made to become what man envisages, as his space-drift glides down into the exact spot he imagined for it.

Yet there is a paradox here, for science itself is an art, as Polanyi reminds us.

> There are rules which give valuable guidance to scientific discovery, but they are merely *rules of art*. . . . The rules of scientific enquiry leave their own application wide open, to be decided by the scientist's judgement. . . . It includes the finding of a good problem, and of the surmises to pursue it, and the recognition of a discovery that solves it.
>
> (*Science, Faith and Society*, p. 15)

Science is a manifestation of a passionate pursuit of truth, and the scientist bears a heavy burden of responsibility to his faith. Yet while science remains the passionate pursuit of human truth (even itself debating whether its "facts" can be "objective") many in the Arts are declaring that they will have nothing to do with truth, morality or values at all. By contrast the purity of science can be compared with the church at its best: as Polanyi says of his disciplines.

> This is the way of acquiring knowledge, which the Christian Church Fathers described as *fides quaerens intellectum*, "to believe in order to know" (*ibid.*, p. 15).

The endorsement of science in our time manifests, as Polanyi says in his essay, a profound act of faith in science, not least in the *authority* of science.

> The authority of science resides in scientific opinion. Science exists as a body of wide-ranging authoritative knowledge only as long as the consensus of scientists continues. It lives and grows only so long as this consensus can resolve the perpetual tension between discipline and originality.

227

At the root of these disciplines and the consensus is a belief in "the reality of emergent meaning and truth": sustaining the self-renewal of science is, Polanyi says a "fatal responsibility". There is, inherent in science, a belief in human nature, and man's future (as there is not in the Arts today).

Polanyi declares that it is "fatefully urgent" to keep the disciplines of science maintained as a disinterested pursuit of meaning and truth. When science is mocked, as it was by Nazism, darkness threatens to descend on the world. But what about the Arts? Isn't it no less important to sustain the pursuit of meaning and truth in the subjective disciplines of symbolism? If we were to see huge areas of science corrupted by commerce or political expediency would we not invoke questions of values and responsibility? Yet in many areas the Arts have completely broken away from responsible concern with that "tension" of setting meaning against "nothingness", and consider themselves above critical and moral discrimination.

To deal with all these problems adequately will require an immense "conceptual recovery". In the present catastrophe in the Arts we have a manifestation of what Martin Buber called the problem of *seelenge-schichtlich* "having to do with the soul's history", and

> Man's tendency to "lag behind his works" . . . his increasing inability to master the world which he himself has brought into being. . . .
>
> (*The Philosophy of Martin Buber*)

With science man gained power over the world (as over disease) but in the resultant growth of mechanism as a philosophy he lost his sense of respect for the mystery of himself. The dangers are as grave as that of our offences against the ecological balance. They have been clearly expressed by Jose Ortega y Gasset:

> While the tiger cannot cease being a tiger, cannot be detigered, man lives in the perpetual risk of being dehumanized. With him, not only is it problematic and contingent, whether this will happen to him, as it is with the other animals, but at times what happens to man is nothing less than *ceasing to be a man*. . . . Each of us is always in peril of not being the unique and untransferable *self* which he is. The majority of men perpetually betray this self which is waiting to be. . . .

228

No human acquisition is stable. Even what appears to us most completely won and consolidated can disappear in a few generations. This thing we call "civilization" . . . like a raft in the initial shipwreck which living always is, . . . all these securities are insecure securities which in the twinkling of an eye, at the least carelessness, escape from man's hands and vanish like phantoms. . . . The fate of culture, the destiny of man, depends upon our maintaining that dramatic consciousness ever alive in our inmost being, and upon feeling, like a murmuring counterpoint in our entrails, that we are only sure of insecurity. . . .

(Jose Ortega y Gasset, *The Dehumanization of Art,* p. 191)

The prevalent blackness and nihilism of our time is really a defence against this need to recognize always that physically and spiritually "in the midst of life we are in death", and that every betrayal of civilization menaces survival.

Strangely enough, what is needed is virtually a biological theory of culture, by which to develop a truthful sense of man's *primary need to exert his higher nature* as stressed by Abraham Maslow. Only such a complete change of the sense of what is "real" can redeem the arts from their present course of humanistic failure, poetry especially. As the philosophical biologists discussed by Marjorie Grene in *Approaches to a Philosophical Biology* demonstrate, in his biological growth man is inherently and primarily a cultural being. Culture is as important, as primary in our being, as that. The essentially human attributes of standing upright, speech and rational action distinguish man from the animal, and his capacities as *animal symbolicum* early in his embryonic and post-embryonic stages of development. Even before he is born he is embodied with a cultural responsibility to his world. Looked at by the biologist in the "new way" this primacy of culture is not to be divided from those aspects of consciousness and self-awareness in man that are a development of the "something like consciousness" in all living creatures. In man the most important primary facts are his ethical life, and his capacity to question the meaning of his existence—setting against his awareness of his mortality and "nothingness" a creative quest to "be oneself" and to find a meaning in life. Out of this evolve human freedom and potentiality. If we see these as primary aspects of man's reality, then we need obviously to take the arts more seriously. We need to take

229

them as seriously as (say) Alexander Solzhenitzyn takes them, and we need to insist on the primary value of the imaginative consciousness. Their trivialization and debasement, especially in London, are serious assaults on man's whole existence and freedom.

When the Nazis debased biology, the rest of the world recoiled in horror, from a distortion of truth which had horrible consequences. Yet today we live daily with widespread forms of abuse of human truth in the nihilistic fashionable arts and popular culture, and even in poetry, by which moral inversion and hate distort attitudes and corrupt them. The consequences may be no less disastrous than those of the fanatical immoralism of Nazi thought. This is not to say that there is no room for disagreement about the nature of man: there must be freedom for disagreement, and freedom of enquiry. But this does not mean we should not subject poetry and the other arts to the strongest condemnation if they lose their humanistic bearings. Just as science depends on certain passionately held values, such as the (wholly subjective) belief in the pursuit of truth, so the Arts depend upon the original Telos of Greek philosophy which set out to seek the whole human truth (from which pursuit, Husserl alleges, empirical science deflected the stream of thought, into the narrow paths of objective science).

How radical a change is needed here might seem impossible to convey to our intellectual minority—not least in the universities, and especially the "new" universities whose syllabuses, when examined seem anything but "new", but further from the truth than ever. In truth, many such centres seem to be actually training their students in a deeper and deeper nihilism, because they cling to reductionist, objective and positivist dimensions.

There are political implications in the failure of poetry, and these may be related to the concept of *homo naturans* and its predominance. We have not yet discovered an existentialist politics in which there is an emphasis on the need for meaning, for freedom and authenticity. The underlying model of both capitalism and communism is one which is taken to imply that people must be controlled (or manipulated) for their own good. But how can people find authentic meaning in their lives if their essential meaning-seeking freedom is taken away? They cannot live without meaning: but today are supplied largely with false meanings.

Here we may relate the politics and attitudes to man behind the poetry of Pound and Eliot to wider questions of the "model" of man, the philosophical anthropology, bound up with their positions. In recent developments in psychology many writers have come to declare that the model of man adopted both by Christians and non-Christians, Freudians and capitalist economists is inadequate because it fails to find man's inner sources of freedom in existence. Freud, for instance, says Guntrip, because of his instinct theory, was "betrayed into some premature, rash and socially dangerous generalizations".

> His position differs little from that of Nietzsche for whom the possible alternatives were the superman who is above morality and simply gratifies his instincts because he is strong and no one can stop him, and the crucified Christian with his slave-morality of self-sacrifice and acceptance of suffering. The theory begs the whole question as to whether man is neurotic because he is instinctively anti-social, or whether he is anti-social because he is neurotic: or, to put it differently, whether criminality and neurosis are expressions of natural and vigorous instincts, or whether they are due to early emotional trauma and subsequent immaturity of development.
> (*Personality Structure and Human Interaction*, p. 69)

The same confusion underlies much contemporary debate in the Arts.

Guntrip penetrates to the underlying confusion, in the model of man's structure.

> Freud is landed in the dilemma that the denial of instinct is necessary for culture and civilization, whilst the gratification of instinct and the relaxation of culture is necessary for health. This pessimistic conclusion should arouse our suspicions. Social life, on this view, can never be any other than unending warfare between instinct and morality, the needs of the individual and the demands of the group, or, in another form, the flesh and the spirit (*op. cit.*, p. 69).

Yet this model has become almost ineradicably fixed in our minds today. It provides an essentially mechanistic view, persuading us to accept "functional man" as the basis for moral thinking, assuming a machine-like, quantitative view of the workings of his body and even his psyche. In this view civilization and good qualities are simply *not natural* to man, and he had to be coerced, in order to be made to subjugate his instinctual (real) impulses to civilized values. Or, his "basic" instinctual impulses have to be "released" as far as possible as is reconcilable with "society".

As Guntrip says, by this view, man's best qualities have no real roots in his inner nature:

> the individual . . . is apparently, not formed for society in spite of the fact that on other grounds he needs it. They are simply matters of expediency imposed by external force and authority. One is re-minded of St Paul's view of the unending conflict between "the laws of the mind" and "the law of the members", in which "the law of the mind" is the external authority of God, just as with Freud the law of morality is the external authority of the social group (*op. cit.,* p. 69).

Guntrip seeks to insist, from the point of view of object-relations psychology, that it is natural for man to be sociable, and civilized. In the psychoanalytical theories of Ian D. Suttie, Winnicott, Mel-anie Klein, Maslow, and others, we find a parallel pre-eminence being placed on man's natural capacities to love, to give to others, to serve causes, and to "contribute in" to the group. The origins of his moral impulse are to be found in his need to make "repara-tion", originating in the infant's first discovery of "the other", on whom he depends, and whose independent existence confirms his own. Fearing that his hate and voracious hunger might hurt the mother, on whom he depends, and whom he loves, the infant finds immense joy in giving in love—and this is the basis of conscience, love and social life, which is natural and necessary to man. Exis-tentialist thinkers and psychotherapists go further, and emphasize that giving and creating satisfy not only because they heal others, but because in such ways, as by discovering the uniqueness of the significant other, man is able to create a sense of meaning and of "being there" that can triumph over the voids, of death, and his eventual nothingness. These satisfactions are to be found in love and "encounter": but, moreover, they are experienced in terms of the quest to find and express one's essential "potentia"—that which each one has within himself to become. Here we find the important concept of "intentionality", of which Roger Poole writes:

It is this assertion that a world is brought into being by the kind of intentionality brought to bear upon it, which makes the phenomenological investigation so rich, the behavioural one so barren.

(*Universities Quarterly*, Autumn, 1974, p. 498)

Strange as it may seem, what is lost in the Christian (or Pauline) "model", in the Behaviourist model, in the Freudian (and "permissive") model, as well as the model implicit in advertising and commerce, is this *creative freedom* of man, to define himself and release his potentialities. Because of our education in attitudes to human nature from which many of these concepts of "intersubjectivity" are missing, and because of the exclusion of meaning and the intentional from so much science, sociology, psychology and public debate, we cannot find what Poole calls "the creative presence of human freedom in perception and thought". In such an atmosphere poetry is well-nigh impossible, and the related widespread failure of vision is now an important political problem. We have no idea of our future, and imagination has failed in our society.

The worst effect of this is that, whether we are considering "English", or poetry, or literary criticism, or politics, it seems there is no escape from a view of man or from a world made mundane and limited by natural scientism. This imprisons us in a dehumanization of man, running parallel to his exploitation by the forces of industrialization, commercial exploitation, mass living in megalopolis, and the general schizoid depersonalization of our era. The most serious consequence is the brutalization of man in our thoughts, which exerts a paralysis over our creative powers, and generates the further failure of intentionality. The social and political attitudes of Pound and Eliot belong to this era of depersonalization, and do not fundamentally offer a challenge to it. Their creativity failed because it is only possible for us to rediscover the creativity of man by protecting and releasing his essential personalization, his authentic capacity *to be*, and to throw meaning over the world.[2] It is difficult for us to diagnose this whole disaster, because, in our scientific and technological age, people have in any case, in our minds, tended to lose their personal qualities. Strangely enough, although they are poets, the attitudes to human beings in Eliot and Pound as I have tried to show express a schizoid sense of superiority, and a distrust of creativity itself.

In this they are complementary to the functional attitude to life of our civilization, even as they criticize it. Discussing this problem Professor John Macmurray says:

> The concentration upon instrumental values involves a growing aware-
> ness of and insensitiveness to intrinsic values: and our insensitive-
> ness to intrinsic values is the measure of our civilization.
>
> What is involved can best be seen if we consider our relations to
> other people. What would it mean if we were to adopt a scientific or
> a technological attitude in this field? We should require to be com-
> pletely objective, unemotional, impersonal. Our knowledge of people
> would have to be like that of the scientific psychologist, for whom—
> when he is behaving as a scientist—other people are instances of a
> type, and their behaviour the exemplification of psychological laws.
>
> *(Religion, Art and Science, p. 25)*

We should, says John Macmurray, come to regard people as if they were things for our use—and this, indeed, is how, in the end, *even* poetry comes to regard them (as in Philip Hobsbaum's poem discussed above): while the relevance to Max Stirner's denial of the value of others in his egoistical nihilism is evident. A world in which people are seen in this way as "exemplifications of psycho-logical laws" threatens us with non-meaning. Macmurray goes on:

> I . . . suggest that this spread of the technological mind beyond the
> proper bounds throws light on many of the social problems of our
> time. The growth of juvenile delinquency throughout the civilized
> world, the increase in crime under conditions in which the natural
> incentives to crime are less than they have ever been, and the
> imbecilities of the arms race are obvious instances. But the most
> complete are the fascist societies. For what we have seen in fascism
> is a working model of a society in which the extension of the power
> of the state is the ultimate objective, and any means which is neces-
> sary to this end is legitimate and laudable without qualification
> (pp. 25–26).

The failure of a belief in human nature manifest in poetry, and the failure of creative perception go hand in hand with that reduc-tion of man to his functions that destroys "future", and with the desperations of mental rage which attempt to compensate for the loss, in hate. The dominant instrumental and functional views of man result, as Gabriel Marcel has argued, in a "stifling impres-sion of sadness" in which man cannot escape from his mechanism:

> In such a world, there is something mocking and sinister . . . besides the sadness felt by the onlooker, there is the dull intolerable unease of the actor himself who is reduced to living as though he were in fact submerged by his functions.
>
> (*The Philosophy of Existence*, p. 3)

The uneasiness, says Marcel, is enough to show that there is in all this "some appalling mistake, some ghastly misinterpretation, implanted in defenceless minds by an increasingly inhuman social order and an equally inhuman philosophy (for if the philosophy has prepared the way for the order, the order has also shaped the philosophy)" (p. 3). Tragedy (in the sense that Hardy's poem is tragic) seems impossible, because in this world "death . . . becomes, objectively and functionally, the scrapping of what has ceased to be *of use* and must be written off as total loss" (p. 3). By contrast "life" is "being of use"—and in a world in which "truth lies between your legs"—this is all that one may claim to expect from it. Against this reductionism the poet above all should stand for the depth, perspective and intentionality of creativity, for his view is more whole, and manifests intersubjectivity. As Macmurray says

> The artist is first and foremost the observer, in a manner that leaves the scientist far behind; and he describes the world in the ordinary meaning of the term. Compared with the artistic description of nature, in poetry, for example, or in painting, the scientific is description only in a very Pickwickian sense. The empiricism of art is, it would seem, much more thoroughgoing than that of science. At any rate, the physicist's picture of the natural world—"cold, dark and shaking like a jelly"— *is much further removed from the world as we know it in perception than the wildest fantasy that an imaginative painter can put on canvas* (*op. cit.*, p. 30, my italics).

—which is another way of making Maslow's point above.

So, if science comes to be felt to be "true", and "more true" than poetry, we falsify our relationship with the world, to place the meaningless forbidding "jelly" of physics theory above the evidences of our senses and our real experience of the world. As Macmurray makes clear, this is also an elevation of the coldness and darkness of that dead universe over our delight and joy, in our existence in the senses. And when (as today) art crawls under the burden of the deadness of the "objectively real", and the meaninglessly trembling black jelly of Beckett's world or Ted Hughes's

Crow-world, or the world of the pornographer of *L'Histoire D'O*
or of Genet or of Sartre's *Nausea*—there is no joy, no "overplus",
no sense of organic well-being or harmonious organization.[3] John
Macmurray speaks of art as a "delight in the hearing or seeing",
and his emphasis may be related to that of Maslow above.

> The joy in the life of the senses would seem to be a particular ex-
> pression of something wider—the feeling that it is good to be alive.
> There is a pleasure in the healthy functioning of our bodies, with
> which there is joined that sense of overplus of energy ready to be
> used. We feel fit for anything: and the natural outlet for this energy
> is to shout or sing or dance. One sees this particularly in children.
> The sense of organic well-being tends to express itself in rhythmic
> movement. It is natural to suppose that the origin of this external-
> izing of rhythm, this natural expression of harmonious sound, lies
> in the rhythms of the bodily life itself, and in the smooth and har-
> monious interplay of all organic functions. It is certainly the case
> that there is a close and constant relation between art and the
> organic aspect of our own experience (p. 31).

To realign our bearings, we may go back to the Romantics and
Blake, because it was at that time that the crucial battles were
fought—even though some of them were lost.[4] Not even Blake's
transcendent vision could withstand the onslaught of Newton's
"sleep", and he could not create with whole success within the
boundaries of eighteenth-century "Reason". One other most
important fighter was Coleridge, whom one can see engaged in
trying to preserve his bearings in poetry in *Dejection: an Ode*—
a statement of the agony of being overwhelmed by the cold reality
of the Newtonian universe.

The poem is about what we would call now a loss of intentionality: he is seeking, in some way, to "win" "The passion and the
life whose fountains are within". That is, he is hoping to recover
his capacity to find delight in a world perceived as benign, sympathetic and meaningful. The central problem in the poem is that

> All this long eve, so balmy and serene,
> Have I been gazing on the western sky,
>   And its peculiar tint of yellow green:
> And still I gaze—and with how blank an eye!
> And those thin clouds above, in flakes and bars,
> That give away their motion to the stars;

236

Those stars, that glide behind them or between,
Now sparkling, now bedimmed, but always seen:
Yon crescent Moon, as fixed as if it grew
In its own cloudless, starless lake of blue;
I see them all so excellently fair,
I see, not feel, how beautiful they are!

The things seen *are* beautiful as they are described in the poem:
but the poet has lost faith in his own imaginative powers, as if
under the pressure of Newtonian science. The objects seen are
described as objects moving one against another, in the Galilean
universe: "give away their motion to the stars", "that glide behind them or between", "fixed, as if . . ." Anything poetical about
the heavens is in "as if . . .": and this is contrasted with the
mythical heaven of the old folksong:

Late, late yestreen I saw the new Moon,
With the old Moon in her arms . . .

The moon here is not the moon of *The Ancient Mariner* which is
the mother, pouring benign grace and love on the other heavenly
features, *"with how blank an eye"*. The effect is "dull pain", and a
sense of loss of

This light, this glory, this fair luminous mist,
This beautiful and beauty-making power.

He yearns in consequence for the gale and rain, because their
immediate "reality" would perhaps "Startle this dull pain and
make it move and live!"
    The pain is engendered by his fanciful perception of the moon,
beautiful and magical:

. . . the New Moon winter-bright!
And overspread with phantom light,
(With swimming phantom light o'erspread
But rimmed and circled by a silver thread)
I see the old Moon in her lap . . .

—which cannot, however, be felt to be "true". The poet wants
to see the Old Moon and the New Moon as one woman in the lap
of another, the mother and the love-object. But he cannot sustain
this personification—as he does, for example, in the hanging
footnotes to the passage in *The Ancient Mariner*:

237

everywhere the blue sky belongs to them and is their appointed rest, and their native country and their own natural homes, which they enter unannounced, as lords that are certainly expected and yet there is a silent joy at their arrival. . . .

"Life at home in the universe": but in *Dejection*, in the grip of depression, Coleridge cannot have this feeling: the "tint of yellow green", the "thin clouds above, in flakes and bars", the crescent Moon in "its own cloudless, starless lake of blue" are apart, fragmented, components of an alien universe.

These things should, Coleridge knows, be transformed by human perception: but he realizes this can only be so if the "fountains within" are flowing.

> Ah! from the Soul itself must issue forth
> A light, a glory, a fair luminous cloud
> Enveloping the Earth—
> And from the soul itself must there be sent
> A sweet and potent voice, of its own birth,
> Of all sweet sounds the life and element!

When Coleridge explores the reasons why he cannot send a creative shaft of attention over the Universe, to give it meanings, he speaks of purity: and he also addresses someone—a "lady" (Sarah):

> O pure of heart! thou need'st not ask of me
> What this strong music in the soul may be!
> . . .
> Joy, virtuous Lady! Joy that ne'er was given
> Save to the pure, and in their purest hour,
> Life, and Life's effluence, cloud at once and shower . . .

This purity and this joy are "Undreamt of by the sensual and proud . . ." Yet they can create "A new Heaven and a new Earth". What Coleridge pines for cannot be experienced by those who "attach themselves to the concrete" and so forfeit the future and creative power. Joy and purity are in the transcendent vision: losing this, he falls out of joy and purity, and loses the capacity to rejoice in himself.

He sees that man is being overwhelmed at large by a loveless *inanimate cold* universe. If we would behold anything of "higher worth",

238

> Than that inanimate cold world allowed
> To the poor loveless ever-anxious crowd . . .

a "light, a glory, a fair luminous cloud" must "issue" from the soul. And "from the soul itself there must be sent / A sweet and potent voice, of its own birth".

In this poem Coleridge thus links the capacity to rejoice in oneself; the capacity to relate to "significant other" in love (behind which lies the image of the Old and New Moon in one another's arms—an image of both primary relationship and continuity); and the capacity to throw a joyful perception over a world seen as creative and benign. There was a time when, however much he suffered and however much difficulty he experienced, when

> And hope grew round me, like the twining vine—
> And fruits, and foliage, not my own, seemed mine.

This seems to be a reference to the feeling one has in childhood, that everything in the world hangs there, in its generosity and beauty, for one to enjoy—so ecstatically expressed by Traherne. This is the creativity of intentional perception.

The present afflictions Coleridge was suffering "bow me down to earth". These were, I believe, relational: and these evidently threatened to reduce him to "earth"—in the sense of a feeling that the world is "shoving its meanings down on him". He is afraid of being overwhelmed by the realness of reality, and of the suspension of the "shaping spirit of Imagination" that can make the world *his*, as he wishes it to be. (Al Alvarez took the phrase *The Shaping Spirit* as the title of a book on modern poetry: but he does not discuss the essential problem of the loss of the shaping spirit in our time, and indeed in his influence on Sylvia Plath and Ted Hughes menaced it.)

Now comes the most difficult part of the poem to understand. Coleridge is speaking of the effect on himself of his alienation from the world, and the division in himself, consequent upon his relational difficulties. In this poem, indeed, we find borne out the insistence in psychoanalysis on the connection between relationship and perception. Coleridge's low state of depression and dissociation has meant that he has not been able to think about the feelings that pressed upon him—but went into a state of patient withdrawal:

> For not to think of what I needs must feel,
> But to be still and patient, all I can . . .

His "sole resource", his "only plan", has been to escape into intellectuality with the effect (deliberately resorted to) of denaturing himself. It is as if he is speaking of a schizoid flight from pain-full emotions into abstract, disembodied, thought:

> And haply by abstruse research to steal
>   From my own nature all the natural man—
>   This was my sole resource, my only plan:
> Till that which suits a part infects the whole,
> And now is almost grown the habit of my soul.

Coleridge here speaks of his psychological, philosophical and theoretical investigations as originating in a need to escape painful feelings, but infecting his whole sensibility, and becoming a bad habit of avoiding all naturalness, emotional health, and joy: a forfeiture of the intentional.

In the next stanza he clearly attacks this schizoid intellectual tendency with the overwhelming domination of "reality"—poisonous, viper, thoughts,

> Hence, viper thoughts, that coil around my mind,
>   Reality's dark dream!

By this time, when he analyses the domination of "dark reality", the reality of the coming storm has arrived: he is distracted from his viper thoughts:

> I turn from you, and listen to the wind,
>   Which long has raved unnoticed . . .

Instead of man throwing his imagination over the world the "real" wind plays on the surrounding world like a madman on a lute:

> Mad Lutanist! . . . thou . . .
> Mak'st Devils' yule, with worse than wintry song . . .

And in the midst of this fantasy of mad chaos (closely mingled with his tormented thoughts) we reach (by way of the screaming and moaning of the wind) a *little child*:

> 'Tis of a little child
> Upon a lonesome wild,

Not far from home, but she hath lost her way:
And now moans low in bitter grief and fear,
And now screams loud, and hopes to make her mother hear.

This strange apparition reveals, I believe, the deepest underlying dynamic in Coleridge's own psyche—the "regressed ego", or unborn (psychic) baby self, that has "lost its way" and feels deprived and rejected. She is a she, because, in the situation in which he finds himself, it is his *female element capacities* to *love* and *create* which are suffering and crying out to find their way, to make the mother hear—in the sense of finding the world benign (as the world in *The Ancient Mariner* becomes benign by the moon-mother's healing rays).

In this way, through the present crisis, "this storm" could be a "mountain *birth*". Here (in a poem all directed at problems of relationship) he returns to consider his "friend", the lady. He hopes she isn't being kept awake in tormented thought by the storm

Full seldom may my friend such vigils keep!
Visit her, gentle sleep! with wings of healing . . .

Coleridge goes out from himself, and so he escapes from his morbidity, ending with an image of continuity and of endless joy

To her may all things live, from pole to pole—,
Their life the eddying of her living soul!

Thus mayest thou ever, evermore rejoice . . .

The poem does not end with a triumphant rediscovery of a sense of joy and meaning such as we experience at the end of *Frost at Midnight*. But in his desire that she should be at peace with the world he forgets his own depression and paralysis, and so, in the course of his wishing, the universe becomes incidentally benign:

May all the stars hang bright above her dwelling,
Silent as though they watched the sleeping Earth!

In the context of my general argument, the *Dejection Ode* seems a clear expression of how the poet has been, since the Age of Reason, often *thrown* down, by the pressure of a "reality" that it seems impossible to mollify by the shaping spirit of imagination—a predicament we are only now beginning to understand, and, it is to be hoped, escape from.

241

For encouragement, perhaps, we need to go back further, to learn from Shakespeare, in whom confidence in the power of the imagination is supreme. It struck me, attending an excellent production of *Henry V* by the Marlowe Society, while writing this book, how marvellously Shakespeare expresses a confidence in the primacy of imagination, in such a way as now to be almost incomprehensible to us. Agincourt is no longer in the past, but is about to happen: "For now sits expectation in the air. . . ." The reality is not simply the few relics on the field, or the words in books, but what happens, *here and now*:

> In your fair minds let this acceptance take . . .
> And make imaginary puissance . . .
> Now entertain conjecture of a time
> When creeping murmur and the poring dark
> Fills the wide vessel of the universe . . .
> . . . Yet sit and see;
> Minding true things by what their mockeries be.

"Thus with imagin'd wing our swift scene flies / In motion of no less celerity / Than that of thought . . . O, do but think . . . Grapple your minds to sternage of this navy . . . Work, work your thoughts . . . Still be kind / And eke out our performance with your mind."

There is never a moment in the play when there is any pretence that what is happening is "literally true", or anything other than *an imagining*.

Yet the imagined is physically present *as experience* so powerfully as to be politically and humanly part of one's living, felt in one's senses, seen in one's mind:

> Play with your fancies; and in them behold
> Upon the hempen tackle ship-boys climbing;
> Hear the shrill whistle which doth order give
> To sounds confus'd; behold the threaden sails,
> Borne with the invisible and creeping wind,
> Draw the huge bottoms through the furrow'd sea
> Breasting the lofty surge . . .

The rigging may be felt in the hand: the vertigo is experienced: the sounds are in our ears. By the texture of the words "hempen tackle" the poetry makes the hands feel they have closed on the ropes: the coarseness of hemp makes them "tickle", the hardness comes over from *tack*, the energy of muscles from the verb to *tackle* (something). *Creeping* generates an image in our minds of the patch of roughness on the water moving slowly across a seascape, and the slow burgeoning of sails in it. The physical nature of *creep, draw, bottoms, furrowed* and *breast* give both images and physical feelings of being involved in huge physical movements, of *surge*, wave, wind and way.

Such concentration of meaning was later to enable Shakespeare to engage with some of the most profound themes of human existence. His capacity to engage with them in a truly tragic way required immense positive values—a belief in man. And in *Henry V* we find this, at an emergent stage, in such verse—which conveys a delight in being human and alive, even when

> The nimble gunner
> With linstock now the devilish cannon touches,
> And down goes all before them . . .

Today, teaching Shakespeare, one seems to fight a losing battle, between a departmental obsession with examining and "scholarship" on the one hand, and students' severe difficulties in reading poetry on the other. They have the greatest difficulty in grasping the English Shakespeare uses, and to feel (in the above) the ship drawing through the water, here and now, "in our imagination", as a moment of being, and "being there", in full triumph of the primacy of *my* imagination, *my* consciousness, excited and creating, *now*. And these difficulties are not only difficulties of language, but of being able to *believe in poetry*, to *love* poetry, to be stirred by it, and to "eke out (its) performance with your mind", to believe in the creative power of human consciousness. It is no less than this belief we have to recapture, to recover our bearings in English poetry.

NOTES

1. It need not be laboured, how pornography seeks to reduce the unique creative experience of love to "a moment of the world's".
2. As Leavis says, perhaps the most creative poem of Eliot's in this sense is *Marina*, where the imagery moves into an unknown future.

3. There is a related point, that this is (in the light of my discussion above) a triumph of "false male doing" over the female element of creativity: above p. 115 ff.

4. This is what Theodore Rozsak evidently believes too: see his *Where the Waste Land Ends*.

Select Bibliography

POETRY

Eliot, T. S., *Collected Poems 1909–35* (1936)
—— *Four Quartets* (1936–43)
Hardy, Thomas, *Collected Poems* (1919)
Hughes, Ted, *Wodwo* (1967)
—— *Crow* (1970)
Lupercal (1960)
Johnson, Lionel, *Poetical Works*, with an Introduction by Ezra Pound (1915)
Laforgue, Jules, *Oeuvres complètes* (1901–3; 1922–30)
Larkin, Philip, *The Oxford Book of Twentieth Century Verse* (ed., 1973)
—— *Whitsun Weddings* (1964)
Lowell, Robert, *Selected Poems* (1965)
Plath, Sylvia, *Ariel* (1965)
—— *The Colossus* (1960)
—— *Two Lovers and a Beachcomber* (Poems handed in for the English Tripos, 1956)
Pound, Ezra, *Selected Poems* (1928)
—— *Drafts and Fragments of Cantos CX–CXVII* (1969)
—— *The Women of Trachis* (1956)
Roethke, Theodore, *Collected Poems* (1968)
Rosenberg, Isaac, *Collected Poems* (1937)
Spearman, Diana (ed.), *The Animal Anthology*
Whitehead, Peter (ed.), *Wholly Communion* (1965)
Yeats, W. B., *Collected Poems* (1950)

FICTION

Bellow, Saul, *Mr Sammler's Planet* (1970)
Dickens, Charles, *Martin Chuzzlewit* (1843)

——— *Dombey and Son* (1848)

Hardy, Thomas, *Tess of the d'Urbervilles* (1891)

Plath, Sylvia, *The Wishing Box* (*Atlantic*, October, 1964)

MUSIC

Mahler, Gustav, *Kindertotenlieder* (1905)

——— *Das Lied Von Der Erde* (1908)

——— *Ninth Symphony* (1909)

Ives, Charles, *The Hausatonic at Stockbridge*

LITERARY AND CULTURAL CRITICISM

Davie, Donald, *Ezra Pound: Poet as Sculptor* (1966)

Ford, Boris (ed.), *Pelican Guide to English Literature* (1973)

Henry, Jules, *Culture Against Man* (1966)

Holbrook, David, *Dylan Thomas: The Code of Night* (1972)

——— *English for the Rejected* (1964)

Leavis, F. R., *New Bearings in English Poetry* (1932)

——— *How to Teach Reading: A Primer for Ezra Pound* (1932)

Pound, Ezra, *ABC of Reading* (1934)

Rickword, Edgell, *The Calendar of Modern Letters* (1927–9)

PSYCHOLOGY

Frankl, Viktor, *The Doctor and the Soul* (1969)

Guntrip, Harry, *Schizoid Phenomena, Object-relations and the Self* (1969)

Holbrook, David, *The Case Against Pornography* (ed., 1972)

——— *Human Hope and the Death Instinct* (1971)

——— *Gustav Mahler and the Courage to Be* (1975)

——— *Sylvia Plath: Poetry and Existence* (1976)

Khan, Masud, *The Privacy of the Self* (1974)

Ledermann, F. K., *Existential Neurosis* (1972)

Maslow, Abraham, *Towards a Psychology of Being* (1968)

May, Rollo, *Love and Will* (1969)

——— *Existence: A New Dimension in Psychiatry* (ed., 1958)

Winnicott, D. W., *Collected Papers* (1958)

——— *Playing and Reality* (1971)

PHILOSOPHY

Buber, Martin, *I and Thou* (1937)
—— *The Question to the Single One* in *The Writings of Martin Buber,* ed. Will Herberg (1956)
—— *Distance and Relation* in *The Knowledge of Man,* ed. Friedman (1964)
Cassirer, Ernst, *An Essay on Man* (1962)
Grene, Marjorie, *Approaches to A Philosophical Biology* (1968)
Husserl, Edmund, *The Crises of European Sciences* (1970)
Kaufmann, W., *Existentialism from Dostoevsky to Sartre* (1956)
Laing, R. D., *The Divided Self* (1960)
Merleau-Ponty, M., *The Phenomenology of Perception* (1962)
Mumford, Lewis, *The Myth of the Machine* (1967)
Paterson, A. K., *Max Stirner, the Egotistical Nihilist* (1971)
Plessner, Helmuth, *Laughing and Crying* (1970)
Polanyi, Michael, *Personal Knowledge* (1958)
—— (with Harry Prosch) *Meaning* (1975)
Poole, Roger, *Towards Deep Subjectivity* (1972)
Sherrington, G., *Man on His Nature* (1940)
Straus, Erwin, *The Primary World of Senses* (1963)
Towers, Bernard, *Concerning Teilhard* (1969)

PHILOSOPHICAL BIOLOGY

Buytendijk, F. J. J., *Das Menschliche Wege zu seinhem Verständnis* (1958)

Index

INDEX